WITHDRAWN

The Baroque Theatre

MARGARETE BAUR-HEINHOLD

THE BAROQUE THEATRE

A Cultural History of the 17th and 18th Centuries

Photographs by

Helga Schmidt-Glassner

McGraw–Hill Book Company

New York · Toronto

Translated from the German
Theater des Barock by Mary Whittall

The author wishes to thank Dr. Günther Schöne
of the Theatermuseum, Munich, for his tireless help and generous advice

Frontispiece: I. A. PESNE *The Dancer Barberini*

Contents

Introduction

Baroque theatre is a rich and complex theme – as iridescent as the 'baroque' pearl, the irregularly-shaped gem from which baroque art probably takes its name. It is customary to delimit the baroque in chronological terms by reference to the history of architecture; its development spans roughly two centuries, from Vignola's church of Il Gesù in Rome (1568) to Neumann's great church at Neresheim, completed by his successors in 1792. In theatrical terms, then, the baroque age runs from the building of the Teatro Olimpico in Vicenza (1580–84) to that of the Teatro La Fenice in Venice (1790–92).

But theatrical life in this baroque age was not confined to theatre buildings, which are only a part of the subject of this book. There was theatre at court, in the festivals, the ceremonies, the etiquette. There was theatre in all human activity. At the very beginning of baroque drama Shakespeare, in *As You Like It*, and Calderon, in *El gran teatro del mundo*, gave the clearest expression to a theme that others were to elaborate: 'All the world's a stage, and all the men and women merely players.'

At no other time was life in general so permeated and obsessed by the theatre as in the two centuries, from about 1600 to about 1800, which we intend to cover in this account of the baroque theatre. The period falls into two parts: the high baroque and the late baroque or rococo. The differences between the two are reflected in the theatre, but certain characteristics are common to both phases: the fluidity of boundaries between illusion and reality; and the theatricality of real life: the flaunting of personality, the posturing and gesturing on the stage of life, the desire to sublimate and transcend one's being. This obsessive concept of the 'great theatre of the world' persisted up to the time of the Enlightenment and even to the end of the age of Absolutism, although the kind of play-acting typified by Marie Antoinette and her shepherdesses, reveals a quite different attitude to both life and acting from the stage appearances of Louis XIV.

During these two centuries great palaces were built as the symbols of power, but sometimes the power existed only in the builder's dreams; they were expressions of his desire for wealth and grandeur, and many such palaces remained unfinished because the dreams were inflated, the self-esteem unfounded. The theatre too could be an embodiment of illusions. Courts, particularly Vienna and Versailles, competed to have the most splendid. Renaissance man had stood firmly in the centre of his universe, confident of being the measure of all things in it. Baroque man stood at a frontier, with no such firm ground under his feet. He could include both the heavens and the underworld in his theatre and see his own figure in comparison with, and measured against, divine infinity.

In our eyes there is something basically theatrical about the etiquette which dominated all polite society. The rigid, formalized patterns of behaviour at court developed from the strict ceremonial surrounding the kings of Spain in the sixteenth century. Etiquette did more than specify the forms of intercourse between king and subject, 'the liturgy of court ceremonial, infused with the awe-struck reverence of the subjects, raised the king to the equal of a god'.[1] Etiquette was of the greatest importance at all levels of noble society. The order of precedence dictated the kind of seats, from canopied thrones to footstools, and how they should be arranged at a particular ceremony. The royal *lever* and *coucher* always followed identical forms. The number of steps and the depth of bows at an encounter, the movement of hands and facial expression during a conversation were all governed by strict rules. These rules formed a protective wall about the courtier; covering every eventuality, they enclosed him like a fortress against the brusque demands of everyday life. Etiquette might change its forms, but it did not abdicate its rule. The seventeenth century was marked by chivalry, grave dignity, formality: the manners of the throne room. The eighteenth century, up to the French Revolution, was characterized by gallantry, refinement, grace and intimacy: the manners of the boudoir.

At the great court festivals of the seventeenth century, at Versailles, Vienna, Prague, Dresden and Munich, the full sovereign power was displayed before wide-eyed subjects. At immense expense the arts and sciences – architecture, sculpture, painting, mime, song, dance, light, water, fire and flying machines – were employed in the glorification of the ruling house. And if the prince himself appeared as the sun in a ballet, or as Apollo, enthroned in clouds, in the final tableau, the onlooker must have been overwhelmed by his power and majesty. He did not merely act the part of the sun or the god; he was himself an absolute, the ruler by God's grace.

The changed cultural atmosphere of the eighteenth century was also reflected at court where the pastoral and the idyll came into favour in place of allegories of power and dignity. Heroic heights were abandoned for the gentle slopes of Arcadia. The troubles and responsibilities of reality were hidden behind a gay, vernal backcloth before which youth was eternal, love and friendship were pure, life and dress were simple. Phyllis lived on the stage, Strephon played at life. Marie Antoinette had a shepherds' village specially built; it would hardly have done to live on a real farm.

To us the theatre is entertainment, an object for criticism and public subsidy. The theatre plays a clearly defined part in our lives: professional actors perform on a stage whose conventional illusions we accept; the theatre is open to all classes of people; actors, singers and dancers are admired for their good looks and applauded for their ability, and they are respected members of society. The theatre and the actor's life were very different in the period covered in this book.

The court theatre was maintained at the prince's expense and the nobility were the invited spectators. For a long time the court formed the only audience. Public theatres in towns were sometimes founded by the initiative of the citizens, or the ruling prince granted his privilege to the director of a company of actors or established a theatre for his subjects. The travelling companies performed wherever they could: in noblemen's houses, at fairs, in market-places, on makeshift platforms or in wooden booths.

All kinds of theatre were greatly influenced by the theatres of the Catholic religious orders and the Protestant schools, which both used drama to disseminate education and instruction among a large section of the public. Pupils and teachers, priests and novices presented on the stages of their schools and monasteries classical and Renaissance plays, at first in Latin and later in the vernacular.

There were far more amateur performances then than now. Solid citizens, artisans and peasants joined forces to present the Passion of Our Lord, in productions that sometimes went on for days. The *Comödistadel* ('barn theatre') which still survives at Kiefersfelden on the Inn looks back on a three-hundred-year-old tradition. Local farmers and farmhands still strut and bellow their way through the thrilling, if unsubtle, melodramas of bold knights and mighty monarchs that their fathers performed. The travelling puppet theatres were the most widely-known and most truly popular dramatic entertainment, moving from village to village, from fair to fair, spreading pleasure as they went. Life-size puppets on the stage, voices singing behind the scenes, flying machines and scene changes like those in the grandest of operas, were illusion enough for the people of that era.

Illusion was everywhere. The streets and squares of towns and villages were full of houses to which the skilful use of a paint-brush gave the appearance of carved stone and solid marble. In the churches of the late baroque, congregations prayed beneath painted domes which were not domes at all, and on which the fathers of the church were wafted to heaven on clouds that billowed in perspective.

Baroque theatre declined as cultural nationalism arose, during the second half of the eighteenth century. French drama and Italian opera lost their position of pre-eminence, vernaculars replaced French as the language of polite society and *belles-lettres*, and individual nations created their own drama and opera. National diversity, springing from the demands of a new, middle-class public, replaced the splendours of the international theatrical culture of the baroque age.

LUDOVICO OTTAVIO BURNACINI *Ballet on the lake, palace of La Favorita, Vienna c. 1660*

I The Courts

The marathon festivities of the late middle ages and the Renaissance took the form of a sequence of separate celebrations. Course followed course at banquet after banquet, interspersed with theatrical entertainments, dancing, masques and firework displays, and between the banquets there were knightly exercises: jousting, fencing, tilting and chariot-racing.[1] All the techniques and resources of theatrical art were employed to embellish the public appearances of both temporal and spiritual rulers. The victorious entries of conquerors, like those of the kings of France into the cities of Italy, were made to resemble Roman triumphs with mock fights and allegorical scenes. The surrender of the keys of a conquered city was celebrated with more allegories, and the victor processed through decorated streets and triumphal arches with a huge, gorgeously dressed following. The expense and the splendour recorded in detail in contemporary accounts are almost inconceivable to us.[2]

The baroque age brought with it new possibilities for the staging of such celebrations. The new palaces with their large and numerous rooms could accommodate the festive gatherings, and broad, landscaped parks provided space and background for spectacles on the grand scale. The court of Louis XIV, the Sun-King, was the model emulated by those of other princes, led by Vienna and Dresden. The opulence of court festivities reached its peak around the end of the seventeenth and the beginning of the eighteenth centuries.

There were numerous opportunities for great festivals. Weddings, coronations, the birth of an heir, birthdays and name-days, were occasions for feasts of sight and sound, combining the fine arts with all the techniques and skills of the stage.

In 1662 the Elector of Bavaria and his court celebrated in Munich the birth of Max Emmanuel, the heir to the throne. In extent it was a relatively small celebration, lasting only three days, but it was perhaps the first occasion on which all the theatrical arts of the baroque era were employed together with complete success.[3] The festivities were linked by connected themes. They opened with a performance of the opera *Fedra incoronata* in the opera house on the Salvatorplatz. On the second day the history of Phaedra was continued in the tournament arena with a pageant, *Antiopa giustificata*, and the third day completed the trilogy with *Medea vindicata*.

Scenes in the opera ranged over the entire baroque universe, heaven, earth, the underworld and even the sea-bed. The action included thunder and lightning, wind and rain, and there were gods in the clouds, monsters in the sea, sirens and centaurs on land.

An arena with two stages was built in the palace garden for the second day's pageant. It opened with Medea flying

ANON. *Carousel, Paris, early seventeenth century*

in on a fire-breathing dragon, landing before the royal box and heralding the entry of the knights with an aria. Allegorical tableaux and scenes from classical mythology were drawn across the stages on decorated carts against constantly changing scenery. Knights on horseback and their squires followed, dressed in classical costumes with elaborate plumes on their helmets, and engaged in battle for the honour of Antiope, who had been offended by Phaedra. Members of the most noble families took part in this mock combat, led by the Elector himself in a costume of blue, white and gold, towering above all others with a six-foot-high crest.

On the third day the 'Revenge of Medea' completed the trilogy in yet another dramatic form that included a firework display. A floating stage was moored on the river Isar while the court remained on the bank on a rising semi-circle of seats like an amphitheatre. The play was embellished with all the tricks of baroque stagecraft: scene changes, flying machines and great numbers of fireworks, mirrored in the water. A fire-breathing monster was brought on to end the naval battle at the end of the play, and a final set-piece of fireworks crowned this water-borne festivity. Thus earth and air, fire and water united to pay homage to the Crown Prince.

Opera, knightly skills and the four elements united here on a high artistic level to make perhaps the first of the great baroque festivals, but this was only a pale foreshadowing of the festivals Louis XIV was to mount at Versailles only a few years later, the influence of which spread across Europe as far as the courts of Augustus the Strong, Elector of Saxony and King of Poland, in Dresden and Warsaw.

In May 1664 Louis XIV decreed a festival at his court of Versailles in honour, officially, of his mother Anne of Austria and his young wife Maria Theresa of Spain, and

9

TEATRO FATTO IN FIRENZE NELLA FESTA A CAVALLO PER LA VENVTA DEL SER.º PRINCIPE D'VRBINO
Qui fecero 42 Canalieri diuersi attanimenti e dipoi un balletto ci si uide ancora una bataglia a piedi di 300 persone, oltre i Carri e l'altra gente per diuersi seruitij
Iullius Parigi Inu; Callot delineauit et F

JACQUES CALLOT 'La guerra di bellezza', Florence, Carnival 1616

unofficially of his mistress, Louise de la Vallière. There are several contemporary accounts of the *Plaisirs de l'Isle enchantée*.[4] Previously the one chief event at any festival of the French court had always been a performance by the Ballet de Cour,[5] but on this occasion all the events, plays, banquets, ballets, firework displays and mock combats were conceived as a single work of art.

Louis appointed the Duc de Saint Aignan, the First Gentleman of the King's Bedchamber, as producer-in-chief, and Carlo Vigarani, his court architect and stage designer, was responsible for the decorations. Vigarani's assistant, Israel Sylvestre, recorded the festivities in a series of engravings.

Saint Aignan chose as the main theme the episode from Ariosto's *Orlando furioso* in which Sir Roger (Ruggiero) and his followers are imprisoned by the witch Alcina on her enchanted island. The story was spread over three days.

On the first day the king led the enchanted knights through the park to take part in a *quadrille*. After the performance of p. 11 an allegory there rose through a trap-door a candle-lit banqueting-table at which the royal family and the first peers of the realm dined to music, surrounded by a noble throng. The climax of the second day was the first performance of Molière's comedy-ballet *La Princesse d'Élide*. Elsewhere in p. 11 the park plays and concerts were given. The scene of the third day's performance was an artificial island bearing 11 Alcina's palace. Whales and sea-monsters swam in the lake, giants, dwarves, spirits and demons hindered the knights' escape, and the action was enhanced by lavish ballets. The witch's spell was broken by a magic ring and her palace vanished amid thunder and lightning, or rather, during a gigantic firework display.[6] In addition, on each evening performances were given by Molière and his company.[7]

Vienna, too, was the scene of large, open-air spectacles, combining classical antiquity, the age of chivalry, triumphal processions and carnival. The climax of the celebrations for the marriage in January 1667 of the Emperor Leopold I and the Spanish Infanta Margareta Theresa, daughter of Philip IV, was the cosmic drama *La contesa dell'aria e dell'acqua*, ('battle of the elements'), a glorification of the divine right of princes. In spite of deepening doubts and anxieties about the future of the Hapsburgs as a dominating force in European politics – this marriage was a contributory cause of the War of the Spanish Succession – there was no sign of any uncertainty in the celebrations. The glory of the moment was lived to the full, as if there could be no change.

The greatest artistic talents were assembled for the production of the pageant. The text was by the court poet Francesco Sbarra, and Ludovico Burnacini worked miracles with men and beasts, fire and water, colours and shapes to emphasize the splendour of the occasion. In addition to acting as overall director, Burnacini designed the floats which bore the four elements; the sets and other designs were by Carlo Pasetti and the choreography by Alessandro Carducci.[8]

As for the Roman carnival in honour of Queen Christina, tiers of seats were erected in the main courtyard of the Hofburg and the palace windows served as boxes for the ladies. A great ship 'sailed' through the gate of the Neue Burg, and from its deck Fame proclaimed the theme of the 'Joyous Festival'. The Argonauts challenged the knights of air, fire, water and earth to battle for the Golden Fleece. The four elements quarrelled among themselves, and the knights prepared for battle, but at that moment a splendid temple burst forth from the clouds and from it Eternity addressed the warriors, whereupon 'the guardian spirits of the Roman Emperors of the House of Austria come forth … Thereafter His Imperial Roman Majesty appears at the threshold of the temple as its most invincible genius'.

p. 13

The anonymous eyewitness revels in his description of the magnificent costumes in the equestrian ballet, the curvets, the formation of a double cross and a many-pointed star in the centre of which His Imperial Majesty 'upon his horse curvetted most beautifully without ceasing'. The leading actors in the courtyard of the Hofburg were the nobility, the star was the Emperor. This was the essence of court theatre, the display of power and glory.[9]

Other celebrations on the occasion of this imperial wedding included hunts, sleigh-rides, receptions and performances of plays, operas and ballets by professional artists. The performance of Marc Antonio Cesti's spectacular opera *Il pomo d'oro*, commissioned for the occasion, had to be

Israel Sylvestre *'Plaisirs de l'Isle enchantée'*, *Versailles 1664, first day*

Second day

Ludovico Ottavio Burnacini *Ballet on the lake*, *palace of La Favorita, Vienna c. 1660*

postponed for over a year until the completion of a theatre specially built to accommodate it.

In Dresden in 1676, a family gathering of the royal house of Saxony was celebrated by triumphal processions, tournaments, plays, fireworks and banquets. The festivities culminated in the *Musikalische Opera und Ballett von Wirckung der sieben Planeten*, a ballet of several acts with sung intermezzi, symbolizing the royal meeting by a dance of the seven planets.

The court of Dresden saw many such festivities. The Moorish ballet staged in the Riesensaal for a further assembly of the Saxon princes in 1680, and the procession of the Greek gods, with Endymion and the spirits of the underworld, which marked the accession of Augustus the Strong in 1695, were far exceeded in baroque splendour by the ceremonies devised for the marriage of Augustus' son to the Austrian Archduchess Maria Josefa, daughter of Emperor Joseph I, in 1719.

The rivalry between courts drove them on to ever more dazzling, ever more expensive displays. The *Mercure historique* told the whole of Europe that the pleasure-camp of Augustus the Strong at Mühlberg on the Elbe in 1730 far surpassed that which Louis XIV had held at Compiègne.[10] A series of engravings by the Venetian Andrea Zucchi gives us some idea of Augustus' world.

Every court festival traditionally began with a triumphal procession, designed to overwhelm the spectators from the very start with the magnificence and wealth of the prince. We have Isabella d'Este's account of the fabulous display of the wealth of the two families when Lucretia Borgia married Alfonso d'Este in February 1502 in Ferrara. A gaping crowd

watched the bride's entry into the town accompanied by archers, musicians, ambassadors, prelates, courtiers, her princely relatives and the court fools, all on horseback or in splendid carriages, all dressed magnificently.

The same degree of lavish splendour, but enhanced by the progress of theatrical technique during two centuries, appeared when the Archduchess Maria Josefa entered Dresden in 1719. The *acteurs* numbered nearly two thousand Saxon, Austrian and foreign nobles of all ranks. In Pirna on the Elbe the bride boarded the Bucentaur, a copy of the famous Venetian ship of state, and, attended by a fleet of yachts and gilded gondolas, she sailed down the river to Dresden where she was received by the king. The Postmaster General led the procession into the city, blowing a golden posthorn encrusted with precious stones. He was followed by carriages, huntsmen, archers, the members of the Diet, the General Staff, cavalry, the royal bodyguard, mounted grenadiers, cuirassiers and infantry. The brightly coloured uniforms and liveries were set off by the gold and silver embroidery on the dress of the courtiers. The brilliant climax of the procession was the princess herself, riding alone in a carriage drawn by eight horses, and closely followed by more than one hundred state coaches, each drawn by six horses from the royal stables. Around the carriages pressed footmen, lackeys, Swiss guards and Negro servants.

We can still gain some impression of the splendour of the royal robes, the brilliance of the jewels and the intricate harness from museums, but the exhilarating colours, the movement, music, cheers, salvoes, and the princely self-esteem are lost for ever, only faintly recorded in eyewitness accounts. In our imagination we can still fill the broad

ISRAEL SYLVESTRE AND FRANÇOIS CHAUVEAU *the Duc de Guise in carousel costume as 'King of the Americans', in the Quadrille des Nations, Cour du Louvre, Paris 1662 'Drummer and trumpeter of the Indies' in the Quadrille des Nations, Cour du Louvre, Paris 1662*

II ISRAEL SYLVESTRE *Versailles, 'Plaisirs de l'Isle enchantée'*

Troisiesme

Theatre dressé au milieu du grand Estang
representant l'Isle d'Alcine, ou paroissoit son Palais
enchanté sortant d'vn petit Rocher dans lequel fut dancé
vn Ballet de plusieurs entrées, et apres quoy ce Palais fut
consumé, par vn feu d'Artifice representant la rupture
de l'enchantement apres la fuite de Roger

Journée

Gerard Scitadier, deline, et Sculpsit.

et escudit Cum privilegio Regis.

avenues leading to Louis XIV's palaces with the stately processions that formed whenever the king moved from one to another; a display that was surpassed on greater occasions when, for example, an ambassador was received, not the mere errand-boy of the twentieth century, but the physical embodiment of his sovereign at a foreign court.

Great banquets were an essential part of every festivity, and the joys of the table played as pervasive and universal a role in the life of the seventeenth and eighteenth centuries as the theatre itself.[11] By the end of the middle ages the elaborate dishes prepared for the courts of Burgundy and the Netherlands were internationally famous. Any distinction we might expect to make between gastronomic and aesthetic enjoyment was blurred as song, dance and mime alternated with successive courses. At a dinner given by Cardinal Pietro Riario in honour of Eleanor of Aragon on 7 June 1483, there were 'sugar confections in the shapes of castles, ships and mythological figures, including the tasks of Hercules, artfully contrived'. There were dishes which opened to reveal people inside. Others illustrated the royal visit that was the reason for the feast.[12]

3, pp. 9, 12   Another essential part of each courtly festival was the tournament, though it was in the baroque age a very different affair from what it had been up to the end of the fifteenth century, when the Emperor Maximilian I earned the title of 'last of the knights'. Armed combat had been replaced by trials of skill in tilting and dressage. The ability to batter one's opponent to the ground was no longer prized; one had to impress by the skill with which one handled horse and weapons, and if the skill was concealed by grace and nonchalance, so much the better.

p. 10   The great Italian, and more particularly Florentine, tradition of the tournament lived on in the theatrical display of the Carousel, especially at carnival times. A *guerra di bellezza* took place in Florence in 1616 in honour of the prince of Urbino. Giulio Parigi's fantastic designs for this festival can still be admired in the copper engravings of Jacques Callot. One of the floats carried an island in a vast ornamental pond in which splashed nereids and tritons, to the delight of the spectators.

A more domestic kind of princely pastime had evolved in Vienna since the sixteenth century. The so-called *Wirtschaften*[13] usually took the form of a courtier's idea of a wedding party in a village inn. These parties were particularly popular on Shrove Tuesday, but they were also held for foreign guests, when they would be included among the usual entertainments, sleigh-rides, amateur theatricals and ballets. The royal hosts appeared, suitably dressed, as the landlord and landlady, and the guests and courtiers wore foreign national dress or the costumes of humble tradesmen,

farmers, gardeners, millers, shepherds, cobblers, even of acrobats and pedlars. The hall was decorated as a wood, refreshments were served in booths decked out as farmhouses, and of course there was an inn where the chief guests were entertained. This was more than a fancy-dress party, for the whole was planned like a stage production, with the same attention given to tableaux, entrances, costumes, colours and movement. Leading theatrical designers,

CARLO PASETTI *Equestrian ballet in the Hofburg, Vienna 1667*

including Ludovico Burnacini himself, were employed for the decorations, sets and costumes.

9–11   In countries with the right sort of climate, sledging parties were held, also in fancy-dress. And if the climate was not right, man could assist it. In 1721 Augustus the Strong had peasants bring two thousand cartloads of snow to Dresden so that a sleigh-ride he had planned could take place.

Further south, the equivalent entertainment was the regatta, gondola-racing, which as a spectacle was by no means inferior to sledging. If there was no great lake in the neighbourhood one was created by flooding.   6

Water, flowing or leaping from elaborate and sometimes bizarre fountains, was always to be found in every great park or garden, and was often incorporated into the spectacles. The trick fountains of Schloss Hellbrunn, near Salzburg, concealed in stone seats, were the setting for what we would think a rather coarse comedy performed by the guests for their hosts.   4

In her memoirs Catherine the Great describes a pastoral entertainment she gave in 1758 in the grounds of her Oranienbaum palace to amuse her moody husband Grand Duke Peter Fedorovich.

'I therefore instructed my architect, Antonio Rinaldi, to build, in a distant corner of the wood, a great float which would hold an orchestra of sixty people, musicians and singers. I had verses written by the Italian court poet and music by the court musician, Araja. In the garden, the main avenue was decorated with lights and a curtain was hung, facing the supper table... After the first course the curtain concealing the avenue was raised and we could see approaching from a distance the orchestra on its carriage pulled by a score of oxen, adorned with garlands, and escorted by as many dancers as I had been able to find. The avenue was so well lit that we could see everything clearly. When the float halted, by a happy chance, the light of the moon fell exactly upon it with such exquisite effect that the whole company was amazed... After [the music] had finished we returned to table for the second course. At the end of it we heard fanfares and drumrolls, and a showman made his appearance, crying "Ladies and gentlemen, roll up, roll up, you will find free lotteries in my booths." On either side of the curtains two little curtains were raised and there we saw two brightly lit stalls, in one of which they were giving away lottery tickets for the porcelain ware it held, and in the other for flowers, ribbons, fans, combs, brushes, gloves, swordknots and other knick-knacks of that kind. When the stalls were empty we sat down to dessert, and then danced till six in the morning.'[14]

I, IV   The great popularity of the pastoral in the later baroque age must have been due to its dual function as conscious display and as unconscious escapism. In times of war the idyll was a welcome refuge from realities and gave an opportunity to play at life from a new, amusing angle. Romantic yearnings found satisfaction in Arcadia, melancholy found solace and freedom from care.

Ernst Ahasuerus Lehndorf, a chamberlain to the Queen of Prussia, gives a description in his diary on 26 June 1750 of a pastoral performed at Rheinsberg.

'In the evening the prince gave his last entertainment, which was a feast for the eyes. At nine o'clock Reisewitz, attired as Neptune, went to fetch the Prince of Prussia and Ferdinand in a boat decorated with shells and rushes, lit from stem to stern, and surrounded by boys dressed as tritons ... When we reached the little stage in the hall, we found the Countess Dönhoff dressed as Queen of the Night; she drew a curtain and revealed a marvellous spectacle: Her Royal Highness and her ladies as the nymphs of Diana, little Madame Forcade as the goddess, surrounded by twelve young girls elegantly dressed, standing in niches ... After supper we returned with the same pomp to the water, where we found refreshments in an artistically contrived arbour.'[15]

The lyings-in-state and the funerals of the baroque age were no less theatrical than its amusements, macabre though they may seem to us. Until the French revolution the abbey church of St Denis contained life-size wax models of the kings of France, from Charles VII to Louis XIII, bearing sceptres and wearing crowns and red robes.[16] The wax model would be displayed on a bier in a hall of state, homage would be paid to it, and the court would take their places at a dining-table strictly according to etiquette. A meal was served, but the food was taken away again untouched. Princess Charlotte Elizabeth of the Palatinate had to lie in state herself when her husband, Louis XIV's brother Philip of Orléans, died. On 9 June 1701 she received James II of England and his wife, Mary of Modena, wearing full mourning, lying on a black bed, in a room totally furnished and decorated in black.

When the last surviving Medici, Anna Maria Louisa, sister of the last Grand Duke, widow of the Elector Palatine Johann Wilhelm, died in Florence in 1743, the stairwells and rooms of the Palazzo Pitti were hung with black. The princess herself was placed on a throne in her richest robes, with the crown on her head. For three days she sat to receive homage for the last time, surrounded by ladies-in-waiting and ministers in mourning. Even in death, greatness had to be displayed.

The courts and the nobility were more than passive spectators and amateur actors, carried away by delight in flaunting their own personality: without their patronage and support the art of the professional theatre could never have reached the heights it did in the seventeenth and eighteenth centuries. The theatre was necessary to the prince to embody his vision of himself, to give life to his dreams of power, influence and immortality. The earliest patrons of the baroque theatre were the most powerful of the European courts: London, Madrid, Versailles and Vienna.

While it is true that the characteristics of the baroque theatre first emerged in Spain, perhaps because that country lacked the kind of Renaissance theatre that had established itself more firmly elsewhere, the developments in the London theatre throughout the reign of Elizabeth I, from her accession in 1558 to her death in 1603, were so important for the development of the theatre and of drama that Elizabeth must be considered the first of the great patrons of the baroque theatre.

Her Catholic predecessor Mary I had preferred morality plays, but under Elizabeth secular entertainments, particularly the masque, were favoured at court. Well-known poets were commissioned to write the texts for the allegories, pastorals and masques that the courtiers themselves performed, accommodating their personalities to those imposed by the masks they wore. This informed interest in the theatre on the part of the highest in the land, as actors, spectators and critics, created a climate in which the theatrical arts flourished.

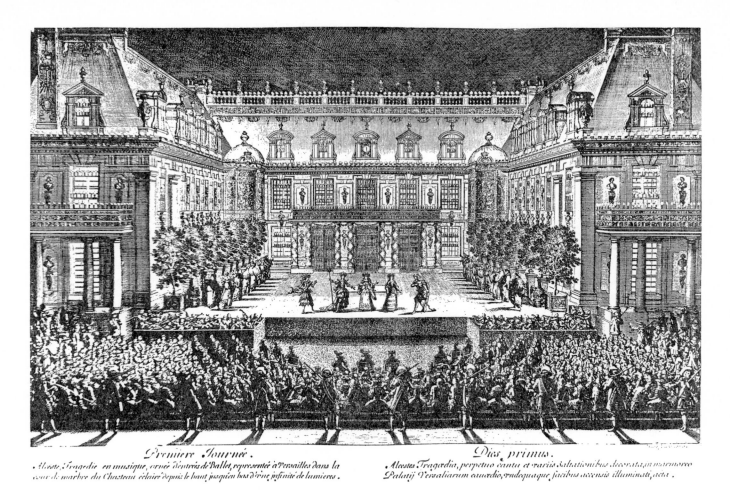

Premiere Journée. *Dies primus.*
Alceste, Tragedie en musique, ornée d'entrées de Ballet, representée à Versailles dans la Alcestes Tragœdia, perpetuo cantu et variis saltationibus decorata, in marmoreo cour de marbre du Chasteau éclairé depuis le haut jusqu'en bas d'une infinité de lumieres. Palatij Versaliarum cavædio, undequaque facibus accensis illuminati, acta.

JEAN LE PAUTRE '*Alceste*', *by Lully and Quinault, in the Cour de Marbre, Versailles 1676*

Elizabeth encouraged dramatic activities in schools and universities, where the emphasis was on the drama of the Greeks and Romans and on the neoclassical drama of the Renaissance humanists. In 1564 Cambridge students were invited to play before her, and her visit to Oxford in 1566 was the occasion of several performances, paid for from the privy purse. Thus undergraduate actors received material support while they learned from experience where they could improve on the neo-Latin drama as well as perfect its performance and production. The stage was erected for the occasion in the college hall, or even the chapel. The monarch, and individual noblemen, supported their own troupes of professional players who were paid a retainer and spent much of their time on tour.

Elizabeth never set foot in a public theatre; it would have been unthinkable for any lady at that time. She neither performed on the stage nor wrote for it but her patronage and

interest played an important part in the creation of the great works of her age. She commanded the writing of a 'Falstaff in Love' which became the exuberant *Merry Wives of Windsor*.

Elizabeth's Stuart successors began to take an active part in plays and masques. Henrietta Maria, the French wife of Charles I, often appeared on the stage at court, and from that time onwards there is evidence that all over Europe royalty appeared with success in both singing and speaking roles, and that histrionic ability became one of the essential courtly arts. Louis XIV danced in ballets, and in the following century the future Empress Maria Theresa took part in pastorals, tragedies and intermezzi, naturally not before the public, but in private performances at court.

In England London was the centre of theatrical activity; in Spain the picture was very different. Many cities and towns besides Madrid had theatres, and support from the court was of less decisive importance than it was in Paris or Vienna. On the other hand the particular development of Calderón as a court playwright would have been impossible without the patronage of Philip IV.

One is liable to think that classical French drama began in the reign of Louis XIV, so closely associated with him are the names of the principal dramatists. But in actively patronizing literature Louis XIV was merely following a precedent set in the preceding reign by Cardinal Richelieu, minister of Louis XIII. Richelieu had a theatre built in his own palace (later the Palais Royal), for which a committee of five distinguished authors, including Pierre Corneille, wrote plays. He carried his interest in the theatre to the point of working on a play himself in collaboration with Jean Desmarets de Saint Sorlin. In 1635 he founded the Académie Française to refine the French language and literary taste. It has exercised considerable influence on the vocabulary of literary French through its famous dictionary; and initially there was even an ill-starred attempt by Richelieu to turn it into an official tribunal of dramatic criticism by requiring it to pass judgement on Corneille's *Le Cid*.

p. 89

Louis XIV's acts of patronage were numerous. He particularly favoured Molière's company of actors and allowed them the use of the Salle du Petit Bourbon. Almost his first act at the beginning of his effective rule, in 1661, was the founding of the Académie Royale de Danse, and his taste for ballet led to the development of a new genre, the *comédie-ballet*. From *Le Mariage forcé* (1664) Molière worked with the court composer Lully, the climax of their collaboration being *Le Bourgeois Gentilhomme* (1670). The operatic and balletic *intermèdes* were performed by the old-established Ballet de Cour, which received a new lease of life from the partnership. After a breach between playwright and composer in 1671, the Ballet de Cour went into a long decline, while the *comédie-ballet* itself strengthened its popularity, maintaining as it did a perfect balance of its two elements. Louis also founded in 1672, at first under the name of Académie des Opéras, the Académie Royale de Musique, which still flourishes as the Paris Opéra. Louis took a close interest in the early development of the French opera, approving new projects and attending nearly every new production. He gave Molière's company the title of Troupe du Roi, and later commanded its amalgamation with the Grands Comédiens de l'Hôtel de Bourgogne; this combined company received a royal subsidy of twelve thousand francs a year, its director was appointed by the king, and it became the official court theatre. From 1689 to the present day it has borne the name of Comédie Française.

5

Louis XV's patronage of the theatre was not on such a large scale as that of his great-grandfather Louis XIV, but he particularly favoured the strolling players of the *théâtres de la foire*, and he had a theatre built in the palace of Versailles, equipped for the production of lavish spectacles. France was not divided into small principalities like eighteenth-century Germany, nor into city states like Italy. Paris was the one focal point to which the great noble families looked for their social life. It was here that *salons* and private theatres flourished in the eighteenth century.

'In the second half of the eighteenth century all classes of French society were stage-struck. The craze reached from the *petits appartements* at Versailles to the dramatic societies of the Rue du Marais and the Rue de Popincourt. A small theatre was installed in every great town house, a large one in every *château*... Society favoured two playwrights: M. de Moissy, who paints a comedy of manners in water-colours, and Carmontelle, a satirist in gouache. Great ladies could no longer survive without their own theatre or stage... At the Théâtre de Monsieur the historical dramas of Desfontaines and the comedies of Piis and Barré were performed; at the Théâtre du Temple, in the residence of the Prince de Conti, Jean-Jacques Rousseau put on his opera *Les Muses galantes*... The theatre of L'Ile-Adam, where Arnaud's drama *Le comte de Comminges* made all the ladies weep. Madame de Montesson acted in her own plays and proved to be no mean actress ... At the theatre of the Duchesse de Villeroy, where the Comédie Française gave a preview of *l'Honnête Criminel* ... At the Duchesse de Mazarin's theatre in Chilly, she had *La Partie de chasse d'Henri IV* performed for her ladies. At M. de Vaudreuil's theatre in Gennevilliers *Le mariage de Figaro* received its first performance; at the theatre of the Duc d'Ayen in Saint-Germain the duke's daughter, the Comtesse de Tessé, and the Comte d'Ayen displayed their talent in a play by Lessing translated by M. Trudaine.'[17]

Italy, unlike France, was a collection of independent sovereign states, each with its court and capital city. The rivalry between them produced an unusually vigorous and varied theatrical life.

Alfonso II d'Este, Duke of Ferrara 1559–97, a great patron of the theatre, employed Giovanni Battista Aleotti (1546 to 1636), a stage designer and architect of genius. His sister Lucretia d'Este, employed Niccolo Sabbatini (c. 1574–1654), another who practised both arts of architecture and stage design, and who probably built the theatre in Modena.

Ranuccio I Farnese ordered the building of the Teatro Farnese in Parma (1618–19), one of the largest and most resplendent baroque theatres in Europe. He commissioned Monteverdi to compose intermezzi and a masque for the wedding of Duke Odoardo Farnese in 1628.

105–7, after p. 160

The meteoric rise of Italian opera would have been impossible without the patronage of the Barberini family. The theatre in their *palazzo* in Rome seated an audience of over

1   FILIPPO GAGLIARDI *Carnival in honour of Queen Christina, Rome 1656*

2   LUDOVICO OTTAVIO BURNACINI *Carnival float,*
Vienna

17

3 ANON. *Sketch for festival costume, Paris seventeenth century*

4 *'Roman theatre' with trick fountains, Schloss Hellbrunn near Salzburg 1613–19*

III GEORGES
DESMARÉES
Maximilian III Joseph,
Elector of Bavaria,
and his theatre
comptroller,
Count Seeau

5 HYACINTHE RIGAUD
Louis XV of France
in his coronation robes

three thousand, and enabled glittering productions of works they had themselves commissioned. They employed Bernini for the decoration of the theatre and Francesco Gutti to design scenery and stage machinery.

'A future pope [Clement IX] writes operas and sends sonnets to opera-singers. Cardinals are librettists, producers, sometimes even costumiers ... Salvator Rosa takes part in comedies. Bernini writes operas for which he paints the scenery, models the statuary, devises the machines, writes the dialogue, sets it to music, all in addition to building the theatre.'[18]

As the French nobility followed the king in supporting private theatres, so in Italy the smaller princes modelled themselves on the great ones and had theatres built in their palaces, partly for amateur performances, partly for the use of professional touring companies. A description of one of these private theatres in the eighteenth century is found in the memoirs of Giuseppe Tomasi, Prince of Lampedusa. Seating about three hundred people, it was decorated in white and gold in the Louis XVI style.

Opera evolved its essential characteristics in the work of Jacopo Peri (1561–1633), *maestro di capella* and theatre intendant to Duke Ferdinand I Medici in Florence. For the celebrations at the wedding of Catherine de' Medici and Henry IV of France in 1600, Peri and the librettist Ottavio Rinuccini wrote the *tragedia per musica, Euridice,* the earliest surviving opera. Vincenzo Gonzaga, Duke of Mantua, was among the wedding guests and was sufficiently impressed by the new genre to encourage it at his own court. Cardinal Ferdinando Gonzaga wrote opera libretti, and Monteverdi began his career at the Mantuan court, and it was Eleanora Gonzaga, wife of the Austrian Emperor Ferdinand II, who introduced the *dramma per musica* to the Viennese court.

Vienna competed with the French court throughout the seventeenth and eighteenth centuries for international preeminence, and the magnificence and variety of its theatre was an important symbol of its power. From the very start opera was a great success in Vienna and for the Emperor's birthday and all such festivities the theatrical entertainment consisted chiefly of performances of Italian opera and of the *commedia dell'arte* by Italian dancers and singers.

Monteverdi's *Il ritorno d'Ulisse in patria* received one of its earliest performances in Vienna – the manuscript score is in the Austrian National Library – and the works of his pupil Francesco Cavalli were very popular there. Ferdinand III summoned the elder Burnacini, Giovanni, as stage designer to the court. Burnacini built the first theatre in the Hofburg and designed a prefabricated wooden theatre for a Diet of the German princes at Regensburg in 1653.

During the reign of Leopold I, from 1658 to 1705, the performance of plays at court became a regular occurrence,

ANON. *Hobby-horse ballet performed by children, Vienna seventeenth century*

whereas formerly they had only been given on special occasions. The ladies of the court, as well as noblemen, took part in plays; and sometimes the Emperor himself conducted an opera. On Fridays plays with a religious subject were performed and a *sacra rappresentazione*[19] was presented in the royal chapel. Puppet plays were given for the children. Previously operas had been written for a particular occasion and received only one performance, but now they were repeated and performances of operas, as of plays, became frequent. This necessitated the employment of librettists, composers, stage designers, singers, costumiers, instrumentalists and conductors. At the time of Charles VI's accession in 1711, the staff of the Vienna court theatre included Ferdinando Galli-Bibiena, one of the earlier members of a family of theatre designers which became famous throughout Europe.

The growth of interest in the theatre did not mean that all theatres were open every night of the year. The theatre

M. BODENEHR *Ballet scene from 'Camillo Generoso', Dresden 1693*

was affected by the seasonal habits of the court. Each summer Their Imperial Majesties, with their entourage including actors, singers, composers and designers, moved out of Vienna to one or other of their country seats. Here the parks and lakes were used to their best advantage as the settings for open-air performances of all kinds, including aquatic operas and ballets. In the autumn the court returned to the Hofburg. During Advent all theatrical performances were forbidden, but from Christmas to Shrove Tuesday was an unbroken carnival in which the theatre came into its own.

p. 225 The crown gave all the most important commissions for theatre buildings, for the enormous theatre on the Cortina, for theatres in the Hofburg, the summer palace of La Favorita, 124–8 and the new palace of Schönbrunn, built in the 1740s. No other capital could rival the theatrical variety of Vienna; but its influence, and the rivalry between lesser courts, served to make standards extremely high.

p. 126 The production of *Il pomo d'oro* with which the Cortina theatre opened on the birthday of Leopold I's Empress, the Infanta Margaret, 12 July 1668, was one of the highest achievements of the baroque court theatre. When Maria Theresa began her long reign in 1740 the great age of the Viennese baroque theatre was over and it was being replaced by the more intimate theatre of the rococo age. Pomp and vast spectacle gave way to sparkle and delicacy. The Empress preferred French theatre and ballet to the Italian, and French replaced Italian as the language spoken at court. Young Austrian noblemen, for whom a visit to Paris was an essential part of their education, gave performances of French plays in the French style of presentation which they had learned there. Maria Theresa commissioned comic operas in the 12 French manner from Gluck, and even took a hand in the planning of the repertory. Even the Viennese tradition of light comedy and operetta owes its existence to her moral rectitude, which caused her to ban the lewd improvisatory theatre which had been the common people's entertainment until then.

49 There is a sequence of paintings on the Narrentreppe ('fools' staircase') in Burg Trausnitz, near Landshut in Bavaria, which shows that the *commedia dell'arte* was established at the Electoral court in Munich as early as the sixteenth century. Thanks to Henrietta Adelaide of Savoy, the wife of the Elector Ferdinand Maria (reigned 1651–79), Italian opera became the principal entertainment at court. The Italian architect Santurini built the Salvatortheater, the first theatre in Germany to stand on an independent site outside the confines of a palace. The Venetian stage designer Francesco Mauro and his sons Domenico and Gasparo came to Munich and helped to inaugurate a great period in theatrical history. Ferdinand Maria's successor Maximilian II Emmanuel (1679

to 1726), however, preferred French theatre and French music and obliged the Venetians to conform to the more severe French style.

Maximilian III Joseph (1745–77) commissioned the building of the theatre in the Residenz, his Munich palace, by François de Cuvilliés. Mozart composed *Idomeneo* with sets by Lorenzo Quaglio for the next Elector, Charles Theodore of the Palatinate, but in 1787 the latter forbade the production of any more Italian operas. Baroque and rococo court theatre in Bavaria came to an end in his reign and henceforth only German plays, *Singspiele* and German operas were allowed. III pp. 181, 183, 177–185, XVI

John George II, Elector of Saxony, had an opera house built in Dresden by Wolf Kaspar von Klengel, which was opened in 1667. For Augustus the Strong the court of Louis XIV was the model; a French troupe was engaged to play Corneille, Molière and Racine, and by 1697 the new Kleines Komödienhaus saw frequent productions of works in the French style. A pioneer of French fashions in Germany, the Saxon court was later one of the first to encourage German drama. The French style lasted longest in Berlin, where Frederick the Great (1740–86) refused ever to see a play performed in German.

The smaller German principalities followed the same fashions as their larger neighbours. One interesting individual development was the so-called Bayreuth Rococo, which evolved through the personal endeavour of the Margravine Wilhelmina. This highly cultured and intelligent woman, the sister of Frederick the Great, played several musical instruments and wrote two operas, *Deukalion und Pyrrha* and *Semiramis*, as well as a number of pastoral intermezzi, in collaboration with the Bavarian court musical director *(Kapellmeister)*, Andrea Bernasconi. Under her patronage the rococo theatre passed through one of its most delightful phases. She was responsible for the picturesque open-air theatres in the park of the Eremitage and the Sans Pareil gardens outside Bayreuth, and her permanent memorial is the lovely Markgräfliches Opernhaus in Bayreuth itself. 89–91 163, 165–175, XIV, XV

Another minor German state, the archbishopric of Salzburg, is thought to have had the very first performance of an opera in any of the German-speaking countries, in 1618. The first German opera was Heinrich Schütz's *Daphne*, the libretto being a free translation and adaptation by the poet Martin Opitz of Rinuccini's text for Peri's *Dafne*. It was written for the marriage in 1627 of George, Landgrave of Hesse-Darmstadt, and Sophia Eleanora of Saxony. A neighbouring prince, Landgrave Maurice the Learned of Hesse, a friend of Henry IV of France, wrote plays after the model of Terence and his palace was famous for the Ottonium, the first structure in Germany built exclusively as a theatre.

GIUSEPPE GALLI-BIBIENA *Scene from the opera 'Costanza e Fortezza', open-air theatre on the Hradčany, Prague 1723*

p. 179 Another early royal patron of the theatre in Germany was Henry Julius, Duke of Brunswick. His own plays, based on Terence, are either heavily didactic or crudely, brutally humorous, and belong to the Renaissance theatre rather than to the baroque. His court was one of the first to be visited by English travelling players in the 1590s, and he employed Thomas Sackville to direct his own court troupe from 1593 to 1598.

It was probably the comparative poverty of the court of Brunswick during the Thirty Years War that caused Duchess Sophia Elizabeth, a princess of Mecklenburg-Güstrow and a pupil of Schütz, to compose herself *Ein neu erfundenes Freudenspiel, genannt Friedens-Sieg* ('A newly invented comedy, called the Triumph of Peace') in 1642, which also gave her sons an opportunity to shine as librettists, directors or singers.

Theatre-mania was as enduring in Germany as elsewhere; the pocket-handkerchief principalities were as stage-struck in the eighteenth century as Parisian *salons* and Italian states.

Gustav III of Sweden (1771–92) was a more than usually keen devotee. He had two theatres, in his palaces of Drottningholm and Gripsholm, and wrote plays far better than anything else that was being written in Sweden at the time, and which were performed until well into the nineteenth century. 158–160, X, XIII

The court in Prague aped Vienna in everything, but apart from the open-air theatres on the Hradčany, the great hill on which stand the citadel and the cathedral, its interest in the theatre was less intense.

A late blossoming of patronage occured among the Hungarian nobility, who were less dependent upon Vienna than the Bohemians. During the eighteenth century many of them built private theatres in their summer residences – of course they spent the winter in Vienna – and employed the best available theatrical talents for their own companies. They also engaged troupes of travelling players, who were only too pleased to find such high-born audiences in summertime. The most famous of these Hungarian patrons were the Esterhazys. Prince Nicholas the Magnificent created a vast fairy-tale palace, Esterháza, on the shores of the Neusiedlersee. His first theatre was built in his park. The stage equipment was designed by Carlo Quaglio, and entertainments as good as any in Europe were given in honour of Maria Theresa, the Archduke Ferdinand and Princess Beatrice d'Este. In 1761, a year before his death, Prince Nicholas' father had engaged Joseph Haydn as his director of music, and Nicholas earned immortality by his continued patronage of the composer. The vast majority of Haydn's works received their first performance at Esterhazy. As well as the main theatres there was a puppet theatre in which Haydn's *Philemon und Baucis* had its first performance.

During the Seven Years War, Augustus III of Saxony, son of Augustus the Strong, and like his father elected king of Poland, moved his seat of government from Dresden to Warsaw. Here the court was able to pursue its theatrical interests in peacetime conditions, and the great Polish nobles – the Branickes in Bialystok, the Lubomirskis in Cracow, the Oginskis in Slonim – eagerly followed suit. The theatre founded by Princess Ursula Francesca Radziwil in Nieswiez is particularly noteworthy because, not content with giving Italian opera and both French and German plays, she set out to introduce the Polish language on to the stage. She translated plays from French and German, notably those of Molière, and in her own comedies she laid the foundations of a national Polish drama.

On his travels in Western Europe, Peter the Great of Russia became acquainted with Italian and German opera and the French *tragédie lyrique*. He was particularly impressed by the German theatre and took back to Russia a company to perform German plays. But a far greater passion for the theatre was shown by his niece, Anna Ivanovna. She even had an astonishing transportable theatre which could be erected, with all its stage machinery and seats for the audience, in whichever of her palaces she happened to be occupying.

Thus we see Russia following the same pattern as other European courts: a progression from Italian opera and comedy to French drama, opera and ballet, and to German plays, all performed by travelling players from the countries of origin. The wealth of the Russian Empire made theatre on the grandest scale possible, and the desire for prestige in the eyes of Europe made it necessary. The Europeanized court theatre in Russia probably reached its zenith under the Empress Elizabeth Petrovna (1741–62). The first permanent theatre in Russia was built in St Petersburg in 1756, and Elizabeth also paved the way for a Russian national drama by her patronage of Alexander Petrovich Sumarokov (1718–77), the leading playwright of the age.

Catherine the Great (1762–96), taking Shakespeare's comedies and histories as her model, wrote elegant and well-turned comedies which in particular ridiculed the reactionary, bigoted, credulous, vain and idle women of her time and country. Her male targets included dandies, fops and socialites. She hoped to reform Russian society and bring it up to date with the changes in European life and thought which came with the Enlightenment. Like Elizabeth, she admitted the general public to the court theatre.

Eighteenth-century monarchs engaged actors and other theatrical personnel, subsidized companies, built theatres and patronized writers and musicians. Their own direct contributions to the arts of opera and straight drama are neglected now, but their example and encouragement were of crucial historical importance. They set their seal of approval where it was deserved and destroyed abuses by the finger of scorn. Theirs was among the most powerful influences on the theatre of the baroque age; although as we shall see, they were not the only arbiters of taste and fashion.

IV JEAN-HONORÉ FRAGONARD *Festivity at St Cloud. Puppet theatre*

6   GIOVANNI PAOLO PANNINI *Aquatic festival on the Piazza Navona, Rome 1756*

7 JEAN MICHEL MOREAU
LE JEUNE
*Festival with
illuminations*

8 GIOVANNI PAOLO
PANNINI
*Concert in honour
of the birth of
the Dauphin, Paris
1729*

9 *Sledge belonging to Frederick II of Prussia, eighteenth century*

10   *Sledging on the Mehlmarkt, Vienna, eighteenth century*

11   *Sledge belonging to Maria Theresa of Austria*

Dessiné par J. M. Moreau le jeune.   et Gravé par de Launay, le jeune en 1777.

14 *Group outside the Chinesisches Haus, Sanssouci, Potsdam 1755*

ANON. *Strolling players, France, early seventeenth century*

II The Public

The masterpieces of European drama were born of the complex interaction of stage and public, élite and common people. Shakespeare's public, for instance, must surely have been endowed with an intelligence and imagination that were themselves creative, for otherwise it is hardly conceivable p. 119 that high drama on a bare stage could have been so successful in a public theatre. By giving his audiences '*What you will*' and '*As you like it*', Shakespeare gathered support from all sections of the public, who not only demanded a steady supply of new plays, but had such good memories that after hearing a play a couple of times they could, and did, prompt the actor who forgot his part.

For Lope de Vega, in Spain, the audience was no less important.

'Off stage, without an audience, without the press of the Spanish public and its restless, sympathetic participation, he lacked something. In the months of court mourning, when the public theatres were closed, it seems that his creative work ceased too. He needed the contact with actors and audiences.'[1]

In Spanish public theatres the men stood in the pit, women were segregated in the galleries, gentlefolk had seats. The prices were low, so that everybody could afford to visit the theatre frequently.

'This inquisitive, thrill-seeking crowd, a thousand people crammed together at a time, was Lope's most important public. Today one might think such people a half-educated, ignorant urban rabble. But it was not so. Today's undiscriminating public, which has heard or read snippets of everything under the sun, has studied nothing in depth; a disparate, atomized public of that kind did not exist in the Spain of Lope's day. The vision of those play-goers was perhaps narrower in range, but it was clearer, more unified, more firmly-based, and their taste and judgment so much the more certain. Their parents and grand-parents and their church had reared them as Christians, Spaniards and patriots. They knew exactly what to think about God, eternity, the state, the nobility, marriage, love and courtship; they knew all about the battles and the legends of Spanish heroes and their deeds, about Spanish supremacy and the Spanish-American empire; grounded on faith, their opinions and concepts were unshakeable. Lope's audience was no proletariat, but a people and, if the play rose to a spiritual plane, a congregation, passionately involved and prayerful.'[2]

This public demanded ever more plays from him, tormented, cheered and inspired him.

Not every country produced a Shakespeare or a Lope de Vega. But even when no poet dominated the stage, when scenery, lighting and stage effects demanded the most attention, the public's taste could still influence and enrich the theatre.

Razullo.   Cucurucu.

JACQUES CALLOT *Commedia dell'arte*

A history of the theatre is also a history of audiences and of their sociology. What does the public want to see? What circumstances in the outside world give rise to which plays? Must plays always provide a contrast to ordinary life, or should they disti its essence? The question might be simplified and answered by statistics (what plays were a success at what time?) But even then, different sets of conclusions could be drawn from the same answers.

For example, in the Elizabethan age, England was enjoying a period of expansion and power, and the public wanted to see great historical subjects on the stage, to share the experiences of heroism and enthusiasm and to condemn villainy. Naturally there could only be praise for the reigning sovereign. On the other hand, when patriotic themes came to prominence in Calderón's plays, the theatre presented a nostalgic audience with a retrospective dream, a substitute and compensation for their country's failing grasp on world power. The plays had similar themes to the English histories, but the climate in which they flowered was very different.

Placards to inform the public that a theatrical performance was to take place were being used in Spain, by Cosme di Oviedo,[3] as early as 1561. Later, from about 1638, it was more common to use a crier, who processed through the town accompanied by actors in costume to arouse interest and curiosity.[4] In London at the beginning of the seventeenth century, a flag was raised at the Globe theatre to announce a performance. Playbills were of course distributed freely; they advertised the programme and time and place of the pp. 98, 99 performance, gave the names of the company and of their patron. Sometimes there was also a short synopsis of the action.

Every member of the audience was an amateur but vociferous and passionate critic. The *mosqueteros*, the Spanish groundlings, were so dreaded that playwrights often wrote placatory prologues. The groundlings in London created similar embarrassments for the actors and even for some members of the audience. To express their disapproval they used all imaginable kinds of missiles, including bad fruit and eggs, and also employed squeaking whistles known as cat-calls. As the theatre spread from the great cities, as professional players began to travel, this boisterous form of criticism spread everywhere too. The public in Southern Europe was always more vehement in the expression of its opinions than the sluggish northerners. In Madrid passions were known to boil over in pitched battles between the supporters of opposing points of view.[5]

Even if not actually shouting or throwing things, members of the audience made no attempt to conceal their mood. If they thought the performance was good they listened, but performances lasting six to eight hours, as an opera might with ballets and knock-about farcical interludes between acts, could not hold the spectator's attention all the time. So he would bring his supper with him, or buy something in the auditorium itself. 'The women put sweets in their purses, to nibble during the action or to throw at the back of the gentlemen's necks, from which the reader can judge that at that time the men sat in front.'[6]

It was a hard time for actors. If the spectators were not eating they were chattering. They received visitors in their boxes while the play was in progress. The pictures of after p. 44, 13 Moreau le jeune give a very vivid idea of the sort of thing that went on in the eighteenth century. They kept their hats on and blocked the view of others, who were doubtless loud in their complaints. The behaviour was the same at all social levels, the differences being only in the volume and the mode of expression. Politeness towards such a low form of social life as the professional actor was not expected, either in the court or in the public theatres, by even the strictest form of etiquette. Only accomplishment could win attention. Madame de Sévigné found it worthy of mention, in a letter to her daughter Madame de Grignan dated 21 February 1689, that at the performance of Racine's *Esther* at Saint-Cyr 'the attention with which the Marshal and I listened to the tragedy was noticed.' A small proportion of the nobility were people of intellect and education, but the greater number of courtiers would take good note of the king's reactions and follow his example. If he laughed, they laughed; if he clapped, they clapped; if he appeared to suppress a yawn, no matter how much they might have been enjoying themselves, they yawned.

Until the end of the eighteenth century, nearly all performances at court took place with the auditorium as brightly lit as the stage. The spectator wanted to be seen and to play his own part. An exception to this rule was found in Venice, where opera audiences put enjoyment of the performance above their own act and the auditorium was darkened.

Theatrical criticism in print started relatively late in the theatre's history, with the *Gazette* founded in 1631 by Théophraste Renaudot under Richelieu's patronage. De Visé's *Mercure Galant* (later *Mercure de France*), founded in 1672 as a social and artistic weekly, gave comprehensive critical reviews of plays, productions and performers in France. Both these journals are important source material for theatrical history.[7] A theatrical paper, *The Prompter*, was founded in England in 1734. It lasted only two years, but from that time theatre criticism appeared in other journals. Discussion of the merit, or lack of merit, of a play or production was not the preserve of members of literary clubs or frequenters of the *salons*, it was wide-spread and general.

One of the most valuable collections of eighteenth-century critical writing on the theatre is the *Hamburgische Dramaturgie* p. 96 of Gotthold Ephraim Lessing (1729–81). Between 1767 and 1769, when he was already established both as a theorist and as a playwright, Lessing was in Hamburg as literary consultant to the newly founded Nationaltheater and published weekly his views on current or forthcoming productions. Often the piece under review was only the pretext for an essay on Aristotelian or other theory. The value of these essays lies in the fact that they are the informed, if biased, views of an eighteenth-century dramatist, criticizing, for instance, what he considered to be the slavish and uncomprehending observance of the unities of time, place and action shown by French playwrights and contrasting it with the spread of time and place and diversity of action of Shakespeare. Lessing was both a representative and a leader of thought in his age, and even if he had been less, the *Hamburgische Dramaturgie* would still be valuable for the picture it gives of a progressive theatre company at the moment when the international theatre of the baroque age was beginning to give way to the national theatres of the romantic era.

Official censorship of the theatre began during the eighteenth century, and its rise was symptomatic of changes in society and the age. In the seventeenth century the sovereign permitted or forbade as he pleased. Then it was still possible to see at a glance just about the whole of what was going on in the theatre. Certain limiting principles were laid down, and followed. Spiritual and temporal authority was sacred, and moral concepts were clearly defined and generally accepted. But in the eighteenth century religious doubt and the obvious decay of political institutions gave rise to attacks on the established order. In the theatre they took the form of satire and burlesque. Abuses were brought to light and discussed, even though in elevated language and disguised in fables. Hypocrisy, false sensibility, social injustice, were held up to scorn on the stage, and even subjects which had hitherto not been presented on stage at all. The authorities instituted censorship to prevent attacks on themselves and on established morality and order. It was introduced in France in 1702,[8] in England by the Theatre Bill of 1736 and the Licensing Act[9] of 1737. As the century wore on, censorship, particularly in France and the German states, became more complete, strict and narrow-minded, necessarily so in view of the crumbling autocracy it was designed to protect. By contrast, in England, where the monarchy was both less powerful and more secure than its European contemporaries, satire and criticism were allowed more freedom.

In sixteenth century England public theatres were hardly ever visited by noblemen and never by noblewomen. The reputation of the theatre was such that no virtuous woman was seen there. When ladies did begin to attend public performances they wore masks to avoid recognition. The ladies

painted on the balcony of the Teatro Olimpico in Sabbioneta are in a court, that is private, theatre, and would not have attended a public one until during the seventeenth century.

The accommodation for spectators in the public theatres of Elizabethan England was arranged with class distinctions in mind, an arrangement that was maintained throughout the seventeenth century. Members of the upper classes were seated in the galleries, the lower classes stood crowded together in the pit, where seats or benches were rare. This made it possible for theatres to hold between two and three thousand spectators. In some theatres gentlemen were given seats on the stage itself, sometimes in such numbers that they got in the actors' way. This absurd practice was continued into the eighteenth century in some of the smaller theatres of Northern Europe, as can be seen from contemporary illustrations.[10]

Ordinary people were hardly ever admitted to court theatres in the seventeenth century. The king or prince sat on

F. Chauvel and N. Cochin *Fair at Guibray, near Falaise 1685, detail*

a throne immediately in front of the stage, his peers about him.

'Let (the prince's seat) be placed as close as possible to the focus point, and on a level with the vanishing point, let it be surrounded by a balustrade of stout wood so that no harm may result from the press of the people, who on such occasions are used to take little consideration. About it may be placed seats for his courtiers or for the soldiers of his bodyguard, as they may please.'[11]

Only in the eighteenth century, as it became more customary for members of the middle classes to be admitted to theatrical events that had originally been reserved for the nobility, did a new kind of seating arrangement become necessary. The seat of the prince was moved to a special box, so that in spite of the crowd he remained splendid and aloof. The earlier arrangement can still be seen in the court theatres at Potsdam and Drottningholm where the king and his most distinguished guests sat in the front row. But these theatres were intended exclusively for performances before the court. The auditoria of most surviving eighteenth-century theatres are dominated by the royal box in the centre, from which tiers of other boxes and seats fan outwards.

The admission of the middle classes to court theatres began at the end of the seventeenth and in the first half of the eighteenth century. The upkeep of a theatre is expensive and the courts could and would no longer find the large sums necessary for the style of theatre to which they were accustomed. The price of a ticket and suitably festive clothing superseded pedigree as the conditions on which people were admitted to the court theatres. It was the money of the middle classes that opened the doors to them, it was their money that maintained the theatres and eventually it was their tastes and standards that prevailed there.

In Vienna it was Maria Theresa, on the advice of her *Intendant*, who opened her court theatre to the paying public. The court theatre in Stuttgart began in 1777 to sell tickets at subscription rates for a whole season's productions as well as tickets for single performances, and in Brunswick, too, the court opera house accepted the support of the duke's subjects.

The distinction preserved between the different levels in the social hierarchy in a court theatre can be seen clearly in the delightful Altes Residenztheater in Munich, designed by François de Cuvilliés in the 1750s. On the dress circle (*piano nobile*), on a level with the royal box, are the boxes for the highest-ranking nobles. Smiling caryatids support the ceiling, red draperies and dainty garlands decorate the front of these boxes. Because of the width of the hooped skirts worn at the time when the theatre was opened there was room in each box for only two seats. The ladies occupied these while the gentlemen had to stand behind them.

In the décor of the tier above, heads peep out of elaborate frames at the lesser nobility, musical instruments recall the function of the room, and weapons the martial feats of the spectators themselves. The uppermost and the lowest tiers were reserved for the newly ennobled, and for court officials and their families. Being of less importance, the decoration for them is correspondingly more modest. These parts of the theatre are the outermost of the ripples spreading from the royal box.

Standing in the boxes was common to get a better view, but in the smaller Zeremoniensaal in the palace of Schönbrunn it was necessary even for members of the imperial entourage to stand, an endurance test that often caused ladies-in-waiting to faint.

While the niceties of social distinction may have been the reason for arranging the seats in court theatres in tiers and balconies, they were also used in public theatres, as in Venice, because a drum-shaped auditorium not only gives a far better acoustic than a flat rectangular hall, but also allows the accommodation of a greater number of people on a smaller site. In the Venetian theatres the boxes were rented by the city's patricians; on evenings when no members of a family wanted to use their box, it could still not be let to anyone else.

The courts and well-to-do townspeople had their own theatres and companies of actors. Monasteries, schools and universities gave their own performances in their own theatres or halls. Poorer townspeople and those who lived in small towns and villages were served by yet other kinds of theatres and actors. In a really large city like seventeenth-century Paris, indeed, there were all the different varieties, to suit all the different sections of society. The Hôtel de Bourgogne was frequented by the *beau monde*, the wits and poets, the lower ranks of the aristocracy and the upper *bourgeoisie*, though these last were rarely seen there on weekdays in the early seventeenth century, since performances began around two o'clock in the afternoon. As a general rule, the more exalted members of the nobility did not visit public theatres but only attended private performances in the royal palaces: the Louvre, Versailles, Fontainebleau or St Germain. For the common people there were the *théâtres de la foire*, opened especially for the visitors to the great fairs, or markets, in the suburbs of Paris, and manned by the many different varieties of strolling players. There was standing room only for the spectators in these popular theatres, whether the performances took place in permanent buildings or on open-air stages in the middle of a market-place.[12]

Of the types of theatre in use in the baroque age, the open-air theatres were the ones with the longest history. In the middle ages religious plays were performed on feast days, at first inside, but later in front of, the churches, then in the market-places and on the streets. The town itself was the backcloth, and the 'auditorium' necessarily a public place. This tradition of staging religious plays continued into the eighteenth century, in Spain at least, with *autos sacramentales*, but meanwhile other forms of open-air theatre developed.

The courtyards of the great houses and palaces of the Renaissance, surrounded as they were by arcades, formed a very favourable setting for the more ambitious musical and dramatic spectacles of the baroque. The aristocratic audience could be seated in the shelter of the branches which twined over the arcades. The courtyard of every nobleman in Europe could be converted to the simplest form of the Roman theatre, where the acting area represented a street and two or three gaps in the curtains that hung at the back were the doors to as many houses as were mentioned in the play. Later, as techniques developed, painted scenery would be used as well,

though for the most part it would be very simple. Performances in places like this are unlikely to have been for the general public. The host would engage a travelling company to entertain himself and his guests, or alternatively they would perform themselves.

Naturally, every large house had not only a courtyard but also a hall, which often proved even more suitable for dramatic purposes.

'Amid the sound of trumpets and drums, the whole company was led into a large dining hall, where the stage had been erected. Isidoro had drummed up the best actors he could find from schools in the surrounding villages. The scenery consisted mainly of curtains and tapestries pasted on to planks. It will therefore be obvious that the machines were very poor and the transformations very few. The stage was constructed upon some raised benches.'[13]

PETRUS SCHENK *Carnival on the Piazza Navona, Rome 1708, detail*

A so-called *Theatrum* dating from 1625 can be seen, though now in a state of disrepair, in Schloss Greinburg in southern Germany. It consists of a hall decorated with mosaics and a semi-circular limestone grotto. It was probably used for festivities and small-scale theatrical productions. Similar theatres were found in most noblemen's residences, even in such castles as survived in the seventeenth and eighteenth centuries. A particularly fine example, with unusual decorations, V, 63 is in the Schwarzenberg palace in Český Krumlov (formerly Böhmisch-Krumau) in Czechoslovakia.

Before the religious orders built their own theatres, they used to play in public squares and were sometimes given permission to perform in private or public halls. On special occasions, such as prize-giving in the monastery schools, they built a stage in the school yard with a temporary roof to shelter the audience. Later, when the Jesuits in particular began to use the theatre a great deal for the propagation and illustration of the faith, they built theatres on a really generous scale. If the hall had to serve more than one purpose, the stage could be hidden by a partition.

But it was the rise of professional actors, earning their living by presenting their plays to as large an audience as possible, that caused the rise of public theatres. The early travelling companies were able to play in the town halls, or had to put up with less suitable halls, a barn or a room in an inn. Goethe gives a very perceptive description of a travelling company, and the conditions in which they worked, in *Wilhelm Meisters theatralische Sendung*.[14]

The first civic theatre in Germany was built in Ulm by Josef Furttenbach between 1640 and 1641, to house performances by the guilds, schools and travelling companies; but this was an isolated example. In the middle of the next century Friederike Caroline Neuber, one of the leading German actresses of her age, was still obliged to perform in the Fleischhaus, the hall of the butchers' guild, in Leipzig; and similar conditions faced travelling companies all over Europe.

These makeshift theatres survived for quite a long time after proper theatres had started to be built in every country. Travelling companies performed at fairs, at markets, in every village, with greatly varying degrees of skill, on wooden

J. PFEFFEL *Festival decoration in the large hall of the Winterreitschule, by Giuseppe Galli-Bibiena, Vienna 1744*

Tom.V. *pag.281.*

La Force
de l'Amour.

LA FORCE
DE
L'AMOUR.

L E Théâtre repréfente un Faux-
bourg de Livourne.

SCENE PREMIERE.

ARLEQUIN, *feul.*

Grace au Ciel, me voici revenu à Livourne en bonne fanté. Le Seigneur
Lélio mon Maître doit m'attendre avec
impatience. Voilà l'Auberge où je l'ai
laiflë... Mais je le vois qui fort.

BONARD *Frontispiece and title page of 'Theatres de la Foire', Amsterdam 1726*

stages of all shapes and sizes. A stage was easily erected. On a few supports – barrels, crates, posts – were laid some planks. Some curtains, behind which the actors could change and wait for their cues and where the few props could be stored, were the only other things needed. The drawing reproduced at the beginning of this chapter, and Callot's drawings of the *commedia dell'arte* show people crowding round this simple stage, ready to fill in the gaps in the illusion with their imagination. The stage in Callot's drawings is built on the same lines as the peasants' theatre in Brueghel's *Village Fête*. Curtains hanging between posts form an easily transported back-cloth. The stage at the fair in Guibray near Falaise in 1685 was no different, and the players of the *commedia dell'arte* were still using this kind of all-purpose stage in the Piazza Navona in Rome in the eighteenth century.

after p. 32, p. 33

p. 35

p. 37

The stage erected by the travelling players on the common in Munich was more solid. There was a roof over the stage and the back and sides were made of wooden flats. But the spectators still had to stand in front of the stage and there was still no fixed charge made: a plate was passed round instead, as at many puppet-shows at present-day fêtes and fun-fairs.

For the common people of Paris there were the *théâtres de la foire*, which play an important part in the theatrical history of France. They were open for the duration of the fairs held in the suburbs of Paris, at St Germain from February to Easter[15] and at St Laurent from July to September. The theatres were small but the sets reproduced in *Les Théâtres de la Foire* (Amsterdam 1722-6) are quite elaborate and ambitious, indicating the use of movable scenery, and trapdoors and flying machines were also employed. Servandoni worked in

18

16

P. 39

German theatre as used by strolling players
in the mid-seventeenth century

these theatres and even Boucher did not scorn to re-create the intimate world of *salon* and *boudoir* in the *théâtres de la foire*. Clearly their artistic standards were far higher than those available to travelling companies in Germany.

A new theatre was built at St Laurent in 1743, and a new auditorium in 1752, so charmingly decorated by Boucher that the king had it built into the Hôtel des Menus-Plaisirs for court productions, after the closure of the Opéra Comique.

The theatres of the St Germain and St Laurent fairs closed for good in 1786, after successive restrictions had been threatening their existence for years: first the companies were not allowed to make music, then the actors were not allowed to speak on the stage, then only one person might appear at a time, all this leading to the *pièce à la muette* or pantomime. During the reign of Louis XV there was also the competition of the Opéra Comique, then enjoying its heyday. After 1791 theatres were no longer confined to the suburbs, whereas before the revolution only those with the king's patent could open in Paris itself.

When markets were held in the centre of Paris, in the Place Vendôme for instance, small booths were erected, 15 inside which the play was performed, while short extracts were played outside to attract the public, rather like the side-shows in today's fair.

While the technical advances made in the theatres of the Parisian fairs were greater than those made by other travelling theatres, these did make some progress. In Germany, by the middle of the seventeenth century, some companies were working with a curtain to divide the stage, allowing the p. 40 scene to be changed as often as was needed while the action went on in front of it. This could have been possible only in permanent buildings, which the travelling companies rarely had a chance to use, normally having to be content with clumsy makeshifts.

15   *Peepshow picture showing 'Théâtres de la foire' in the Place Vendôme, Paris eighteenth century*

16   ANON. *Theatre at the Foire St Germain, Paris late eighteenth century*

Die zwen *Acteurs*.

Ach liebster Printz! Wenn meine Schmertzen,
Euch gar nicht gehen mehr zu Hertzen,
so bin ich auch im Leben todt.
Prinzeßin schweigt von eurer Liebe,
Ihr setzet mich durch solche Triebe,
und Euch zugleich, in große Noth.

Die Vier Narren.

Wer uns nur sieht, der muß gleich lachen,
bloß weil wir das vorstellig machen,
wofür man uns doch selbst nicht hält.
Am Ende: Wenn man es betrachtet,
so ist diß Spiel, zwar ohnverachtet,
mit Narrheit meistentheils bestellt.

17   ANON. *The Comedien–Haus, Nuremberg c. 1730*

18 ANON. *Popular theatre on the Anger, Munich c. 1750*

III The Players

161 JACQUES CALLOT *Players on the road, France, early seventeenth century*

In the Renaissance noblemen and academics made their own theatre at court and in the universities. The amateur court theatres survived till the end of the eighteenth century and the theatres of the Catholic academies made an important contribution to the history of the theatre as a whole. Pupils and priests played all the parts, and, since women never appeared on any stage in the early days, there were no particular casting problems even when the play involved large crowd scenes. The lay public were admitted to these productions, and the demand for this combination of entertainment and religious instruction must have been great; in France alone in the seventeenth century, there were about a hundred Jesuit colleges that gave public performances.[1]

In his *Italienische Reise*, Goethe describes the impressions made on him when he visited a Jesuit theatre in Regensburg on 3 September 1786.

'I went at once to the Jesuit College where the pupils were giving their annual play, and saw the end of the opera and the beginning of the tragedy. They performed no worse than any decent amateur company and were splendidly, almost too richly, dressed. This public performance convinced me, and not for the first time, of the cleverness of the Jesuits. They neglect nothing that might impress, and know how to effect it with loving care and attention. This is not a cold, calculating cleverness, it springs from delight in what they are doing, from enjoyment of their own and others' actions, as if from life itself. This great religious society has among its members organists, woodcarvers and gilders, and there must certainly be some who occupy themselves in the theatre by choice and with professional knowledge, and just as their churches are distinguished by their agreeable splen-dour, so too these intelligent men make use of wordly sensuality to enhance their theatre.'

The language of the Jesuit plays was Latin, but to avoid tiring the spectators there were comic interludes or ballets as well.

p. 117 On holidays and feast days, the members of the guilds used to perform plays with the appropriate religious theme, or occasionally with a secular subject, and ordinary towns-folk and country people, for their own and others' edification, played scenes from the gospels and from the lives of the saints and entertained themselves with rough scenes of farce based on their everyday lives.

A number of these traditional presentations of religious scenes by laymen have survived to the present day. The most famous examples are those performed at Erl in the Tyrol and at Oberammergau in Bavaria, by farmers, craftsmen and local officials as well as by schoolmasters and priests. But in the past every market town or village of any local importance in Germany had its passion play, and the large majority of the population took part in it as a matter of religious duty, either as performers or as deeply involved spectators.

Play-acting comes naturally to the people of the Alps and southern Germany, so theatres run by and for peasants are no rarity, but the three-hundred-year-old tradition of the peasants' theatre at Kiefersfelden on the Inn is nevertheless remarkable. The side of a hill serves as a natural amphitheatre around a stage of scaffolding. Here, as they have for hundreds of years, farmers and labourers portray good men and evil men, their rewards and their punishments, with deep serious-ness. A play is repeated a few or many times, according to popularity, just as it would have been in the early mediaeval

DANIEL RABEL
Costumes: Servant, Fairy,
Innkeeper's wife,
France, early seventeenth century

ANON. *Rustic musicians*
from the ballet
'Les Fées des forêts de St Germain'

theatre, and performances are given only at weekends, because the actors are at work on weekdays.

The evolution of acting as a full-time profession began in the middle ages with the entertainments provided by minstrels, jugglers, tumblers, conjurers and acrobats. The thirteenth-century story *Del Tombeor Nostre Dame* ('Our Lady's tumbler'), is a moving account of the life and art of one such travelling entertainer. The class of professional actors can be seen developing from the merging of these professionals with the artisans who had learnt to act in guild plays.

The mediaeval minstrels travelled alone or in pairs; in the fifteenth century the groups began to increase in size, but only in the sixteenth century can they really be called companies. The development was roughly simultaneous in Spain, Italy and England.

Around the year 1600 there were already eight full companies in Spain, in 1615 there were twelve, and in addition there persisted minstrels and strolling players throughout the land. There were eight categories of actors and companies.

'*Bubulú*: a single player who travels around villages, playing an entire comedy by changing his voice; *ñaque*: two men equipped with a woollen beard and a few musical instruments, who can give an *entremés*, a Corpus Christi play or short episodes from an epic; a *gangarilla* consists of three or four players with a boy to take women's parts. They are able to perform the famous *auto* of the Lost Sheep. *Cambaleo* is the name given to a small troupe of five men and a female singer with a correspondingly larger repertoire and more properties.

The *compañía de garnacha* numbers five or six men, a woman and a boy; they are capable of performing about four comedies, three *autos* and *entremeses*, and consequently can stay in the same town or village for a week at a time. The *boxiganga* consists of six or seven men, two women and a boy; they perform their range of six comedies and three or four religious plays until late into the night, and tour the country with two great chests and four hired horses. The *farándula* has still more players, as well as having a larger wardrobe and repertoire, and the *compañía* proper may have as many as thirty members, among them real artists whose accomplishment and ability demand respect. A *compañía* keeps its repertoire of about fifty plays fresh by regular rehearsal, and settles in a town for several months.'[2]

In the middle of the seventeenth century more than three hundred travelling companies were counted in Spain. They remained in the same place for varying periods, months or even years, if their reception was profitable. Rojas describes their restless life with sympathy and declares: 'In Spain there is no Negro, in Algiers no slave, who does not live more comfortably than the unfortunate comedian.'[3]

Like the Puritans in England, the Catholic church in Spain saw fit as early as the end of the sixteenth century to attack the immorality of the theatre, and to rule against breeches-parts for women, indecent costumes, lewd subjects and morally offensive dances. A law of 1641 lays down that no girl under twelve may be employed as an actress, unless she is married. It repeats the insistence on propriety in dress

mention of the Comédiens françois du Roy, a company with a royal patent, in the Hôtel de Bourgogne. There were women among the Comédiens, but they played only gentle-women: old hags were played by men even in Molière's day. The great age of French plays and ballet, when French travelling companies were in demand everywhere, came at the end of the seventeenth century. In the eighteenth century no self-respecting court in Europe could be without its French actors. In Germany, Austria, Denmark, Sweden and Russia, noblemen great and small had a permanent company, or at least engaged a guest company for a period. Over and above their theatrical functions they were apostles of French culture and the French way of life.

In England, in the early days, a company consisted of four men and a boy. With such small numbers every member had to play several parts.[4] The number of professional actors increased steadily during the sixteenth century and numerous companies were formed. Some occupied the newly built theatres in London, some played in the houses of noblemen, and others continued to tour the country. In 1574 the Puritans banned nearly all the companies in and around London, driving them to seek their living further afield. Only the leading companies, and those with the most influential patrons, were able to stay in London.

When English actors began to travel on the continent around 1600, they had a far-reaching influence on the development of the theatre there. The first country to welcome English actors was the Netherlands. Dutchmen joined their companies, learnt from them and after a time were able to develop their own professional theatre. Then they too began to travel. Because of the similarity of language the Dutch companies stayed mostly in the Low German region: Holstein, Flensburg, Hamburg and Denmark.

The English themselves travelled further. From 1592 onwards they were found in all the capitals of Sweden, Denmark and Germany, and they also presented their plays at fairs and markets. As long as they continued to speak English they were confined to an educated public, or were driven to the extremes of mime to make themselves understood. From about 1605 they began to use German.[5] They were pre-eminent in Germany up to the outbreak of the Thirty Years War but by then German actors had learnt enough for them to be able to start travelling about Europe themselves, particularly in the north and east.

The peculiar social status of actors in the early years is hard for us to understand today. As they had developed from jugglers, wandering minstrels and acrobats, for a long time people continued to class them with such itinerants. To start with, in nearly every country the aristocracy and the middle classes both took the same attitude towards actors.

and includes general regulations against excessively rich costumes.

Long before the actor's art was practised professionally in France and Germany, or even in England, Italy had the *commedia dell'arte*. As early as the beginning of the sixteenth century troupes of comedians had already been in existence for several decades and before the end of the century these masters of the impromptu had hauled their wagons across the Alps and appeared in Vienna and soon after in Munich. The pleasure they gave is plain to see from the pictures on the walls of the so-called 'Fools' Staircase' of Burg Trausnitz. The troupes were geared to an Italian-speaking public, which presented no difficulties at the Viennese court, where Italian was customarily spoken in the seventeenth century; but they had relatively less success with the general public. Nevertheless the Italians and their improvisatory theatre made their way all over Europe from Spain to Russia.

Hiring companies from so far away must have been expensive for the courts and gruelling for the players, but neither seemed to mind. The importance and number of foreign touring companies only declined towards the end of the eighteenth century, as the indigenous drama gained ground in every country in Europe. Eventually only Italian singers were left, at those courts where music was taken particularly seriously.

In France, too, professional acting evolved at first in a modest, unimpressive way. In 1600 the Théâtre du Marais moved into the Hôtel d'Argent in Paris. By 1607 there is a

49

JEAN BÉRAIN *Costumes: Neptune, Diana, Zeus, France, late seventeenth century*

Members of the profession were admitted into bourgeois and court society to practise their art, but remained socially outside. Occasionally the emergence of a particularly eminent figure like Molière improved the social status of actors in general, but as late as 1641 a decree had to be published to establish that to follow this profession was no longer a disgrace.

For a time, in the middle of the seventeenth century, the Catholic church took a more tolerant attitude towards actors: they were allowed to take the sacraments and might act as godparents and as witnesses of marriages. But the immorality of certain actors, or perhaps Molière's supposed attacks on religion in *Tartuffe*, led the church to revert to its former attitude, and the sacraments were refused to actors, a situation which persisted on the continent into the eighteenth century.

The Lutheran church, at times even less tolerant of the theatre than the Catholics, refused communion to the actor-manager Johannes Velten on his death-bed in Hamburg in 1695. Caroline Neuber was buried at night and in secret, like Molière, and even Adrienne Lecouvreur, fêted in her time in the most aristocratic circles, was denied burial in consecrated ground. In spite of Voltaire's efforts on behalf of his friend she was given a nameless grave somewhere beside the Seine.

Principals of companies made countless efforts to regulate the behaviour of their actors, but it was precisely the most talented, and therefore those most in the public eye, who disregarded middle-class manners and morals. The churches could hardly allow one set of standards for the real world and another for the world of shadows.

The conditions under which actors were engaged, and the payments they received, were at first the same within each country. Later, as actors began to tour abroad, they expected the same conditions they had had at home, and so several different rates might obtain in one country. In the early days of professionalism, in Spain, an actor's contract lasted initially one or two years. The actors received a fixed wage or took a share in the profits, according to their status in the company. They were expected to prepare a new production each week. In Shakespearean England the actors formed share-holding, self-governing companies. The chief actors were the 'housekeepers', joint owners of the theatre and sharing one half of the profits between them. The other actors, the 'sharers', divided the rest of the profits. Hired men were taken on as supernumeraries at an agreed wage for very limited periods.

Travelling companies placed themselves under the protection of a prince or lord. The right to use their protector's name enhanced both their social position and their profits.

The king's players received a regular honorarium. Henry VIII had a company of eight players, who not only performed before him but had the right to undertake other engagements. Like many Continental aristocrats of the eighteenth century, sixteenth-century English noblemen had companies, which may in some cases have worn livery, but were not full-time employees. The important thing, so far as the actors were concerned, was the letter of recommendation which their protector would send to a town, asking the authorities to admit his players and to pay them appropriately. Only thus could a company raise itself above the status of vagabonds, acrobats and bear-leaders. There were about one hundred and fifty such companies in England at the end of Elizabeth's reign.

Elsewhere and later too, Molière needed protection for his company, as did the German actor-managers, Caroline Neuber, Johannes Velten, Johann Friedrich Schönemann and others.

In Molière's day, all the members of a company were engaged on equal terms, except for the director. The small provincial companies were composed of about five or six players, the Parisian companies of between twelve and fifteen. With such small groups specialization was out of the question. Versatility was essential, and the ability to play both comedy and tragedy. The administration was undertaken by such actors as were most capable, and above all the company needed an eloquent *orateur*, responsible for public relations, advertising and keeping order in the auditorium.

Good actors could earn a lot of money in Paris, but they were all obliged to find their own very expensive costumes. The leading actors in the Comédie Française company were sharers (*sociétaires*) and received a share of the profits, while supporting players, musicians and singers had a fixed wage. The *sociétaires* had the right and the duty to read any new play offered to the company, and the decision whether or not to perform it was taken jointly by them.

Molière's was the first company to establish a pension fund for actors or their dependants in the event of their death. This was much earlier than in England, where David Garrick first introduced pensions, or Germany, where Konrad Ackermann started to promise his actors a support for their old age to keep them in the company, in 1767. Molière's actors had to finance their pension scheme entirely by their own contributions.

In Vienna the imperial household included a number of leading actors in permanent posts, and others were engaged for individual productions, receiving a fee from the privy purse. In addition, several members of the imperial family had their own musicians who could be brought together on special occasions to form an orchestra.

A unique kind of professional theatre, the serf theatre, evolved in Russia towards the end of the eighteenth century. This was the period when the national theatres were rising elsewhere, but the serf theatre was distinctly a phenomenon of the baroque, rooted in the absolute power that Russian noblemen had over their serfs. The training was anything but gentle. Only the abolition of serfdom brought this particular branch of the theatre to an end. Serf actors were a source of income, as well as of entertainment, to their owner, since he could hire them out to a public theatre.

The careers of a few outstanding personalities illustrate the actor's existence, his social position and the gradual development of the profession throughout our period.

William Shakespeare (1564–1616) was not the manager of a company or director of a theatre; he was a sharer and a part-owner of the Globe. He began as an actor, did some doctoring of plays already in the repertoire and then began to write his

JEAN LE PAUTRE *Dancer of the Opéra, Paris, seventeenth century*

FRANCISCUS LANG *Poses from 'Dissertatio de actione scenica': position of limbs, entrance, emotion, Munich 1727*

own plays. He took a part in repertoire planning, received a share of the profits and thus had a direct financial stake in the success of the theatre. The actors commissioned and bought plays and had the parts copied but not printed. There was no effective copyright law, and other companies would play anything that appeared in print, or would even have surreptitious transcripts made of unprinted plays. Playwrights were not generally well paid, and were considered to be of less importance than the leading actors; but as a successful dramatist, actor and sharer in the Globe, Shakespeare gained wealth and position and died a respected citizen, which would hardly have been possible outside England.

The leading Spanish dramatists of the seventeenth century, too, were more than playwrights. Lope de Rueda, Lope de Vega, Calderón de la Barca, Tirso de Molina, all directed as well as writing, some in the public theatres, some, Calderón for one, at court. A large number of the names of the earliest Spanish actors have been preserved, which is the best proof of the regard in which their public held them.

The life of Jean Baptiste Poquelin de Molière (1622–73), one of the most famous figures in the whole history of the baroque theatre, illustrates by his success as an actor and leader of a company the functions and achievements of the seventeenth-century theatre. No other actor, however,

reached Molière's position of eminence in France or anywhere else. Having abandoned his legal studies, the young Molière, together with Madeleine Béjart, founded in 1643 the Illustre Théâtre, which made its Paris début in a rented tennis court near the Porte de Nesle. In spite of some successes and the patronage of Louis XIII's brother Gaston d'Orléans, giving the right to call themselves Comédiens de Son Altesse Royale, the company could not compete with the larger theatres of the Hôtel de Bourgogne and the Théâtre du Marais. A move to another tennis court, in St Germain, did not relieve their financial difficulties, and the Illustre Théâtre and the Comédiens de Son Altesse Royale foundered. Molière was committed to a debtor's prison from which his father had to redeem him.

A lack of self-criticism, over-estimation of his own capabilities at that stage, and a youthful refusal to assess realistically the competition of the established theatres had led to this fiasco. Thirteen years of hard work in the provinces – Bordeaux, Nantes, Limoges, Toulouse, Narbonne, Poitiers – with an ever-changing troupe, enabled Molière to find where his genius, both as actor and dramatist, really lay: in comedy. The Prince de Conti and the Duc d'Anjou took him into their service and the company's reputation began to grow. Their first appearance before the king was on 24 October

1658. They played Corneille's tragedy *Nicomède*, followed by Molière's own *Docteur amoureux*, and Louis XIV was so well entertained that he gave the company the title Troupe de Monsieur le Frère unique du Roi. From then on they had the use of the Hôtel du Petit Bourbon and, from 1660, the Palais Royal. Molière was more than a playwright of genius: as the best actor and producer in his own company he had a completely professional knowledge of the needs and potentialities of the theatre. He steered so skilful a course through the troubles, threats and controversies that arose around the banned *Tartuffe* that he enjoyed Louis' favour until his death. The church, however, denied him Christian burial.

The outbreak of the Thirty Years War in 1618 drove German companies abroad, particularly into Northern and Eastern Europe. The most notable among the early principals was Michael Daniel Treu, who took over the plays with which the English companies had been so successful and introduced the Spanish baroque dramatists. He may be said to have been the first to present a cross-section of contemporary European drama on the German stage. From that time on the number of companies was constantly increasing, as they divided and sent out offshoots.

From the English and Dutch companies, whom language difficulties had obliged to use coarse and obvious effects to make their meaning clear, the Germans could hardly have inherited a subtle technique. Scenes of horror, murders and executions were shown with plenty of stage-blood. The Thirty Years War brought a general coarsening of manners and sensibilities; it made the life of the travelling players even more uncertain and the need to avoid the battlefronts kept them constantly on the move.

Magister Johannes Velten (1640–95), a man of culture and education, was the first of the German actor-managers to depart radically from tradition. Female characters were no longer portrayed by male actors in his company, he trained young players, and took steps to reduce the amount of cheap sensationalism, excessive erotic and scatological realism, and crude declamation. He put on the works of the great dramatists: Shakespeare, Calderón, Molière, and had the reward of his efforts when engaged by the court of Dresden in 1685.

A great, though tragic, figure in the history of the German theatre in the eighteenth century was Friederike Caroline
37 Neuber (1697–1760). Born Weissenborn, she ran away from her strict middle-class home to marry a former law student, Johann Neuber. Together with Johann Christoph Gottsched (1700–66) she undertook a reform of the German theatre. Impromptu comedy, which had been witty and elegant, had sunk to the coarse effects and smutty jokes of Hans Wurst. She tried to free the German stage of this kind of crude interlude.[6] An educated woman, speaking French and Latin, she

played Corneille and Racine and the first German plays to be written in alexandrines. She wanted plays on significant subjects, written in a German free of French and Italian expressions, which would yet be suitable for serious plays. Goethe used her ideas as a basis for his *Regeln für Schauspieler* ('Rules for actors', 1803), in which he tried to create a language and a pronunciation that would be free of regionalisms and so could be used on stages all over the German-speaking countries. German theatres still use a standardized 'stage German', essential in a country where it can still be difficult for, say, a Holsteiner to understand a Bavarian. One result of Caroline Neuber's efforts was that polite society, which had been completely oriented to the French theatre, once more took an interest in the German.

By taking over a company to which it had been granted, Caroline Neuber acquired a patent issued by the Elector of Saxony, and in 1736 she received the Schleswig-Holstein privilege from Duke Charles Frederick. But these entailed only very small subsidies, and although she could count the

GERARD DE LAIRESSE *Polite and vulgar manners from 'Groot Schilderboek', Amsterdam 1707*

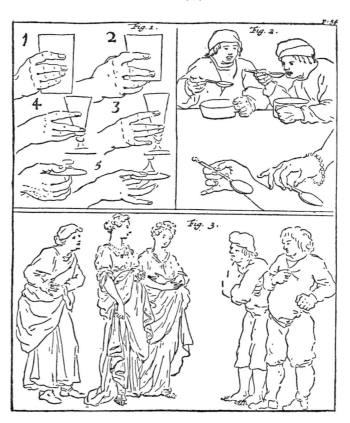

educated classes as her audience she was never free of financial difficulties throughout her life. Clowns and players of farce continued to draw the largest audiences and make the greatest profits. In spite of the strength of her claims to wield a valuable influence upon the behaviour and morals of the public, the Hamburg city council could not be persuaded to place a permanent theatre at her company's disposal. She was compelled to keep on the road, travelling as far as the court of Catherine the Great.

Caroline Neuber is generally considered to be the first great actress of the modern German theatre; she also wrote passable plays that were frequently performed, but she was no Molière or Shakespeare and her company could not build an entire repertoire from them. Gottsched's arid, pedantic translations from the French and his own anaemic plays were also unsatisfactory: the German drama that she wanted and needed did not exist. Therein lay the tragedy of her life and the cause of her own failure. When her ideas for reform eventually began to bear fruit, it was too late for her. She was trapped in the conventions of her maturity, and died, lonely and obscure, fleeing from the Seven Years War. A memorial was erected to her soon after.

The eighteenth century saw a proliferation of actors and principals who influenced the development of the theatre in Germany, and who deserve individual mention for their part in the improvement and refinement of German dramatic art.

p. 98 Heinrich Gottfried Koch (1703–75) started as a member of Caroline Neuber's company and for twenty years was her closest and most active collaborator as director, scenery and costume designer, actor and repertory planner.[7] Johann Friedrich Schönemann (1704–82) showed originality in his programmes and in his discovery and manipulation of new talent. Cautiously and very deliberately he introduced 'regular drama' into a repertoire which long remained dominated by the crude and vociferous figure of Hans Wurst. The year 1750 saw a decisive innovation in the German theatre; Schönemann's company was engaged as permanent comedians to the court of Schwerin with permission to make guest appearances elsewhere. This was the first step towards a more secure existence for the travelling companies, and towards a drama of literary merit and permanent value, as distinct from the farce and blood-and-thunder of the commercial theatre.

There is a clear relationship between a man's dress and bearing and the impression he makes on other people, and this is even more obvious in the case of an actor on stage. The majestic dignity of seventeenth-century baroque called for a different style of acting and costume from the graceful wit of the rococo. A few perceptive actors give a form and a style to what lies as a potentiality in the spirit of the age.

When Hamlet is instructing Polonius to look after the actors, Shakespeare has him say, 'Do you hear, let them be well used; for they are the abstracts and brief chronicles of the time.'[8] Later he gives the actors advice which tells us a lot about the dramatic styles of Shakespeare's age and what his own opinions were.

'Speak the speech, I pray you, as I pronounced it to you, trippingly on the tongue: but if you mouth it, as many of your players do, I had as lief the town-crier had spoke my lines. Nor do not saw the air too much – your hand thus: but use all gently: for in the very torrent, tempest, and (as I may say) the whirlwind of passion, you must acquire and beget a temperance, that may give it smoothness. O, it offends me to the soul, to see a robustious periwig-pated fellow tear a passion to tatters, to very rags, to split the ears of the groundlings… Be not too tame neither, but let your own discretion be your tutor: suit the action to the word, the word to the action; with this special observance, that you o'erstep not the modesty of nature; for anything so overdone is from the purpose of playing, whose end, both at the first, and now, was, and is, to hold, as 't were, the mirror up to nature; to show virtue her own feature, scorn her own image, and the very age and body of the time, his form and pressure.'[9]

There were routine methods for expressing emotions; in pain the actor threw himself on the ground, in anger he tore his hair and dealt out kicks and cuffs, in silent sorrow his head was lowered, his back bent, and so on. In Shakespeare's day the stage was almost bare and the only lighting usually daylight. The size of the theatre made broad, clear gestures necessary, and attention was drawn to facial expressions, only visible at close quarters, by the words of the other characters.

Acting on the baroque stage was never naturalistic; on the contrary, it was always emphatic and grandiose. Gesture, movement, voice and mime all underlined emotions heavily, and this was common to all nations. It started in Spain with particular vehemence; the French were more restrained and the serious theatre in Germany learned from them.

Throughout the whole baroque age, book after book on dramatic technique appeared, among them the *Groot Schilderboek*, (Amsterdam 1707), by Gerard de Lairesse, and Franciscus Lang's *Dissertatione de actione scenica* of 1727. p. 51
p. 50

Gerard de Lairesse's book is about the techniques of the professional theatre, and the publication of English, French and German translations shows that what he wrote did not apply only in the Netherlands.[10] He discusses the significance of gestures in detail. The different ways in which members of each social class hold their glasses and spoons, how they eat, stand and pass things to each other is minutely described, explained and illustrated. It may well be that a book of this kind had an influence on manners in real life.

19 DANIEL RABEL
*Entrance of the esperlucattes
early seventeenth century*

20 LUDOVICO OTTAVIO
BURNACINI
*Grotesque masks and
allegorical beasts
late seventeenth
century*

21–2   LUDOVICO OTTAVIO BURNACINI *Male and female grotesques*

23–4   LUDOVICO OTTAVIO BURNACINI *Spanish court costume: Male and female figures*

25 JEAN BÉRAIN
*Turkish costume,
end of seventeenth century*

26–8 JEAN BÉRAIN *Ballet costumes: Neptune, Hymen, dancer*

30–2 ANON. *French costume designs for Pan (or a faun) and dancers with castanets*

29 JEAN BÉRAIN *Lady in court dress*

33 NICOLAS DE LARGILLIÈRE
Anne-Marie Chateauneuf-Duclos
in the title role of Corneille's
'Ariane', 1714

34 JEAN ANTOINE WATTEAU *Love at the Comédie francaise, c. 1720*

35 JEAN RAOUX
Mlle Prévost
as a Bacchante,
1723

Franciscus Lang summarizes the development over a hundred years of techniques in the theatre of his own order, the Jesuits. He asks his readers to avoid the kind of mechanical effects produced by the conventional routines of professional actors, and to give their portrayals depth by penetrating the real nature of the character. His first requirements are the carriage and manners seen in polite society and natural, expressive speech, for which he lays down the exact accentual stresses heard in joy, sorrow, equanimity and frenzy. The gesture of command is described down to the index finger, and Lang also gives detailed advice on the representation of pain and grief.

The rococo stage required a different style of acting and different techniques. The index finger was no longer pointed imperiously, but the little finger was crooked with delicacy and grace, perhaps a little affectation. Sweeping gestures, emphatic self-confidence, the embodiment of dignified gravity, which lent drama even to the act of standing still, were replaced by balletic lightness. Intimacy invaded the spaciousness that was so essential to the baroque stage, the theatre reflected the general social and intellectual withdrawal from the rigid etiquette of the great royal palaces to the smaller, more relaxed world of the *salons*. Heroism gave way to gallantry,

C. Dauphin and J. Thourneysen
French actor at the court of Munich

Johann Messelreuther
Actor and actress in 'Roman costume'

61

heroes became lovers, goddesses were endowed with *esprit*. The baroque superman left the stage, and wit, gaiety, ambiguity, scepticism and irony, all the nuances of human personality were seen instead.

In his *Paradoxe sur le comédien, c.* 1778, Denis Diderot calls not for passion and emotional involvement but for perception observation and judgment. Hogarth drew not only caricatures of theatrical life but also patterns for gestures.[11]

Individual actors of outstanding skill grew in public esteem and pictures of them became more numerous, no longer intended just to show costumes and characteristic poses, but as portraits of complex personalities.

The progress from the declamatory diction of Corneille's age to a more natural delivery, still of course very different from everyday speech, began with Molière. As a director he tried to achieve a more naturalistic style in movement and gesture, in the number of steps taken and in the smallest detail of facial expression. Every director trains his actors in rehearsal, but there were also regular schools of acting. Lope de Vega, who participated in every aspect of theatrical life, founded his first school in 1588; Landgrave Maurice the Learned of Hesse had his pupils instructed by English actors in the early years of the seventeenth century; and in 1770 a ballet school was founded in Stuttgart, where the curriculum included music and dramatic art.[12] The first fully-fledged dramatic academy in Europe was founded by Konrad Eckhof in 1753; it survived only fourteen months, but it led to further refinement of the art and to an improvement in the status of the profession.

The fact that players were usually on the move kept their stock of properties and scenery to a minimum and made them rely on costumes to dazzle the spectators. The costumes were a company's most valuable property. But this practical factor is not the only one to take into account: the spirit of the age is expressed in theatrical costume.

The costumes of the Shakespearean stage were extremely grand. On the almost bare stage there was nothing to distract the spectators' attention from the actors; their imagination, their creative intelligence, was helped to transcend the limitations of everyday reality only by the splendour of their costumes. In the early seventeenth century it was the same everywhere: the plainer the stage the richer the costumes, in Holland and Spain, in England as in Italy. The conventions of costume, found everywhere, though varying from one country to another, are particularly interesting. Some attempt was made to indicate the period of the play in the costume, but only very approximately. Armour was worn when the action was supposed to take place in the middle ages, and particularly bright colours were reserved for noblemen. Townspeople and peasants were shown in what would be the Sunday-best appropriate to their station. Beside these general rules, there were some specific conventions.[13] Whores wore dresses with very full skirts, usually of red taffeta; Jews wore long coats and masks with big noses and red beards; pagan priests wore mitres.

Inigo Jones (1573–1652) borrowed from classical costumes in his designs for mythological characters, but the whole thing was adorned in early baroque fashion with tucks, ribbons and lace. Contemporary dress was always what would be worn on a gala occasion, only more striking and extravagant, with lower *décolletés* and more vivid colours. Actresses always wore contemporary dress, and for tragedies were sometimes lent dresses by the court where they were appearing; only the male costumes indicated the period and locality of the play. Whatever time and place, the actors wore their fashionable periwigs, which, like the stetsons in cowboy films, had a symbolic value: heroes wore white and villains wore black. It was essential to the dignity of tragedy that the heroine should wear a long train. Baroque costume came to its full splendour with the introduction of artificial light, at first only candles, which made jewels glitter and brightened the colours. For plays and operas alike, stage costumes were always richer and more magnificent than in real life. Loose robes were worn over a *justaucorps*, great plumes nodded on hats and helmets, and ladies wore their hair piled high. According to Fénelon's *Aventures de Télémaque* (1695–96), there were seven social classes whose different styles of dress had to be taken into account on the stage. French costumes had long replaced Spanish styles, and even Caroline Neuber played her parts in modern French dress. The prevalent style of acting was also French and every actor claimed to be French.

We can see the influence that stage costumes had on fashion in general in the seventeenth century. The *fontange*, for instance, the towering hair-style, originated on the stage. In the eighteenth century, however, the close relationship between on-stage and off-stage dress began to give way to a quest for authenticity. This was a slow process, as the memoirs of Charles Simon Favart (1710–52) reveal.[14] Country girls still appeared in expensive jewelry, court shoes and hairstyles, and ancient Greeks happily wore silk stockings and knee-breeches, or pearl-encrusted robes over hooped skirts.

Favart's wife Marie Justine Favart (1727–72), one of the most famous French actresses of her day, set a precedent in 1753 by appearing in *Bastien et Bastienne* with her hair down, wearing a plain woollen dress and clogs. Other actresses and opera-singers rushed to follow her example, and efforts to attain authenticity became even greater. Genuine costumes were even sent for from distant countries.

LOUIS RENÉ BOQUET *Costumes for the ballet 'Medusa'*

p. 65 Costumes were usually designed by the stage designers. p. 47, 19 Callot depicts only those of the travelling players, but a large number of Daniel Rabel's sketches survive from the beginning of the seventeenth century, before the full flowering of the baroque. p. 48, 25–9 The drawings of Jean Bérain (1637–1711) show baroque magnificence combined with the supple French elegance which the Germans hardly ever attained. Messel- p. 61 reuther's engravings of an *Actor and Actress in Roman Costume*, 20–4 1720, are stiff by comparison. Ludovico Burnacini, who worked principally at the imperial court in Vienna, gives a more powerful, and often cruder, impression in both his festival garments and his costumes for grotesques, but in any case he remained longer under the influence of Spanish fashion because of the Hapsburgs' connections with Spain.

The activities of the great costume designers were no more confined to the land of their birth than those of set p. 63 designers and architects. Boucher's pupil, Louis Boquet

(1717–1814), for instance, whose sketches show the lightest perfection reached by rococo costume design, was summoned to Stuttgart for several months each year by Duke Charles Eugene and his designs were circulated widely.

For functional reasons, ballet costumes in the eighteenth I, 35, 46 century followed a slightly different path from other theatrical costumes. Skirts had to clear the feet and ankles, and male dancers, too, needed greater freedom. At the beginning of the seventeenth century when dancing was more staid and steps were restricted to a dignified circling and turning, freedom of movement was less important and there was no need for dresses to be noticably different from those worn by p. 49 any lady in polite society. The stage presentation of country dancing was not, of course, affected by any of these fashions. 19

Two great costume reformers paved the way for later developments: David Garrick in England and Konrad Eckhof in Germany. Both were notable actors, perhaps the best

JOSEPH LANGE *Scene from J. G. Noverre's ballet*
'*Alexander and Campaspe*'

For some time no one in England dared to go as far as Madame Favart, but costumes became more simple in their cut and ornament. Although Garrick played Shakespearean roles in *habit habillé*, in up-to-the-minute French fashions, the extra touches which he added to characterize a part, like an ermine cloak for King Lear, were still a significant innovation. Costumes were no longer intended purely to impress but also to tell something about the wearers. Nationality was at least hinted at. Roman generals no longer wore full-bottomed wigs, and not every female character wore hooped petticoats. Garrick also persuaded people that witches did not necessarily have to wear white lace and powdered wigs. Surprisingly, however, his efforts in the direction of verisimilitude did not have the same wide and permanent influence in England that they had in France and Germany. The strength of his personality was such that the social position of the acting profession was markedly improved; he became a respected member of society and was buried in Westminster Abbey. Like Molière he founded a pension scheme for old actors.

Konrad Eckhof (1720–78) was already called the 'Father of German dramatic art' in his lifetime. Short, ugly, almost deformed, he first had to work hard to overcome his physical disadvantages, to allow his outstanding talents, his intelligence, his beautiful voice, his expressive features and his ability as an actor to develop. He made an intensive study of literary drama and works on acting theory, and became a most influential actor, director, principal and teacher. As a member of the Schönemann troupe he had the support of Konrad Ackermann and Sophie Charlotte Schröder. His first ambitions, influenced by Caroline Neuber's reforms, were to play French drama and the plays of Gottsched, and to preserve some remains of the impromptu theatre. But he soon outgrew the ceremonial aspect of French classicism and, like Garrick, turned to realism and natural characterization. It was no longer good enough to present a stereotype, each character had to be developed as an individual. An actor's intelligence and intuition became more important than elegance and ceremony.

The purposes of Eckhof's dramatic academy were to raise the artistic standards and social status of professional actors, to create a native German art and tradition, and to turn strolling players into artists with prospects of secure employment. The building of a repertoire, production, self-criticism and the study of human nature were among the things the academy tried to teach, but it was the following era that was to see the fulfilment of its aims.

The baroque theatre was truly international. Not only were the plays of the great Spanish, English, French – and later German – writers widely known, but also the comedy

of their age, and both reformers in more than one aspect of theatrical life. They and Madame Favart represent the new trends.

39   David Garrick (1717–79) took over the artistic direction of Drury Lane in 1747, became a shareholder, and determined the progress of this famous theatre for thirty years. He was strict in enforcing his directions and allowed no improvization. He trained his actors in simplicity, permitted neither exaggerated mime or grimaces nor melodramatic gestures, and made a characteristically eighteenth-century attempt to return to nature. He played Hamlet without the usual wig.

of improvization that delighted the ordinary people was played at fairs the length and breadth of Europe.

The origins of the *commedia dell'arte* are obscure. There seems equally good reason for tracing it from the extempore debates held by courtiers and academics before audiences of their peers, as from masked carnival parades. The regional nature of the stereotypes suggests a purely folk origin. The trail can be followed for about two thousand years, from Greek mime, through Rome, Byzantium and the Turks to Venice. There are obvious connections with puppets and shadow-theatres. Perhaps all we can do is to compare the *commedia dell'arte* to a tree, spreading its branches and throwing a broad shadow for two hundred years and nourished by numerous roots in its native soil.

During the baroque age the plays of the *commedia dell'arte* consisted of improvization within the prepared outlines of an action. Detailed scenarios, the *canevas*, were posted back-p. 68 stage. Soon there were also published stock texts of useful monologues and dialogues appropriate to all sets of circumstances and all character types: love and hate, cunning and stupidity, knavery and boorishness. Like a kaleidoscope producing an infinite number of patterns from the same pieces of coloured material, this kind of improvization continually produced new plays and original comments on real life. The character types remained the same, and the actors – who from the earliest days of the *commedia dell'arte* were professionals – opted for one or the other type at the beginning of their careers. They were thus able to present their chosen type with the ever-increasing virtuosity and refinement that came from continuous practice. Italians are articlate and inexhaustible talkers, given to expressive gestures, and born mimics – a combination that was extremely favourable to the development of the *commedia dell'arte*.

The first professional *commedia dell'arte* companies were in existence by the middle of the sixteenth century. Angelo Beolco (1502–42) started the establishment of the different regional types: Pantaloon (Pantalone), the old Venetian merchant, the Doctor from the university city of Bologna, and the 'zanies' (*Zanni*), Harlequin (Arlecchino) and Brighella, from the city of porters, Bergamo. Thus regional types were established and mercenariness, pedantry, frivolity and peasant cunning were personified. The names of the best 48 known Roman companies have been preserved: the Comici Gelosi and the Comici Accesi. Famous actors and actresses like Isabella Andreini (1562–1604), whose careers are known to us, were evidently well-educated in literature and music. Unlike later German and Dutch improvizers, they also possessed the mental agility necessary for quick-fire repartee.

There was little room for serious characters in this genre whose only aims were fluency and wit, though tragicomedy was not unknown. The fashionably dressed juvenile lead p. 65 usually bore the name of Lelio or Flavio, the ingénue or *comica innamorata*, the object of his affection, was called Flaminia or Isabella. The *canterina* ('singer') was a dancer too, and performed in the musical interludes. Foremost among the comic masked characters were the *Zanni*, usually servants with wit, impudence and ingenuity, who were not too particular about loyalty or honesty to their masters but were always ready to help young lovers and to play tricks on the self-satisfied. There was a whole family of 'Harlequins', who might sometimes bear the names Bagatino or Truffaldino instead. Harlequin's patchwork costume consisted of a loose jacket, tight trousers, a tall hat, a black half-mask and a wooden sword. At first a simple rogue, he later developed wit and intelligence. His female counterpart was the soubrette, Columbine, always the pert maid. p. 67

JACQUES CALLOT *Young lover from the Commedia dell'arte*

Mezetain · La Chanteusse · Le Docteur Baluardé · La Marquise de Noirchignon

Amarante · Arlequin · Isabelle · Scaramouche ·

Marinette · Octave · Colombine · Pierot

Théâtre Italien:
Commedia dell' arte characters
in France

Pulcinella was a Neapolitan, an intriguer, impudent, avaricious, drunken and a womanizer, who bequeathed various parts of his nature to Mr Punch, Jack Pudding, Polcinello and Hans Wurst. Capitano Spavente was a braggart, forever boasting of brave deeds he had never actually performed. Pantaloon, the miserly, distrustful, unscrupulous Venetian merchant, appeared in every play, looking for a young bride or a rich son-in-law. Brighella, to begin with, was a hypocritical scoundrel, but later came on to the side of the angels, his personality being split up to a certain extent among Scapino, Mezzetino and Flautino in Italy, Sganarelle in France and Figaro in Spain. His original costume consisted of a tight jacket, wide trousers, a cloak, a hat and an olive-coloured mask, but as Mezzetino he gradually assumed the red and white striped suit of Harlequin. The Doctor from Bologna might be physician, philosopher, lawyer or classical scholar, and varied his dress accordingly, pulling a tall hat down over his brows when representing the medical profession and stuffing documents into his belt when cast as a lawyer. Until the mid-seventeenth century his basic costume

ANON. *Catherine Biancholelli,*
of the Théâtre Italien, Paris,
as Columbine

was a black suit and starched ruff; later he also wore a striped coat. The greatest of all aphorists, Scaramuccio, evolved from Capitano Spavente; his servant was Pasquino (Crispin in France), and among the other comics were Tritellino, Tabarino and Tartaglia.

47 One absolutely essential, never-failing property was the mask. The comic characters wore half-masks of fine leather, appropriate to their stereotype, with forehead, eyes and nose but no expression. Laughter, weeping, despair and happiness were expressed by the actor's body, and if the mime

was good the fact that half the face remained totally immobile actually increased the effect. The basic nature of the stereotype was fixed in the mask, and the body provided the variety of expression.

The early troupes had about twelve members. The *concertatore* was leading actor and producer, devised the *canevas* and usually ran the company's administration as well. He was a virtuoso to whom mime and physical expression were all-important and he constantly invented new tricks and pieces of business of which he held, in a sense, the copyright, and which he could use time and again in new combinations. His playing became more and more refined and proficient, the display of his technical skill became so much more important than the plot of the play, that the literary theatre in Italy suffered a decline from which it was rescued by Goldoni, who incorporated the best of the *commedia dell'arte* in his new straight comedy.

pp. 66–7, 77, 50

In France, the *commedia dell'arte* was assimilated as the *comédie italienne*. Some of its stock types found their way into native written plays, including those of Molière. Harlequin was no longer a crude glutton but a homespun philosopher, original and comic, and much closer to Shakespeare's fools than to his Italian model. The *comédie italienne* did not use masks, and so the actor's face took over a large part of what had previously been left to the body to express. The emphasis on caricature and stereotype became less, and verbal wit gained greater prominence.

Traits of the English clown, the Low German Pickelhäring, the French Gros-Guillaume, Arlecchino, Harlequin are all found in the south German Hans Wurst. He specialized in belly-laughs, and even in tragedies he was allowed to introduce the broadest, and by today's standards most obscene jests. He so exceeded the bounds of licensed folly that in Austria improvization was eventually banned altogether. p. 80

The *commedia dell'arte* appears again and again in paintings from the sixteenth century onwards. Paintings of the *Comici Gelosi* and the *Comédie Italienne au cour de Navarre* are early evidence of the importance and popularity of the Italian improvizers, as are the frescoes of Burg Trausnitz. Antoine Watteau painted them with French style and elegance. In the Residenz in Würzburg there is a huge tapestry, dating from *c*.1745, showing Harlequin's entry into Venice; and above all there are numerous eighteenth-century porcelain 48, 50 49 51 54

III.

HEspero adveniente, dum Isabella, ad nutum Cynthii sui in hortum venisset, eumque in tabernaculo frondeo jam diu latentem offendisset, forte fortuna accidit, ut paulo post fastidiosus centurio Rodomondus, sonum percipiens citharizantis Prigatellæ, pariter hortum adiret, spe bona fretus, se Isabellæ gratum fore, quam gratissimum; ille vero non solum a Columbina ludibriose exercetur, sed etiam a perdilecta sua Isabella inopinatam fert repulsam. Præsens autem Arlechin, verberum in ædibus Doctoris acceptorum, haud immemor, dulcissima ulciscendi libidine eundem ad discessum stylis circumscribit ulmeis.

Joh. Jacob Schübler del.   Joh. Balth. Probst Sculpsit   Cum Pr. Sac. Cæs. Maj.   Hæred. Jer. Wolffii excud. A.V.

MJttler Zeit der Abend heran genahet, und nach erhaltener Ordre Isabella sich in den Garten bey ihrem in dem Lust-Hauß versteckten Liebsten dem Cynthio eingefunden hatte, füget sichs ungefehr, daß ihr verdrießlicher Liebhaber der Capitain Rodomondo dem Hall der Music nachgegangen, weil die Prigatellin auf der Lauten gespielet, und wider Verhoffen auch in den Garten gekommen in Meinung bey Isabella willkomm zu seyn; allein der gute Capitain wird nicht allein von Columbina mit einem spöttischen Compliment ausgelachet, sondern Isabella befiehlet ihm, ihr nicht mehr hinfüro beschwerlich zu seyn, biß er endlich von Arlechin von wegen der unlängst in des Doctors Hauß um des Capitains willen, empfangene Schläge folgends erbärmlich seine ruckständige Capitains-Gage auf den Buckel ausgezahlet bekommet.

JOHANN JAKOB SCHÜBLER
Scene from German improvized comedy, Augsburg c. 1720

36 NICOLAS LANCRET *Scene from 'Le Glorieux' by P. N. Destouches, c. 1738*

37 ELIAS GOTTLOB HAUSMANN *Friederike Caroline Neuber, alias 'Die Neuberin'*, 1744

69

38 ANTON
RAPHAEL
MENGS
*The singer
Domenico
Annibali,
1750*

39   John Joseph Zoffany *Garrick, Aicken and Bransby in 'Lethe'*, *c. 1766*

40 FERDINAND
DIETZ
*Minerva,
Veitshöchheim near
Würzburg c. 1768*

41   *Detail of a costume in the theatre museum, Drottningholm*

42   *Tunic for a 'Cavalier à la romaine', Drottningholm*

43   G. SHEMCHUGOV
Russian serf actress
as Eliane in Grétry's 'Mariages Samnites',
c. 1770

74

45 SEBASTIAN LE CLERC
*Mlle Clairon as Idame
in 'L'Orphelin de Chine'*
1779

44 *Russian stage helmets*

46   Louis Carrogis de Carmontelle *Pas de deux from the opera 'Sylvie'*   VI Linzer Kasperl: *Marionette*

figures of *commedia dell'arte* characters. The exuberant *Harlequin and Columbine* in the Rijksmuseum in Amsterdam, was made by J.J.Kaendler in 1744, but it seems almost crude when compared with the restrained gaiety and grace of F.A. Bustelli's figures, the most valuable examples of their kind. Each figure is a separate piece but they are so formed that any two may be paired. They may have been commissioned as a table decoration, or even so that their owner, moving them about, could play at *commedia dell'arte* by himself.

The theatre of improvization has always been closely related to the puppet theatre, and indeed many of the travelling players were also puppeteers. Puppet plays of all kinds were known in nearly all countries from very early times although such varieties as rod-puppets, flat-figures and shadow-puppets, of non-European origin, were only adopted in Europe after substantial modifications. The glove-puppet had been widespread since the fourteenth century, a source of

entertainment for the common people on fairgrounds and for the upper classes alike, as in the Guardis' *Parlour of the Convent of San Zaccharia in Venice* (1745–50). The children in the picture are as thrilled by the play of the glove-puppets, doubtless very similar to that of the *commedia dell'arte*, as today's children at fêtes and fairs. Harlequin, Punch or Kasperl, whatever his name may be, still carries on his rough and ready comedy act. Cheerful, always ready to help others, and at the same time to help himself, for which he always gets punished at some stage in the action, he nevertheless triumphs in the end. These puppets are manipulated by at most two people and they usually follow the broad outlines of the standard plot, improvizing dialogue.

Puppets manipulated by strings attached to limbs and joints were known in the Byzantine Empire, though the term 'marionette' to describe them was not used in England until the seventeenth century, and later in Germany.

Théâtre Italien: Harlequin discovered in the Seraglio, Paris c. 1690

LUCINDE. DONNA PETRONELLA. DONNA MARTINA. LALAGE. SIEUR ANSELMO. SIEUR GERONTE BRIGELLA.

LE SCAPINE. DONNA ANGELICA LISETTE LE ARLEQUIN BERGAMASEO. LE MESETIN.

Turba levis lepidos risus spectanda theatris
Excitat; ast caveat, seria quisquis amat.
Cum Pr. Sac. Cæs. Maj.

Martin Engelbrecht excud. A.V.

MARTIN ENGELBRECHT *Commedia dell'arte characters, late eighteenth century*

Cervantes' Don Quixote meets the puppeteer Don Pedro travelling with his theatre on a cart. The stage is quickly set up, and wax candles lit to make it look rich and dazzling. The puppeteer controls his figures from behind the scenes, while beside the stage 'a boy appeared, Master Pedro's servant, to act as interpreter and expositor of the secrets of the puppet-play; he held a baton in his hand with which he pointed to each character as it made its entry and named it'. IV We may suppose that the young man in Fragonard's painting of puppets at St Cloud performed a similar function. In this kind of marionette play the whole action was narrated by the speaker, and lines were not put into the puppets' mouths. Drums, trumpets and gunfire were sounded, and scenery and stage machines were used, to give the same illusions as in real theatres. The plays, too, were the same as those performed on larger stages: semi-historical plays about kings and political intrigues, biblical stories, legends of the saints, straight histories and comedies.

The fact that Don Pedro had to protect his head against the blows from Don Quixote's sword indicates that he moved his puppets from below. They would have been held upright by a stand at their backs or a stick inside them, wires would have been threaded through loops somewhere on the upper parts of their bodies and would have hung down to be pulled from beneath.

The hanging marionette, manipulated from above by 55 wires or strings, was capable of much freer and more realistic movement, creating an illusion more in keeping with the spirit of the baroque theatre generally. The seventeenth and eighteenth centuries were the golden age of the hanging puppet; it was a genuine form of folk-art practised by travelling showmen, jugglers, bear-leaders and the like, and at the

MAD.^{lle} COLUMBINE   MAD.^{lle} ARLEQUINE.   MAD.^{lle} LUCINDE, *fille de* GERONIE.   IL DOTTORE   SCATALON BOLOGNESE.   IL CAPITANEO SPAVENTO NAPOLITANO.   IL ARLEQUIN.   MONS.^r OCTAVIO.

LA DONNA IULIA   LA CORINNE   LE SCARAMOUCHE   LE SIEUR PANTALON.

Non oculos modo, sed loculos quoq3 Comicus arte
Haud raro petulans vexat et evacuat.
Cum Pr.Sac.Cæs.Maj.

Scaramuz und Arlequin kan manches ding ergötzen.
Dabey sie auch das Hertz und Beutel offt verletzen.
Mart.Engelbrecht excud.A.V.

MARTIN ENGELBRECHT *Commedia dell'arte characters, late eighteenth century*

same time a source of entertainment for the nobility in their palaces and at court. In Paris, a regular opera house for marionettes, the Opéra des Bamboches, was opened in 1674 with all the stage machinery and resources of a real theatre. The parts were sung off-stage, and it was so feared as a rival for real opera that Lully caused a ban on music in the puppet theatre after a production of *Les Pygmées*.[15] Plays from the repertoire of ordinary theatres were performed as well as improvizations including an orthodox Harlequin with halfmask and wooden sword. In Martin Engelbrecht's engraving of 1730 the puppeteer can be seen peering through the curtain at the orchestra in front of the stage. The great puppeteers, the Italian Pietro Aggimondi, the Hilverdings, and Josef Anton Stranitzky, travelled over half Europe from Vienna to Stockholm, with their *bambocci* ('dolls') or *bamboches*. Princes like the Esterhazys had their own theatres

built in their palaces, and Haydn wrote operas for them.

Very few of these marionettes survived their decline in the nineteenth century; but a figure from Linz, the 'Linzer Kasperl', is an exception. In his expressive, pensive and sceptical face the lower jaw and eyes are movable, giving some idea of the skill of his maker and his manipulator.

Another toy which enjoyed great popularity with princes and common people was the mechanical theatre. One example which survives is at Schloss Hellbrunn near Salzburg. The figures in it are driven to perform their fixed movements by water-power. Dolls propelled by machinery were also popular at fairs, but their actions would have been based on different themes or stories. At Hellbrunn the mechanical theatre reproduces the original owner's state: a prince – Archbishop Andreas, Count Dietrichstein – holds sway over a host of servants and vassals in his own palace.

ANON. *Josef Martin Menninger as Hans Wurst*

MARTIN ENGELBRECHT *Hans Wurst, the Salzburg pork butcher*

47   *Commedia dell'arte : Three masks*

48   ANON.
Commedia dell'arte :
'I Comici Gelosi' with Isabella Andreini
c. 1580

Overleaf:

52   FRANZ ANTON BUSTELLI *Commedia dell'arte figurines: Ottavio, Isabella and Julia, c. 1760*

53   JOHANN JOACHIM KAENDLER *Harlequin and Columbine, 1744*

57 G. A. AND F. GUARDI
*Parlour of the convent
of San Zaccharia, Venice 1745–50*

54 ANDREAS PIROT *Harlequin's Entry into Venice, tapestry in the Residenz, Würzburg c. 1745*

86

55 *Marionettes:*
Brighella and Arlecchino
eighteenth century

56 MARTIN ENGELBRECHT
Puppet theatre (Policinello), c. 1730

58 *Mechanical
theatre
in the park of
Schloss Hellbrunn,
near Salzburg c. 1750*

FRANCIS HAYMAN
Scene from Shakespeare's
'A Midsummer Night's Dream',
1743–44

IV The Plays

Title page of 'Mirame', by Jean Desmarets de Saint-Sortin and Cardinal Richelieu, showing the proscenium of the theatre in the Palais Cardinal, Paris 1641

Drama, which had flourished in ancient Greece and Rome, was reborn around the eleventh century; in every country its source was the Christian church.[1] Probably the earliest and most remarkable extant mediaeval play, the French *Jeu d'Adam*, dates from the middle of the twelfth century. At first plays were performed in churches, then at church doors, and eventually in the market-places. Gradually the whole story of man's redemption came to be played, scenes in heaven and hell were included and legends of the Virgin and the saints performed. Performances of a whole cycle of scenes might last for hours, so to keep the audience's interest short comic interludes were inserted.

These plays, first called mysteries in France and later in Germany and England also, became associated in the late middle ages with traditional festival plays, which in turn can be linked with pre-Christian rites; Shrove Tuesday plays derived from springtime processions, with participants rousing life from its winter sleep by blowing on squeaking blades of grass and driving away demons. The plays of the mummers were a popular art, dramatic, luridly imaginative and sometimes grotesque.

The morality play was born of the attempt to instil a Christian and social moral sense into the layman by means of allegories of Virtue and Vice, Wealth and Poverty, Life and Death.

In the Renaissance the classics were rediscovered, Plautus and Terence were performed, and the neoclassical, humanist Latin drama was created. The religious struggles of the Reformation and Counter-Reformation in Germany saw the establishment of the theatre as a medium of education and propaganda in both Protestant and Catholic schools.

By the seventeenth century the theatre and drama of three countries – Spain, England and France – towered above that of all other countries, dominating Europe until the second half of the eighteenth century. Mystic faith, Christian transcendentalism and humanist secularism, *religio* and *ratio*, society and individuality, ethical norms and personal responsibility – the drama of the age grew from these divergent elements, bursting forth in the sixteenth century, reaching its highest point in all three countries in the seventeenth. Germany was left behind; torn by religious and civil wars, she was incapable of producing drama of comparable stature and endurance until Lessing's day.

The development of the drama in Spain owes a great deal to the *autos sacramentales*. These thrilling spectacles, played

ANON. *Jean Racine*

with the greatest pomp and display in streets and squares, were religious plays for the festival of Corpus Christi. During the Counter-Reformation they received particular attention and improvement,[2] but since the fourteenth century processions had been held with giant models of animals symbolizing various sins. This brilliant use of image and spectacle to illustrate abstract ideas reached its peak during the seventeenth century, between Lope de Vega, to whom about four hundred *autos* have been attributed, and Calderón de la Barca.

The pastoral poems of Juan del Encina (1469–1529) had begun the development of a secular theatre with graceful pastoral comedies performed privately at court. During the course of the sixteenth century Rodrigo Cota de Maguaque and Ferdinando de Rojas wrote the earliest dramas with murder and intrigue as their subjects, and Bartolomé de Torres Naharro's division of his plays into *jornados* (meaning 'days', but in effect, 'acts') was an important structural innovation. The final stage in these formative years of the Spanish drama came with the comedies of Lope de Rueda (*c.*1510 to 1565). Written for the general public, not just for court society, their strength lay principally in racy dialogue rather than in carefully thougth out action.[3]

Lope Felix de Vega Carpio (1562–1635), commonly known as Lope de Vega, was Spain's first great baroque writer. The most important and influential dramatist and poet Spain has ever known, his output was tremendous and his fame universal. He worked extremely fast, under pressure from the public and his patrons. He took his material from wherever he could find it, from history, myth and legend, popular ballads and lives of the saints; his plays were pirated and other men's plays were fathered on him, and so no one has been able to say with absolute certainty how many of the plays attributed to him he actually did write. The legends and the hero-worship surrounding him have made it difficult to arrive at an exact assessment of him as man or as artist. 'In his lifetime he was a legendary figure, and almost a symbol of his nation's glory.'[4] He was no rebel, no outsider; he knew that in his country he could live and work only within the bounds set by church and state. Religious faith and the monarchy, patriotism and honour, chivalry and love were the mainsprings of his writing and his life. As reformer and innovator he virtually created the drama not only in Spain but far beyond her borders.

Juan Ruiz Alarcón y Mendoza (*c.*1580–1639) had a lasting influence on French and Italian comedy of character, and introduced moralizing tendencies and genuine human characteristics into the genre. Tirso de Molina (the *nom-de-plume* of a priest, Fray Gabriel Tellez, ?*c.*1580–1648) created *Don Gil de las calzas verdes* ('Don Gil of the green breeches')

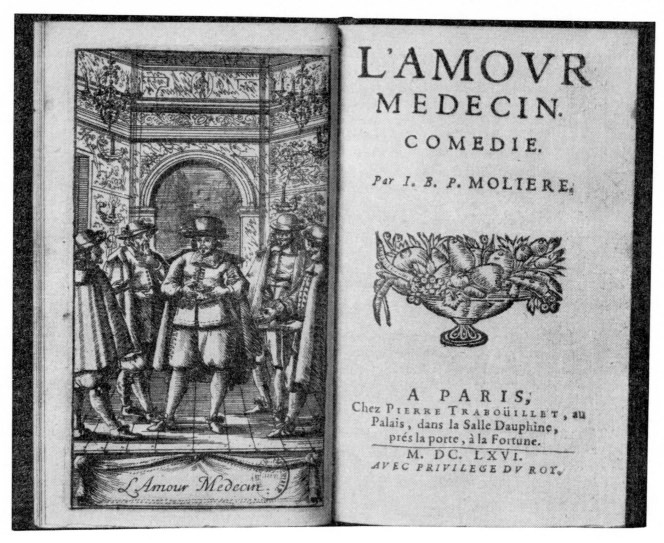

Title page of Molière's 'L'Amour Médecin', Paris 1666

who still struts the stage. He dramatized the legend of Don Juan with *Don Juan, el burlador de Sevilla y convidado de piedra*, the first of a long line of versions which includes Molière's play, Gluck's ballet and Mozart's opera.

Spanish drama reached its highest point in the work of Pedro Calderón de la Barca (1600–81).[5] This was baroque theatre with all the stops out; stage techniques had been fully mastered and were used to the best advantage. Calderón was poet and magician; the *deus ex machina* and the *diabolus ex machina* join, put asunder, preserve and destroy by turns. Heaven descends, and hell ascends, on to the stage; light

exalts and casts down; thunder, lightning and storms sweep the stage; song and music embellish the action.

Calderón was virtually the creator of the *zarzuela*, the Spanish operetta, combining spoken dialogue and sung arias. The genre owes its name to Zarzuela, the royal pleasance where Calderón's *El golfo de las sirenas* was first performed in 1657.[6] He was moreover the last and the greatest writer of *autos sacramentales*.

In a welter of sometimes vulgar pomp and overblown allegories a few works – *La vida es sueño* ('Life is a dream') and *El gran teatro del mundo* – stand out as great poetry and undying contributions to world literature. In Calderón Spanish drama is at its most intensely baroque; life and dream, reality and illusion are closely mingled and fused.

Lope de Vega's nature was restless, turbulent, full of exuberant curiosity, impatient, constantly bringing him to the verge of disaster and, even after he had entered the priesthood in his fifties, involving him with women. Calderón was by contrast silent and secretive. Lope de Vega was close to the common people from whom he drew his energy and for whom he wrote. Calderón was a courtier and an aristocrat, a reactionary in his belief in Spain's lost hegemony, behind the times also in his unquestioning acceptance of the authority of the Catholic church, undermined though it had been by the enquiring spirits of Renaissance and Reformation. Calderón was first and last a court poet, enjoying the favour of Philip IV, during whose forty-four year reign he wrote all his plays.

Calderón's achievements were never surpassed in Spain. His successors were competent enough dramatists, but on a more realistic level, sometimes satiric and crudely humorous, and sometimes blood-curdling and horrific. The prevalent types of play were the *comedias de capa y espada* ('cloak and sword plays') which purported to reveal the private lives of the nobility, and *comedias del teatro* which were based on the public lives of princes and on history as well as on mythology and legend. Equally popular were *comedias de santos*, drawn from the lives of the saints, farcical *burlescas*, and *fiestas*, spectacles with ballet and music devised for festivals at court. The wealth of Spanish drama lastingly influenced the rest of Europe, but by the seventeenth century her 'golden age' was past, her dramatic invention dried at the source, and the tide began to turn. By the end of the seventeenth century, Corneille, Molière and Racine were being performed in Spain.[7]

Neither Worcester nor Coventry is very far from Stratford on Avon, and it is quite possible that the young William Shakespeare saw and was influenced by the mysteries and miracle plays performed there. He would also have known the moralities of the sixteenth century, although their days were numbered and the new drama was beginning to rise in the histories of John Bale.

after p. 88 Only two years younger than Lope de Vega, Shakespeare is first mentioned as actor and playwright in 1592. In an active career spanning hardly more than twenty years, he carried to its perfection the noblest of dramatic genres, the tragedy of character. His histories, tragedies, comedies and 'problem plays', with their complex characterization and motivation and their rapid transitions of mood between tragedy and comedy, are the supreme achievements of an age which was surely the most brilliant in the history of the European theatre. In theatrical terms his work spans a transition from the Elizabethan plain stage, for which his earlier plays are written, to the more elaborate 'baroque' style of production, with masques and apparitions, which is called for in *The Tempest* (1611).

Although Shakespeare towers above his contemporaries in retrospect, he was by no means the only gifted or successful dramatist of his age. His exact contemporary Christopher Marlowe (1564–93), a precocious genius, was the first great English poet to turn to tragedy; and Ben Jonson (1572/3 to 1637) numbers among his achievements the virtual creation of the classical comedy of satire in England. Younger men, Francis Beaumont, John Fletcher, Philip Massinger and Thomas Middleton, wrote melodramas and comedies of manners and intrigue which are still excellent theatre.

The great age of English drama came to an abrupt end in 1642, when the Puritans closed the theatres. When the lights went up again eighteen years later the theatre found itself catering for the very different social and intellectual circumstances of Restoration England. A courtly, aristocratic audience demanded principally heroic dramas. Shakespeare had to be adapted and set to music, to come to terms with new production methods. The heroic play portrayed the audience's ideal world, full of noble sentiment and sentimentality. The comedy of manners, as represented by the works of William Wycherley, William Congreve and John Dryden,[8] mocked human hypocrisy and the folly of courtiers, while the pomposity of Nathaniel Lee's florid historical dramas was very popular in his day. In the middle of the eighteenth century Oliver Goldsmith (1730–74) contrived to rescue English comedy from the extreme sentimentality into which it had fallen, by infusing it with natural gaiety and an occasional touch of bawdy. *She Stoops to Conquer* can still delight a twentieth-century audience and so too can *The School for Scandal* by Richard Brinsley Sheridan (1751–1816), England's last great comic dramatist of the eighteenth century.

English actors took the English theatre to North America. The first known play by an American was *The Prince of Parthia* by Thomas Godfrey (1736–63), performed in 1767 in the Southwark Theatre, Philadelphia.

In France, the transition from the university plays of the Renaissance to the tragedies of the seventeenth century took place largely in the works of Robert Garnier (1544–90), whose work leans heavily on Seneca and Ariosto. Jean de la Taille (1533–1617) was the first to call for Aristotelian unity of place.[9] Antoine de Montchrestien, Sieur de Vasteville (1575–1621) was the first to dramatize a piece of very recent history in *L'écossaise*, based on the life of Mary, Queen of Scots.

The heroes in the plays of Pierre Corneille (1606–84) are stirred by great passions, not of love alone, but also of ambi- *33*

FRANÇOIS BOUCHER
Scene from Moliere's
'Le Bourgeois
Gentilhomme',
eighteenth century

93

tion and pride. Mere human feelings tend to be regarded as weaknesses, and heroic ideals are invoked in elevated language by larger-than-life characters.

Corneille was presented to Richelieu in 1634. As the ablest dramatist of the age, he presided over the adoption by all his colleagues of the principles of classical drama: the unities of action, time and place, and the strict separation of comedy and tragedy, rules which condemn, for instance, Shakespeare's entire output.

p. 90 The latter part of Corneille's working life was overshadowed by the rise of a new tragedian, Jean-Baptiste Racine (1639–99). Literary tastes were changing. Racine analyses the inner torments and desires of sensitive people with whom the members of his sophisticated audience could identify themselves. From *Andromaque* to *Phèdre* the Racinian tragedy of love was refined and perfected; within the formal bounds of the alexandrine the French language was for him an instrument of unprecedented beauty and subtlety. Corneille's heroes rise above their weaknesses; in Racine's plays we see men and women destroyed by their passions.[10]

pp. 91, 93 Jean-Baptiste Poquelin de Molière, born midway between these two great tragedians, gave to the world a comedy which, though firmly placed in his own age, by its themes and situations is valid for all time. He took Italian farce with its dependence on situations and mistaken identities, and transformed it into the comedy of manners and character, equal in literary stature to tragedy. He created the shrewd, cowardly comic servant Sganarelle, on the model of the Spanish Gracioso, and played the part himself with consummate skill. It is impossible to place all his comedies in one category; verse plays constructed according to the classical rules alternate with carefree farces, *comédie-ballets* and prose comedies, and even within these groups there are plays which are a mixture of more than one type. In his greatest plays the comedy arises simultaneously from character, situation and manners. He ridicules the latest intellectual fads, and exposes the weaknesses, injustice and abuses common to all men of all classes at all times, and his characters are rounded human beings.

After Molière's death in 1673 there were others who wrote light comedies of situation, brilliant enough when they were new, but of no permanent influence. The next really great writer of comedy in France was Pierre Carlet de Chamblain de Marivaux (1688–1763), whose works reflect the spirit of the age of the rococo. Marivaux portrays the most delicate vagaries of the heart and mind in an elegant, allusive, bantering style which has become known as *marivaudage*. His female characters are even more subtly drawn than Molière's servants and maids are drawn closer to the centre of the action, as confidantes, even to impersonate their masters; he is closer to the realities of the human heart.

Johann Esaias Nilson *Children's company in Augsburg*

The authors who wrote for the *théâtres de la foire* had to be versatile and turn out comedies, librettos for *opéra comique* (which evolved here), comic songs or *vaudevilles*, as well as scenarios for *pièces à la muette*, mimed to a sung ballad. Alain René Lesage, Charles François Papard and Alexis Piron fulfilled these requirements with ferocious wit in plays whose view of society was cynical rather than pious. Their plays were designed to please a wide public and mark the beginning of a retreat from the comedy written solely for and about the aristocratic and wealthy classes. Peasants and common people were portrayed with moving honesty and simplicity whereas in earlier comedy they had been clumsy, crude stereotypes. *Comédie larmoyante*, sentimental comedy, became popular, and the time was ripe for Rousseau.

Charles Simon Favart (1710–92) catered for the public's taste for rustic idylls in his light musical comedies and songs. His plays, set in the light-hearted, delicate world of Watteau

94

JOHANN ESAIAS NILSON *Scene from Gottsched's 'Atalanta'*

and Boucher where the sky is always blue and life a game, set him and his wife, the actress Marie Justine Favart, on a pinnacle of success and popularity for half a century. In a manner that appealed greatly to the public he combined the two main dramatic themes of the age: the rococo theatre of a carefree aristocracy, and the theatre of sentiment, full of middle-class virtue and the sorrows that beset the common people. Aristocracy and common people alike were enthralled.

One of the outstanding figures of the Enlightenment, possessed of tremendous erudition and a keenly analytical, questioning mind, one of the greatest intellects of his age, 61 François-Marie Arouet de Voltaire (1694–1778) was honoured as a national hero at the first performance of his tragedy *Irène* in Paris in 1778, but he is at his best only in his prose writings; his verse dramas, written according to the classical rules of the preceding century, lack poetic vigour.[11]

Pierre Augustin Caron de Beaumarchais (1732–99) was the last great French playwright of the baroque age. The voice of revolution, already heard as a murmur here and there, speaks loud and clear in *La folle journée, ou Le Mariage de Figaro*. A rotten society, its privileges, its way of life and its attitudes are put on trial publicly with dazzling wit and destructive scorn; and yet to those who were the principal objects of condemnation the play was just a successful, if titillating, play, although performances were twice forbidden by the king.

There was a free exchange, theatrically, between nations throughout these two centuries. *La verdad sospechosa* ('Truth suspected') by Alarcon y Mendoza was the model for Corneille's *Le Menteur* ('The liar'), Tirso de Molina put the Don Juan motive on the open market, Moreto y Cabana's *El destén con el destén* inspired Molière's *La Princess d'Élide*. Molière's *Misanthrope* became Wycherley's *Plain Dealer*, and Corneille was a model for the heroic plays of the English Restoration theatre. Elements of Calderón's *El magico prodigioso* are found in Goethe's *Faust*, and the influence of *La vida es sueño* reaches through Holberg's *Jeppe paa bjerget*, through Grillparzer (*Der Traum ein Leben*), to Gerhart Hauptmann and Hofmannsthal (*Der Turm*) in the twentieth century. Hofmannsthal's *Grosses Welttheater* clearly derives from Calderón's *Gran teatro del mundo*. Shakespeare and his contemporaries became known all over Europe through the travelling players; later, Voltaire translated Shakespeare. The *commedia dell'arte* made a rich contribution to the theatre in every country they visited; where Italian was not understood they concentrated on pantomime and acrobatic agility and made greater use of music and singing in their programmes.

The *commedia dell'arte* was not the only forerunner of the modern theatre and drama which we owe to sixteenth century Italy. The *Sofonisba* of Giangiorgio Trissino (1478 to 1550) is generally acknowledged as the first tragedy in modern literature, while the *Aminta* (1572) of Torquato Tasso (1544–95) was the model for all future pastorals, and remains one of the finest examples of the genre. Throughout the baroque age classical literature, and in particular Greek and Roman tragedy, was a source of inspiration and material, as well as providing formal models.

By the beginning of the eighteenth century the dominant style in European drama was that of French classicism, 'classical' drama at at least two removes. Once again new movements in the theatre began in Italy. Scipione Maffei (1675 to 1755) used Greek tragedy as the model for his *Merope* (1713). *62, p. 97* Carlo Goldoni (1707–93) took the best elements from the *commedia dell'arte*, which by now had lost its original invention and freshness, and raised comedy to new heights. The *commedia dell'arte*'s reliance on improvization was superseded

*Title page of Lessing's 'Hamburgische Dramaturgie',
Hamburg 1769*

trated in Germany, between the coastal plains of the north
and the mountains of the south, between Protestants and
Catholics, between mercantile, republican Hamburg and
imperial Vienna.

The magnificent spectacles at the Viennese court were
first devised by Nicolaus Avancini (1611–86), a Jesuit and
a nobleman from the South Tyrol. Over a period of forty
years there grew up beside the simple Latin plays performed
in the Jesuit schools the famous *ludi Caesarei*, court festivities p. 122
glorifying the reigning dynasty in scenes drawn from classical mythology and the Old and New Testaments.

Folk-tales, folk-songs and folk-plays were the means by
which gospel stories and the legends of the saints were hand-
ed down among the common people.[12] In contrast to this
rustic simplicity, the Jesuit theatres throughout Catholic
Europe presented both religious and classical material with
all the wealth and splendour they could command. Their
theatrical achievements were among the most resplendent of
the seventeenth century. Well-endowed monastic orders
could afford to be lavish in equiping their theatres: they were 161
often richer than many a petty prince, not to speak of travelling professional actors.

One of the most notable of the writers of Latin baroque
Jesuit drama was Jakob Bidermann (1578–1639), who wrote
for the Jesuit theatre in Munich. His *Xenodoxus* is an 'Every- 59
man', presenting, with a penetration that can still be appre-
ciated today, the worlds of 'being and seeming' and the
vanity of ambition. The play borrows from Plautus and
Terence and moves swiftly, calling on all the stage resources
of the day, including comic relief.[13]

The centre of the Jesuits' theatrical activity later moved
from Munich to Vienna. The magnificence of the Vienna
productions made those in Munich look insignificant, but
the increased emphasis on spectacle, typical of the baroque
theatre, brought with it a decline in literary quality.

In Switzerland the Jesuit theatre based on Fribourg flourished from 1620 to about 1700. In Italy the outstanding centres were Rome, Naples, Bologna, Florence, Parma and
Milan.

Germany had not only the Jesuit theatres but also the
Protestant school theatre, which aimed to spread knowledge
of all spheres of life, history and mythology, and to teach its
audiences morals, by means of exemplary tragedies, pastorals and comedies. The chief writers for this theatre came
from Silesia, a region which suffered less during the Thirty
Years war than the rest of Germany. Daniel Caspar Lohenstein (1635–83) used the most lurid means to serve his ends;
his heroes are whiter than white, his villains of the blackest
dye. Venus, Mars and Mors are presented with macabre
relish. His tragedies and those of Andreas Gryphius (1616–64)

by Goldoni's literary humour, and situation as a source of
comedy was replaced by the human character.

p. 97 Among Goldoni's contemporaries, Pietro Chiari (1711 to
1785) was both rival and imitator, but he joined forces with
Goldoni as a rival to Carlo Gozzi (1720–1806), who in his
turn continued to write for the old *commedia dell'arte*, and
also achieved great public success with a new form, fairy
tale comedy. His *Principessa Turandot* (1763) was translated
by Schiller and, eventually, set to music by Puccini.

The terrible wars and plagues of the seventeenth century
left Germany with a desperate craving for pleasure, security,
wealth, splendour and beauty. The fear of death, the intimate knowledge of decay and destruction gave rise to the
contradictions of the age. The most delicate sensitivity existed side by side with brutal cynicism, dreams of an idyllic
'simple life' beside boundless ambition and ostentation, the
desire for classical discipline beside uncontrolled emotion
and the heights and depths of passion. The differences between Northern and Southern Europe generally are concen-

IL FILOSOFO
D I
CAMPAGNA
DRAMMA GIOCOSO PER MUSICA
DI POLISSENO FEGEJO
PASTOR ARCADE
DA RAPPRESENTARSI
NEL TEATRO GRIMANI
DI S. SAMUEL
L' AUTUNNO dell' ANNO 1754.
Dedicato all' Eccellentissime
DAME VENEZIANE.

IN VENEZIA , MDCCLIV·
PRESSO MODESTO FENZO.
Con Licenza de' Superiori

Theatralische Werke
von
Carlo Gozzi.

Aus dem Italiänischen übersezt.

Erster Theil.

Bern,
bey der Typographischen Gesellschaft.
1777.

Title page of Goldoni's 'Il Filosofo di campagna',
Venice 1754

Title page of Gozzi's plays in a German translation,
Berne 1777

and Johann Christian Hallmann (1640–1704) are full of torture and violent death; but these writers laid the foundations of later German comedy. The vision of Gryphius and Lohenstein was naturally darkened by war and its aftermath, but their verse, though ponderous, is often extremely powerful.

The plays presented by the travelling companies at this time lacked any poetic or literary virtues and were even more bloodthirsty and horrific. Martin Opitz (1597–1639) had tried to bring German literature up to the standards of other nations. He received a poet's crown from Ferdinand II in Vienna in 1625. In fact his own plays, unoriginal adaptations of Seneca, like those of his pupil, Johann Rist, are academic, flat and totally without poetry.[14]

By the eighteenth century the repertoire of travelling companies in Germany consisted entirely of French plays or plays in the French style. Friederike Caroline Neuber had translations made of Corneille and Racine, and herself wrote curtain-raisers and pastorals. It is clear from contemporary playbills that every serious drama had to be accompanied

by a short comedy. Johann Christoph Gottsched (1700–66) p. 95 was another who worked to reform the German theatre along the lines of French classicism. In his efforts to create a comedy that would be according to the rules and yet would appear easy and natural he was supported by his wife, Luise Adelgunde Gottsched, who translated Molière, Destouches and Addison, and wrote realistic, satirical social comedies after the model of the French and the Dane Holberg. It is clear from her translations that German was still a much more elaborate, ornate and indeed baroque language than French.[15]

The German playwrights mentioned in Lessing's *Ham-* p. 96 *burgische Dramaturgie*, written between 1767 and 1769, are largely forgotten today and are far outnumbered by the French, and it was only at this time that Shakespeare was re-discovered for the German stage. Gotthold Ephraim p. 99 Lessing (1729–81) was the first German to write plays of more than academic interest. His tragedies of middle-class life, still something very new in the mid-eighteenth century, his *Nathan der Weise*, set in the Palestine of the Crusades but imbued with the best human principles of the Enlightenment, p. 100 and his comedy *Minna von Barnhelm*, are still performed today. German audiences were not really ready for drama of this quality, and at the first production of *Minna* in Hamburg in 1767 acrobats had to perform between acts to fill the theatre.

The international theatre of the European courts began to lose its grip on Germany in the second half of the eighteenth century. The 'storm and stress' of Goethe's *Götz von Berlichingen* burst upon the dainty world of the rococo in p. 98 1774, and German *Singspiele* and operas began to rival the

Playbill of the 'Electoral Court Comedians' of Saxony, Leipzig 1766

Mit gnädigster Erlaubniß
wird heute
von den Churfürstl. Sächsischen
Hof-Comödianten
auf dem neuen Theater,
nach einer vorhergegangenen Rede in Versen
zum Erstenmale aufgeführet:
Herrmann.
Eine Tragödie in fünf Acten, und ein Originalstück in Versen vom Herrn Prof. Schlegel.
Personen:

Herrmann, Herzog der Cherusker.	Der Fürst der Carten.
Sigmar, Herrmanns Vater.	Varus, Prätor in Deutschland.
Flavius, Herrmanns Bruder.	Marcus, ein junger Römer.
Segest, ein Fürst der Cherusker.	Adelheid, Herrmanns Mutter.
Siegmund, Segests Sohn, ein Priester Augusts.	Thusnelde, Segests Tochter, Herrmanns Braut.
Der Fürst der Chauzier.	

Stumme Personen:
Sechs Römer, die dem Varus in Ketten gebunden ne Weile vortragen.
Einige Catten.
Einige Deutschen, die dem Herrmann die eroberten Adler und die Waffen nachtragen.
Der Schauplatz ist ein Hayn, mit den Bildern des Thuiston und Mannus.
Darauf folgt ein Ballet:
von vergnügten Schäfern.
Den Beschluß macht:
Die unvermuthete Wiederkunft.
Eine Comödie des Herrn Regnard in einem Acte.
Personen:

Geronte, Clitanders Vater.	Der Marquis.
Mad. Bertrand, Lucilens Tante.	Merlin, Clitanders Diener.
Clitander, Lucilens Liebhaber.	Herr Andres, ein Wucherer.
Lucile, Clitanders Geliebte.	Jaquinet, Gerontens Diener.
Cidalise, Lucilens Freundinn.	Lisette, Lucilens Mägdchen.

Der Anfang ist nach 5. Uhr.
Der Preiß der Logen und Plätze ist dieser:

Geschlossene Logen des Ersten Ranges.	Logen des zweyten Ranges.	Logen des britten Ranges.
No. 1 u. 14. jede zu 8 Person. 8 thl.	No. 20 Große Mittel-Loge, auf Stühlen, die Person 1 thl.	No. 26 Große Seiten-Loge, die Person 8 gr.
No. 2 u. 13 jede zu 7 Person. 7 thl.	welche statt der bisherigen großen Loge dienet.	No. 27 Große Mittel-Loge, die Person 12 gr.
Die übrigen Logen zu 6 Personen jede 6 thl.	Die übrigen geschlossenen Seiten-Logen, alle zu 6 Personen 4 thl.	Die übrigen geschlossenen Seiten-Logen zu 6 Personen 3 thl.

Im Parterre 6 Gr. auf der Gallerie 4. Gr.
Und die Billets können im Quandischen Hofe in der Nicolaistraße vorne 3 Treppen hoch abgeholet werden.
Man ist genöthiget sehr zu bitten: sich gütigst gefallen zu lassen, daß künftig unter währender Action kein Zutritt aufs Theater erlaubt werden kann, weil sowohl die Enge des Raums, als auch das Machinenwerk solches bey mehrmaliger Verwandelung wegen Verhinderung und zu besorgenden Schadens nicht gestattet; da überdiß noch der enge Raum zur Zeit zum Ankleiden muß gebraucht werden.
Leipzig, Freytags, den 10. Oct. 1766.
Heinrich Gottfried Koch.

Italians and the French. Gradually one court after another began to include more and more German works in its programmes. The foreign theatre kept its footing longest in Berlin, where Frederick II refused ever to visit a theatre where works were performed in German.

An earlier German counterbalance to the Italian and French court theatre was created in Vienna in the popular theatres. The Kärntnertor theatre became the first permanent theatre for the common people in all the German-speaking countries. It opened in 1711, under the direction of Josef Anton Stranitzky (1676–1726) who had started as a puppeteer and is credited with the invention of Hans Wurst. Philip Hafner (1731–64) contrived to preserve the improvizatory comedy of Hans Wurst within comedies of character and thus created the Viennese popular comedy which depicted everyday life, in the local dialect, yet avoided the obscenities of an earlier age. His plays remained the model for all Viennese *Singspiele* and popular plays until the rise of Raimund and Nestroy in the following century.

As a province of Spain, the Low Countries were initially under predominantly Spanish influences in the theatre, but they were the first foreign land to be visited by the English travelling players. Later French plays, particularly those of Molière became very popular. In the golden age of the Dutch Netherlands, in the century following their independence, there also arose a native literature. Their greatest playwright was Joost van den Vondel (1587–1679) whose plays, based on Seneca, Euripides and Sophocles, are a product of their age, combining humanist scholarship with the baroque sense of the dramatic. Vondel was famous not only in the Netherlands but abroad, and had a particularly strong influence on Gryphius. His tragedy *Gysbreght van Aemstel* is still performed. p. 178

Vertooningen, *tableaux vivants*, were a product of the baroque theatre that was particularly popular in Holland; and so were spine-chilling horror plays. By the eighteenth century Dutch theatres performed mainly French and German plays; the great age of Dutch influence was past.

As for Scandinavia, Norway and Finland at this time had little or no theatre of any kind, while in Denmark and Sweden the picture was the same as in the rest of Europe. For a long time they were visited by French, Italian, English and German travelling companies, performing the drama of their own and each other's countries, and only later were plays written in Danish and Swedish. Ludvig Holberg (1684–1754) is called the Father of the Danish Theatre. Like many of his contemporaries his plays and style owed a lot to Latin, French and Italian drama, but he created original comedies of character and intrigue, about national folk-heroes, such as the tragicomic peasant farmer, Jeppe of the Hill (*Jeppe paa bjerget*).

Playbill of the 'Electoral Court Comedians' of Saxony,
Vienna 1697

ANON. *Gotthold Ephraim Lessing*

Independent national theatres arose in the Scandinavian countries, as elsewhere, only in the last thirty or forty years of the eighteenth century. The theatre in Sweden remained predominately French in style until the reign of Gustav III, who came to the throne in 1771. Russia, too, for a large part of the seventeenth and eighteenth centuries, relied mainly on travelling companies from Western Europe; the plays performed by the native troupes of serfs were also foreign. Original Russian plays first began to be written during the reign of Catherine II. p. 108

The perfect baroque art-form is opera, in which music, poetry and the plastic arts combine to please all the senses of the enthralled audience. Opera as we know it is the product of a long evolutionary process. Music and song had formed a part of theatrical performances from the early middle ages. One can perhaps see pointers to later operatic forms in Adam de la Halle's *Jeu de Robin et Marion*, first performed in Naples around 1233,[16] in which the simple action, the wooing of Marion, is performed by four solo singers, or even in the earlier *Aucassin et Nicolette* which originated in Hainault at the beginning of the thirteenth century and in which the narration, the *chantefable*, alternates spoken prose and sung verse.[17]

Music flourished as much as literature in Shakespeare's England. Instrumental music formed a prelude to every theatrical performance and music and singing permeated the plays themselves. A song might point a dramatic situation or prolong the action; folk-songs, drinking songs, funeral marches, military drums and trumpets, serenades and music lessons were all means of adorning the play with music.

The triumphs and pageants of Florence and Venice were another preliminary stage in the evolution of opera, and musical intermezzi came to be more complete works of art in themselves. A significant formal advance was made between the madrigal comedies of Adriano Banchieri (1567 to 1634) and Orazio Vecchi (1550–1605), with their polyphonic choruses and *commedia dell'arte* action, and the pastoral *Dafne*, with music by Jacopo Peri and text by Ottavio Rinuccini. In this work the music is subordinated to the words and the action; solo voices sing in recitative above a very simple accompaniment. *Dafne*, which is acknowledged as the first real opera, received its first performance in the Palazzo Corsi in Florence in the spring of 1598[18] before the *Camera fiorentina*, an association which wanted to revive classical drama, proceeding from the assumption that the parts in Greek tragedy were originally sung.

The music of this, the first opera, has been lost, but its influence was felt as far away as Germany. The oldest opera to have survived is *Euridice*,[19] also by Peri and Rinuccini. The term 'opera' was not yet in use, and it was designated a

**ACTE I. SCENE VI.**

**MINNA DE BARNHELM**
ACTE I. SCENE II.

**ACTE II. SCENE II.**

DANIEL CHODOWIECKI *Scenes from Lessing's 'Minna von Barnhelm'*

dramma per musica. The original score has no specific orchestration; the choice of instruments was left to the performers and depended on what was available. There would have been a *basso continuo* of harpsichord, lute and double-bass with a few strings and wind instruments. At that date it was quite usual for the musicians to play on the stage.

The first work of major importance in the new genre was the *favola in musica, L'Orfeo* by Claudio Monteverdi (1567 to 1643), whom his contemporaries called the 'oracolo della musica', the 'Divino Claudio'. His secular music had a decisive influence on baroque music. Opera houses sprang up in Venice to accommodate his *drammi in musica.* There was far less recitative, and arias, duets and trios formed an increasingly large part of the works. *L'Incoronazione de Poppea* and *Il ritorno d'Ulisse in patria* are the greatest music dramas of the age. They effected a real union of words and music.

p. 102

Monteverdi remains the outstanding figure in the history of Venetian opera. The first opera house in Venice, the Teatro San Cassiano, built in 1637, opened at the beginning of a period of great activity. One of Monteverdi's most talented pupils, Francesco Cavalli (1602–76) composed forty-two operas of great charm, all but two of which received their first performance in Venice. His *Ercole amante* was commissioned for the wedding of Louis XIV of France in 1660, though its first performance was delayed until 1662. Francesca Caccini (1581? – *c.*1640) the daughter of the Roman singer and composer Giulio Caccini, who contrived to interpolate some of his own music into Peri's *Euridice,* composed among other works *La liberazione di Ruggiero dall'isola d'Alcina* (1625) which was the first in a long line of operas and ballets on this extremely popular subject performed at many different courts – notably Paris and Vienna – during the next hundred years. Marc Antonio Cesti (1623 to 1669), another composer of the Venetian school, was a master of the idyllic mood and sensuous melody. Credited with over a hundred operas, very few of which have survived, he composed his masterpiece, *Il pomo d'oro*, for the wedding of the Emperor Leopold I in Vienna in 1667.[20]

p. 126

The chief male roles in these early operas were frequently written for *castrati* who, in spite of a certain lack of verisimilitude, retained their popularity on the stage until the second half of the eighteenth century.

In Venice opera evolved in the form of works principally for solo singers, with passages of recitative, with the chorus kept very much in the background, if not totally suppressed. In Rome, on the other hand, early baroque opera made more use of the chorus, with crowd scenes, as well as lavish stage settings to delight the audience's eyes, and comic *intermezzi*. Domenico and Virgilio Mazzochi and Stefano Landi contributed to the achievements of opera in Rome with their pastorals, spectacular operas, music dramas and comic operas.

Italian operas were performed in Paris under the patronage of Cardinal Mazarin, but they did not gain a firm foothold in France. They inspired Robert Cambert (1628–77) to write the first French operas, but opera in France really begins with Jean Baptiste Lully (1632–87).[21] Although he was an Italian by birth, Lully's music is completely at one in spirit

pp. 104, 107

with the language of Corneille and Racine, and is the expression of its age, the self-confident, 'classical' era of Louis XIV, whose reign spanned Lully's creative years and to whose wishes he had to conform, while enjoying the king's protection against his numerous enemies.[22] In Lully's operas the declamatory *arioso* is balanced by instrumental music, solos, choral songs and balletic interludes. He took up motifs from popular music and originated the modern overture. His fruitful collaboration with Molière gave rise to the *comédie-ballet*, which developed from the *intermèdes* danced by the Ballet de cour, and which in turn led to the *tragédie lyrique*, a specifically French genre which was the main achievement of Lully's later years.

The Italians made greater inroads in Germany and Austria than in France, and German composers travelled to Italy to learn their craft, among them Heinrich Schütz (1585–1672),[23] whose stay in Venice made him familiar with the works of Monteverdi. It is unfortunate that the music of his *Daphne* (1627), the first German opera, is lost. Martin Opitz's libretto, partly a translation, partly a refashioning of Rinuccini's text, makes it appear likely that it consisted of a sequence of rather static set-pieces for chorus or soloists, a cantata rather than a *dramma per musica*.[24]

In Vienna the musical scene was completely dominated by Italians in the seventeenth century, particularly by the Venetians. The works of Cavalli were very popular, the court commissioned works from Cesti, and Marc Antonio Ziani (1653–1715) spent over twenty years there. The versatile Giovanni Andrea Bontempi (1624–1705), an architect, singer, conductor and theorist, as well as a composer, spent many years in Dresden, as did Carlo Pallavicini (*c.* 1630 to 1688). Both were successively assistant to Schütz, who was court director of music (*Kapellmeister*) there, and Pallavicini occupied this post after Schütz's death. In Munich the same position was held from 1674 to 1732 by a father and son in succession, Ercole and Gioseffo Antonio Bernabei from Rome.

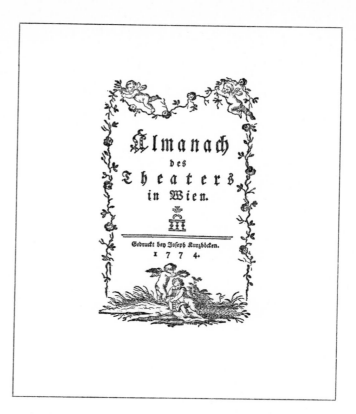

Title page of 'Almanach des Theaters in Wien', Vienna 1774

Title page of French edition of Pergolesi's 'La Serva Padrona', Paris 1752

First page of Monteverdi's manuscript of 'L'Incoronazione di Poppea' (above) and a page by a copyist

The earliest surviving opera with a German libretto was first performed in Nuremberg in 1644: *Seelewig* ('Soul eternal'), 'a spiritual pastoral or comedy, set for singing in the Italian style' by Sigmund Gottlieb Staden (1607–55). It consists mostly of strophic songs and *ritornelli*.[25]

An independent German baroque opera flourished for a time in the northern city of Hamburg, where the first public opera house in Germany was opened in 1678. The leading composer who wrote for the Hamburg opera in its early years was Johann Sigmund Kusser (1660–1727), a friend and pupil of Lully, whose influence is discernible in his melodic p. 105 writing. Reinhard Keiser (1674–1739) wrote over a hundred operas, rich in melody, and on all kinds of subjects, mythological, historical and pastoral as well as using more popular, not to say vulgar, material. German opera in Hamburg reached its final peak with Georg Philipp Telemann (1684–1767). His operas leave the formality of the baroque behind and move into the rococo world of gallantry and grace. Well before Gluck and Mozart he tried to characterize people and actions by a more subtle treatment of instrumentation. In addition to his own numerous operas he adapted works by Keiser and Handel, who went to Hamburg in 1703 and composed four operas in the three years he spent there, reflecting the taste of the times by mingling Italian and German styles. The Hamburg opera house had to close in 1738, by which date German opera had been completely superseded in public favour by French and Italian opera.

After the deaths of Cesti and Cavalli towards the end of the seventeenth century, Venetian opera went into decline, and pre-eminence passed to Naples. Pietro Alessandro Gaspare Scarlatti (1660–1725) had a far-reaching influence on eighteenth-century opera, up to the time of Mozart; his development of the *da capo* aria, his instrumental writing and use of musical expression were widely emulated. He wrote over a hundred operas of which a characteristic is the clear distinction between recitative and aria. There are many names, famous and obscure, in the history of Neapolitan opera, contributing particularly to comic opera and above all to the *opera buffa*, a genre of purely Neapolitan origins which evolved from the comic intermezzi. The best-known p. 101 is *La Serva padrona*, an *intermezzo buffo* written by Giovanni Battista Pergolesi (1710–36) to accompany his *opera seria Il prigioniero superbo*. Good and bad human qualities are exaggerated to the point of the grotesque, but it is because it depicts a real and not an ideal world that this opera has lasted so well.[26] The melodic wealth is not surpassed elsewhere by Pergolesi, nor indeed by any of his contemporaries. Short but meaningful thematic ideas characterize the arias and carry the action forward in the recitatives. His use of ornament is restrained. Recitatives are accompanied only by the continuo and the small orchestra consists only of a *basso continuo* and strings. 'All the subsequent masters of *opera buffa*, Galuppi, Piccinni, Paesiello, Cimarosa, Rossini himself, are faithful disciples of Pergolesi.'[27]

In 1752 *La Serva padrona* was performed in Paris by an Italian company whose eighteen month stay there set off a revolutionary revival of all French opera writing and performance. Realism in the *opéra comique*, even criticism of contemporary *moeurs*, constituted a reaction against the stylization and formal posing of Lully's *tragédie lyrique*. This had been developed further by Jean-Phillippe Rameau (1683–1764), a greater composer than Lully. He retained the mythological subject matter, the ballet and the chorus, but his melodic writing was more sophisticated, and the introduction of horns and clarinets gave his instrumental music more colour.[28]

Jean-Jacques Rousseau (1712–78) wrote his *intermède*, *Le Devin du village*, in imitation of Italian *opera buffa*. It was greeted with enthusiasm by the champions of the new fashion and with obloquy by its opponents. Rousseau applied his famous principle of 'return to Nature' in opera as well. In his opinion the human voice was 'natural' while instrumental music was not, and should be subordinated to the voice in a manner that should be '*ni forcé ni baroque*' but uncontrived and pleasing to souls who yearned for the simplicities of pastoral life.

In the *opéra comique* and the *théâtres de la foire* composers like Egidio Duni, Pierre Alexandre Monsigny, François André Philidor and André Grétry had great success with hilarious satires, romantic idylls, tales of fairies, magic and myth, many of which had libretti by the same man, Jean François Marmontel. Grétry composed an *Aucassin et Nicolette*, harking back to one of opera's earliest ancestors.

The outstanding English composer of the seventeenth century was Henry Purcell (1659–95), who was alone among his contemporaries in being able to absorb both French and Italian influences and yet produce specifically English music. He wrote one opera, *Dido and Aeneas*, and a large number of semi-operas, based on straight plays in which the dialogue is spoken but interspersed with arias, choruses, instrumental pieces, pantomime and ballet. Among these lavish and ingenious hybrids, typical products of the baroque theatre, are *King Arthur*, in which Purcell collaborated with Dryden, *The Fairy Queen*, derived from *A Midsummer Night's Dream*, and *The Tempest*, also based on Shakespeare. Purcell's evocation of Arcadian landscapes and pastoral bliss, his imaginative, stylized effects and his sensitive treatment of the English language were unsurpassed.

No national opera evolved to survive Purcell's death: the scene was dominated by Italian opera until the arrival in

ACADEMIE ROYALE DE MUSYQUE

ARMIDE

JEAN BÉRAIN
*Frontispiece
of libretto
of Lully's 'Armide'*

p. 106, 65 London in 1711 of George Frideric Handel (1685–1759). His first triumph was the opera *Rinaldo* (1711), and the foundation of a 'Royal Academy of Music' under Handel's direction began a new chapter in the history of opera in England. Handel wrote about forty Italian *opere serie*. Only one, *Serse*, has some *buffo* scenes and departs from the rather stilted pattern of the other operas in favour of a more plastic use of various aria forms. One of the reasons for Handel's great success may have been the fact that he wrote for specific singers, and even for whole companies, whose abilities he knew. In spite of rival operatic activities sponsored by the Prince of Wales, Handel flourished in London for seventeen years, until a reaction set in against the gods and heroes, the solemnity and the mythological backgrounds, that were the very stuff of *opera seria*.

64 *The Beggar's Opera* (1728) by John Gay and Christopher Pepusch, had an immediate and enormous success, and set a fashion for the ballad opera. In this genre spoken dialogue linked songs set to folk-tunes or popular tunes of the day. Set in contemporary London, its characters thieves, whores and beggars, *The Beggar's Opera* satirized politics, society and *opera seria*. Its success was at least partly responsible for the bankruptcy and closure of Handel's Academy.

English travelling companies took the ballad opera to Germany where it became naturalized as the *Singspiel*,[29] and where, too, its popularity represented a middle-class reaction against court fashions. A similar development occurred in Spain, where the *zarzuela*, a small-scale entertainment originated by Calderón, with songs, spoken verse and ballet, became more generally popular. Like the ballad opera and the *Singspiel* it was frequently set among the lower classes in the large cities.

Meanwhile *opera seria* was reviving, not least thanks to the most versatile and influential of all librettists, Pietro Metastasio (1698–1782) who recognized and expressed the spirit of the rococo.[30] It is hardly possible to describe the development of opera in terms of individual nationalities. Metastasio, a Roman, lived and worked for fifty-two years p. 107 in Vienna, the Florentine, Lully, created the opera of France, opera in England was revived by the German Handel, and Johann Adolph Hasse (1699–1783),[31] who was born in Hamburg, became a pupil of Scarlatti and an outstanding exponent of the Italian court opera style of the mid-eighteenth century.

The formal conventions of seventeenth-century French and Italian opera had gradually fossilized. The most important developments in opera since Monteverdi were introduced by Christoph Willibald von Gluck (1714–87). His reforms resulted in music being made to serve the dramatic action, instead of being a succession of virtuoso show-pieces. He strove for simplicity and truthfulness of expression, 'he did away with the superfluous coloratura on which the *da capo* aria relied for its effects, gave greater depth and significance to the plot, and eliminated excessively large-scale scenes for the chorus',[32] which he tried to use more in the manner of classical drama. As a young man Gluck travelled widely. He studied with Sammartini in Milan and many of his operas are in the Italian heroic style, even some written after the first 'reform' operas. He also visited London, where Handel made a great impression on him, Hamburg and Copenhagen. He eventually settled in Vienna in 1750, though he maintained contacts with Favart in Paris and the *vaudeville* and the *opéra comique* were not without influence on his music and his attitude to his work. Marie Antoinette, who had been his pupil, summoned him to Paris, and *Iphigénie en Aulide* became the first of his works to enjoy a great success at the Paris opera house, although written in a style very different from any grand opera that had been heard there before. A new German singing style began to evolve, and for the first time German opera began to enjoy European approval and importance. Vienna was the centre of the new

Playbill for Keiser's
'Das zerstörte Troja', Hamburg 1716

Julius Cæsar:
AN
OPERA.
Compos'd by
G. Frederick Handel,
of London, Gent.
donné le 20 février
1724

LONDON,
Printed at Cluer's Printing-Office in Bow-Church-Yard,
and sold there, and by B. Creake at ij Bible in Jermyn street, S^t.

*Title page of Händel's
'Julius Caesar', London 1724*

opera whose reviving effects were felt all over Europe. The opera house in Bologna was opened in 1763 with Gluck's *Il trionfo di Clelia*, his influence was felt by the national Danish opera and his works were performed at the court opera in Stockholm. In Paris his reform operas were violently opposed by the admirers of Niccolò Piccinni (1728–1800). Piccinni's comic opera *La cecchina ossia la buona figliuola*, with a libretto by Goldoni based on Richardson's *Pamela*, was one of the great international successes of its day, transforming a Neapolitan *opera buffa* into a musical comedy oozing with middle-class sentimentality. Although he was the 'Italian' faction's chosen hero, Piccinni himself admired Gluck, and was made the centre of the dispute against his will.

The light-hearted musical comedies of Giovanni Paesiello (1740–1816) demand from the singers an almost balletic agility and grace.[33] The *stile galante* of court opera began to penetrate the *opera buffa* too. Paesiello carried it as far as St Petersburg, where he was director and inspector of the Italian opera at Catherine the Great's court.

The Pantheon in Rome places the bust of Domenico Cimarosa between Paesiello and Antonio Sacchini. Throughout his life he was on the move, as was not unusual at that time, settling wherever his works were being performed. For the performance in Vienna of his opera *I due baroni di Rocca Azzura* (1789) Mozart wrote the soprano aria *Alma grande*.

When one looks at the work of even the few composers mentioned here one is amazed by the sheer quantity, as well as by the receptiveness of the contemporary audiences and the facility in learning and performing that was required of the singers and actors. The number of Italian opera composers in the eighteenth century is enormous and it would be impossible to arrange them in any order of merit.

p. 105 The most popular operatic works in Germany in the second half of the eighteenth century were the many *Singspiele* or operettas. *Doktor und Apotheker* by Carl Ditters von Dittersdorf (1739–99) still retains some of its original appeal. Its humour, naturalism and lively melodies pointed the way forward to comic opera in Germany.

66 Franz Joseph Haydn (1732–1809) wrote the greater part of his twenty-four, mostly Italian, operas for the opera house or the marionette theatre in the park at Esterhazy. *Il mondo della luna* has remained the most popular.

A formal step towards the development of German opera was taken in Vienna when the Emperor Joseph II ordered the establishment of a *Deutsches Nationalsingspiel* ('German national musical theatre'). From now on German operas were to be performed in the court theatre, which was open to the public, and Italian and French operas were to be sung in German.

The operatic climax of the eighteenth century came at its end with Wolfgang Amadeus Mozart (1756–91). He was no reformer like Gluck but all the elements of the age are gathered together and transformed in his work; *opera seria*, *opera buffa* and *Singspiel* are imbued with a richness and beauty they had never known before. After some youthful comic operas. Mozart's first full-length essays were *opere serie* in the Neapolitan style with their stereotyped characters and situations; in accordance with the usual practice recitative, *arioso* and *da capo* arias carry the action and present the character's state of mind, while the expression of strong emotions is left to the instrumental passages. But in *Idomeneo*, his most important *opera seria* and first major opera, Mozart was already no longer interested in the singers and arias alone, but turned his attention to the plot, collaborated in

JEAN BÉRAIN *Title page of Lully's 'Phaëton', Paris 1683*

Bilingual playbill for Manfredini's 'Charlemagne', St Petersburg 1764

the text, and evolved a freer, more dramatic action which is supported and carried along by the music.

Mozart's early comic operas were also written in a conventional style, using stock characters. But then ensembles and instrumental music grew in importance in relation to the set-piece arias. Beaumarchais' vituperative political satire *Le Mariage de Figaro* becomes a human comedy; the music does not so much prophesy the downfall of the *ancien régime* as demonstrate how love is the prime mover, forming and transforming all men. The characters are clearly defined individuals behaving in a credible manner. The balance between arias and ensembles becomes more effective, characters are revealed by their relationships and behaviour towards each other. An ever-recurring theme of European drama, the legend of Don Juan, was treated by Mozart in a way that wove together comic and tragic strands in a superb

fabric. That comedy of errors, *Così fan tutte*, clearly belongs in the *buffo* tradition but it is developed on a higher plane than *buffo* had ever reached before; actions and situations arise from the characters, genuine and simulated emotions can hardly be distinguished. *The Seraglio* derives from another established form, the *Singspiel*, with spoken, vernacular dialogue to carry the action between arias and ensembles, but again Mozart goes beyond the basic pattern and 'through-composes' the dramatic climaxes.[34]

All the elements of the baroque musical theatre are united in *The Magic Flute: opera seria, opera buffa, demiseria, Singspiel*, big choral scenes, solos and ensembles. For the first time a German text (Emmanuel Schikaneder's passport to immortality) is used in an opera with a serious purpose and a cosmic theme. The last baroque opera is also the first romantic opera.

VIII GIOVANNI BATTISTA TIEPOLO *Rinaldo under the Spell of Armida*

MORS PECATORUM PESSIMA

59   ASAM BROTHERS
St Bruno and Xenodoxus,
over a confessional
in the Asamkirche,
St Johannes Nepomuk,
Munich 1733

60　C. Frusotte *Scene from 'Les deux solitaires', Théâtre de l'Ambigu-comique, Paris*

61 ANON.
*Voltaire receives
a laurel wreath
from Mlle Clairon,
Paris 1778*

Aux yeux de Paris enchanté   Pour jouir de l'honneur de l'immortalité,
Reçois cet hommage   Voltaire reçois la couronne
Que confirmera d'âge en âge   Que l'on vient de te présenter,
La sévère Postérité.   Il est beau de la mériter,
Non tu n'as pas besoin d'ateindre au noir rivage,   Quand c'est la France qui la donne.

64   WILLIAM HOGARTH *Scene from Gay's 'Beggar's Opera', 1729*   65   PHILIPPE MERCIER *George Frideric Handel, 1730*

66 ANON. *Final scene from 'L'Incontro Improvviso', with Haydn at the harpsichord, Esterhaza c. 1775*

<small>L</small>UDOVICO <small>O</small>TTAVIO <small>B</small>URNACINI *Set for 'Il Fuoco eterno', Vienna 1674*

V The Stages

The sophistication of the baroque stage, with its complicated machines and elaborate scenery, was not attained overnight. Permanent stages and scenery were relatively new, and their development was gradual.

The mediaeval idea of simultaneous stages, so that different scenes could be played in different places at the same time has its parallel in mediaeval art, when several different events are shown happening in the same picture. The simplest kind of simultaneous stages were those erected on carts, or 'pageants', in England, before the emergence of professional actors. Curtains hung from the floor of the stage to form changing rooms, wardrobes and a place for storing properties. By lining up a number of carts in a row a wide variety of locations was obtained, and in addition the space in front of the carts could be used. The players were members of the craft guilds, who also provided the carts.

p. 117

For the English mystery *Mary Magdalene* a number of stages each representing a different place were arranged in a circle. Perhaps unexpectedly, there is little scenery to differentiate between the different locations. For the palaces of Caesar, Herod and Pilate, and for the world itself, a chair is the only stage property; there is no apparent difference between the inn and Simon's house, and only heaven and hell have a roof and curtains.

p. 118

An engraving of 1547 records the stage-settings for a passion play in Valenciennes. The different scenes of the action are arranged in a row: paradise, Nazareth, the temple, Jerusalem, the bishop's house, the golden gates, the sea, limbo and hell. By this date several of the scenes have elaborate settings, making quite clear the place they are meant to be.

p. 118

The *carros* in Spain, the carts for the *autos sacramentales*, were built with great art by the best master carpenters and the costumes were equally lavish and effective.

'The platform is firmly mounted on wheels, and upon it there rises in several stories an ingenious construction of movable and fixed scenery and machinery for transformations, which make it possible not merely to suggest, but to present physically all the symbolic and allegorical trappings of this kind of religious drama. The carts are pulled by oxen, which, when greater expense is possible, are covered with rich cloths and their horns are gilded and adorned with flowers. When one cart is not enough several are used in a line and for some of Calderón's *autos sacramentales* no less than five are necessary ... The multitude and variety of men and beasts, heavenly and infernal spirits, personified virtues and vices, grails, crosses and sacraments, suns and moons, clouds, rainbows, lightning and thunder, smoke and fire, and above all the miraculous transformations, are astounding.'[1]

The first performance of each *auto* was given outside the

ANON. *Mediaeval English 'pageant'*

royal palace. Scaffolding was erected to seat the noble audience, with the king's canopied throne in the centre. The ladies watched from the windows, behind *jalousies*.

When the *autos sacramentales* were banned in 1765, the wheeled stages also lost their significance in Spain. Fixed simultaneous stages of the kind illustrated at Valenciennes continued to play a part in the theatres of the religious orders until the eighteenth century. The scenery was in a more or less contemporary style. Non-religious plays needed a stage on which the scene could be changed, for a single, all-purpose set could not adequately have transmitted the dramatic impact or the writer's ideas.

The English stage during the reign of Elizabeth I was open on three sides, while the wall at the back, or a curtain hanging slightly in front of it, so that actors could move behind it unseen, was part of the scene. Since the view from all three sides had to be left clear, large pieces of scenery were out of the question. It is possible that in the early days the audience occupied the galleries on the fourth side also, as they would have done when actors played in inn-yards, but they were cleared from there so that the back wall of the stage could be used at two levels. By ringing the changes on windows, balconies, doors and curtains the number of possible entrances was increased. A roof supported by pillars projected over part of the stage, dividing it into two parts,

p. 119

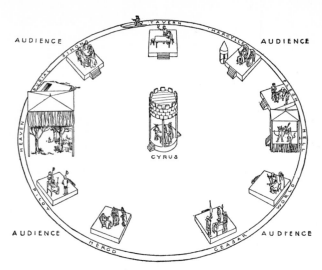

Setting for the English mystery 'Mary Magdalene'

HUBERT CAILLEAU *Simultaneous stages at Valenciennes, 1547*

and when necessary sheltering the actors from the rain. The name of 'heaven' for this canopy was taken from the mystery plays, as was 'hell' for a trap-door, but the significance of these names was soon lost. A hut was built on above the canopy in which heavenly apparitions could be prepared, gods and spirits stood ready to descend by means of flying machines and trap-doors to intervene in human affairs.

There was little essential difference between the stages erected in the courtyards of English inns and those of the Globe and Swan theatres. There was the same bare apron stage, curtains hanging at the rear, and if there was enough clearance there was an upper stage. The *corral* theatres in Spain were similarly set in a courtyard surrounded by buildings on three sides. The upper windows served as boxes for the more wealthy spectators. A difference was that while the English stage projected into the pit and was surrounded by spectators on three sides, the *corral* stage lay across one of the narrow sides of the yard, with the audience all in front.

There were few properties. Short scenes made numerous changes of scenery necessary, and since the shifting had to be done in full view of the audience, rocks, trees, tombstones, tables and chairs had to be easy to move. In the Spain of Lope de Vega, as in Shakespeare's England, the apron stage remained bare while the upper level at the back of the stage could be used as a balcony, or a window and backcloths painted with trees, houses, springs or rocks could be changed to indicate a change of place. It was not until about 1620 that public theatres began to use the more elaborate means of creating effects which had long been used in the court theatres and for the *autos*. The audience's imagination was helped out by descriptive passages in the play's text. In Cervantes' *Rufián dichoso*, Comedy addresses Curiosity:

> Upon our stage a map is spread,
> Where London, Rome and Valladolid
> Lie but a fingersbreadth from Ghent.
> The hearer marvels when I fly
> Without removing from this stage
> From Germany to Guinea far.
> Thought is winged and with its aid
> You can travel far and wide;
> Only let me be your guide.[2]

The spectators also had to imagine the time of the day, for public performances were given in the open air by daylight; there was no lighting apparatus to reproduce grey dawn, twilight, blood-red sunrise or sunset. Thunder and lightning were the only effects the writer could call upon to create illusion; the rest he had to write into his text.

Even so Lope de Vega complained about extravagance in the production of his plays, though he may have been a little flattered as well: 'Our theatre has dwindled into a frame for painted cloth and joinery'. His poetry was fully able to transport the audience without the help of 'the carpenter with his ingenious craft'.[2] His own words had the descriptive power to free the spectators from the limitations of the bare stage, and he felt that as scenery became more elaborate it impressed the eye but left the mind and imagination less receptive to his poetry.[3]

The theatre of the Greeks and Romans was re-discovered during the Renaissance, and the attempts of humanist scholars to revive it provided foundations for the development of stages and scenery in the secular theatre as a whole. In the ancient theatre the action took place between the *parascenae* in front of a fixed back wall which enclosed the scene horizontally.[4] This was soon felt to be inadequate in the sixteenth century. An important innovation in the Teatro Olimpico (1584) in Vicenza is the way in which the back and sides of the scene are interrupted at five points, the centre of the back being emphasized by a wider opening. In the Teatro Farnese (1619) in Parma the centre opening is even larger, and what would have been the back wall has become the architectonic frame for a panoramic space which appears to stretch back beyond the limits of the stage. In the course of time this frame became less obvious and was pushed further aside, changing as contemporary theories changed, but the principle of it was never totally abandoned. Because there was not necessarily very much space behind this frame the illusion of space had to be created by scenery. The first painted perspective scene on record was in Ferrara in 1508.[5] In 1513 Pellegrino da Udine had parts of his perspective scenery built in plaster. This scenery was immovable, permitting only one setting for an entire play.

67, 76, 101   The Teatro Olimpico in Vicenza still has a permanent set on the stage, which it would have been impossible to change during the course of a performance, even if there had been a curtain. From the five entrances to the narrow acting area streets appear to lead back to a great depth, as the stage rises steeply and the buildings are foreshortened at a sharp angle. The set is built very solidly of wood with firm supports and decorated in relief with wood and stucco. The five streets cannot all be seen from all sides so could not have been used

as part of the acting area. The whole effect of this scene is permanent and weighty; at the time of its building stage design had not evolved easily movable sets. There was as yet no scene-shifting apparatus above or below the stage: all the settings had to be moved into position from the sides.

Sebastiano Serlio (1475–1554) also based his sets on the principle of a fixed framework. The lines of his houses, parks and streets converge strictly according to the rules of perspective. The second volume of his *Architettura*, published in Paris in 1545, gives his theories on stage design. Tragic and heroic sentiments and deeds were only possible among men of noble rank, so a tragedy had to be set in a street of great palaces. Comedy could take place in the country or in front of inns or the houses of ordinary people, because such people were fit subjects for laughter.

In the baroque drama plays could no longer be confined to one scene; stage-settings had to be more adaptable. Already on the stages of Renaissance Italy some use had been made of *periaktoi* or *telari*, triangular prisms erected at the sides of the stage, which turned on an axis to allow three changes of scene, or more if the frames were covered with painted canvases, which could be changed quickly, instead

p. 121

JOHANNES DE WITT *The Swan Theatre, London 1596*

GEORGE WESTCOTT *Reconstruction of an Elizabethan theatre*

Giacomo Torelli *Set for 'Venere gelosa', Venice 1643*

of with fixed boards. The sides of the triangles were of different lengths so that turning the prisms also altered the size and shape of the acting area.[6]

The *periaktoi* were still only a little more adequate than the permanent sets to meet the needs of the baroque theatre. The next step was to find a means of changing the perspective back-scene. The Italian designer Niccolo Sabbattini devised several possible methods. The back-scene could be in two parts, each of which could run on or off sideways along a groove, or they could open and shut like doors, or it could remain in one piece and be raised and lowered like a curtain. A painted back-scene could give an illusion of great depth and width, and also made it possible to use the space behind the stage. A raked stage developed, which could be divided laterally at two or three points, so that scenes could be played on the fore-stage while scenery was being changed behind a curtain. All these innovations, which quickly followed each other, spread throughout Europe in the course of the seventeenth century.[7]

p. 123

On the almost bare stage of sixteenth century England and Spain a front curtain was hardly necessary – there were no visual surprises, no illusions to be preserved other than those created by the text of the play and its speakers. But now, at this later stage, after all manner of exciting sound effects, 'the curtain falls away at that moment, and there is presented the heroic perspective of the *scena di comedia*; but already the Prologue, the first of the actors, is walking to and fro on the stage'.[8] The curtain might either fall into a pit (the *Graben* of Furttenbach's diagrams) which also held the orchestra, or 'after all things had been made ready, music struck up behind the stage, during which the curtains were swiftly raised'.[9]

p. 121

The front curtain was in general use during the central and late baroque period, and to increase the element of surprise it was lowered between the acts and during changes of scenery.

Baroque man needed magic. As the anxieties of everyday life became more oppressive and the need to escape from

120

them became more urgent, his craving for more convincing, and at the same time more extreme illusions caused the arts of illusion to play an increasingly important part in stagecraft. The stage designer had to create what was now beyond the ability of the spectator to imagine. The descriptive, scene-setting passages in sixteenth century plays were superseded by stage sets which established time and place at a glance. The spectator's imagination no longer participated in the creation of the marvels spread before his eyes. The illusions he craved had to come from outside.

p. 139, 72-3 The invention of wings at the beginning of the seventeeth century is ascribed to Giovanni Battista Aleotti. He began to experiment with them as early as 1606 in the Teatro dei Intrepidi in Ferrara, but only brought them into fully effective use in the Teatro Farnese in Parma in 1619.[10] Canvas-covered flat wooden frames ('flats') were fixed on a 74-5, 78 wheeled undercarriage which ran on rails in the cellar below-stage. They were handled from below and pushed backwards and forwards as needed in slits in the stage floor. With the appropriate scenery painted on the canvas the flats were arranged symmetrically in groups of four (or sometimes three, as at Český Krumlov). Joseph Furttenbach's drawings p. 121 of the stage at Ulm show that the *periaktoi* did not disappear from use immediately. Both types of side-scene were found for some time, but eventually wings won the day throughout Europe. Besides the carriages for the wings, the cellar had to accommodate the traps which were essential to the baroque theatre. The sinner's descent to hell must be made visible, the devil had to be seen to shoot up from the nether regions.

The space above the stage was as useful as the cellar. Here the flies and the grid with their network of ropes and pulleys raised and lowered hanging scenery and platforms, 77 disguised as clouds, bearing the *deus ex machina* or even a whole pantheon. Flying machines were indispensable in the baroque theatre as evil spirits darted through the air showering pestilence, while angels descended on errands of mercy. When Shakespeare's plays were revised or turned into operas for the Restoration stage his witches and fairies had to fly like everybody else's.

Furttenbach, Sabbattini and others gave plentiful instructions for the use of flying machines and trap-doors and for p. 134 all the possible effects to be made with fire, water, smoke and steam, but as time went on it became necessary to employ a specialist engineer, a *capomaestro delle teatri*, to invent the many different machines that were necessary for the staging of complicated, astonishing, bizarre and lavish scenes and actions.

Sound effects were always easy to execute. Thunder, the alarums of battle, animal cries required only the simplest

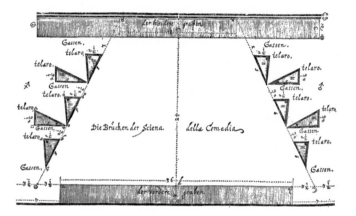

JOSEF FURTTENBACH *Stage with periaktoi, Ulm 1663*

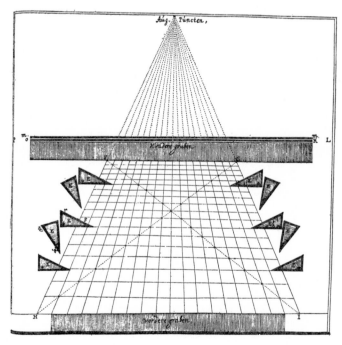

'Ludi Caesarei' in Jesuit theatre, Praque 1617

GIUSEPPE GALLI-BIBIENA *Set for Otway's 'Titus and Berenice',*
Vienna 1719

instruments. Light was more difficult to handle. At first plays were performed by daylight, and the spectator had to manage as best he could to visualize the ominous red dawn, nightfall and flashing lightning when the actors spoke of them. When performances began to be held in closed halls the stage and auditorium had to be lit with candles, oil lamps and torches; it is hardly surprising that only a small number of these early theatres escaped destruction by fire.

Candelabra were used both on the stage and in the audi- p. 140 torium. Footlights were usually oil lamps, and there were sometimes torches or oil lamps standing on wooden pillars on either side of the proscenium arch. Lighting effects in the early seventeenth-century theatre were rudimentary. Lights placed behind the proscenium arch, the *periaktoi* or the wings threw heavy shadows. Sudden darkening of the stage could be achieved by simultaneously lowering little cylin- p. 137 ders suspended above the candles.

A more dynamic and imaginative use of light began during the 1630s. Clouds gleamed as if made of gold, or were pierced by lights carried within them. Lights were shone on stars in such a way that they reflected the ray and appeared to emanate from the god they surrounded. Clouds reddened and glowed in bengal fire, the flames of hell danced orange and crimson. Parigi and Torelli were the new magicians, conjurors with cloud machines, light and shadow. Colour and light played on each other, increasing the illusion and the enchantment, and mirrors reflected and multiplied the brilliance. There was nothing static on the stage; variation and movement were the only constants. Bright lights also enhanced the actors' glittering costumes; the audience gasped as gold and silver ornaments, shining silks and coloured stones flashed and gleamed.

It became possible to accentuate an important entrance, emphasize a particular action, by lighting, while the rest of the stage was cast into shadow. The baroque theatre was able to anticipate all the lighting effects of the modern stage, long before gas, let alone electricity, was introduced. There was even the magic lantern to throw the image of a city or a moonlit landscape on the back-drop.[11] There was a constant flow of new ideas to overcome the stage's limitations and increase its apparent breadth and depth.

By the end of the seventeenth century, stages capable of division by act-drops at three points, and steeply raked to increase the perspective effect of the backcloth, were the general rule. There was usually a broad opening at the back to allow the entrance of carriages and animals. Stages were deep enough to allow great variety of manœuvre. On every stage in Europe *periaktoi* were turning, wings sliding in and out, divine apparitions ascending and descending on

Title page of first edition of Sabbattini's
'Pratica di fabricar scene e machine ne' teatri', Ravenna 1638

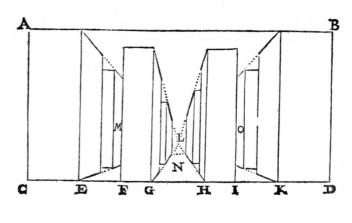

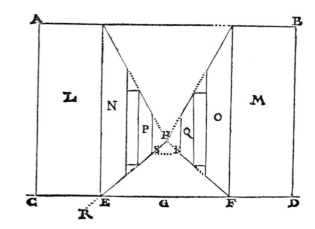

NICCOLÒ SABBATTINI *Diagrams for sets with three streets and one street*

flying machines; the earth was opening, spewing forth devils and demons, and swallowing the damned; the sea raged and the heavens stormed. Space had broken its bounds and become indeterminate.

The baroque splendours of the age of Absolutism faded in the Enlightenment of the eighteenth century. Exaggerated gestures, pathetic declamation, overpowering sets and costumes, were out of tune with the spirit of the new age. There was no longer any great desire to be amazed by the splendours of heaven or thrilled by the horrors of a stage designer's hell. Once again the spoken word and the actor took the centre of the stage, attention was once more focused on men, not the gods. The old-fashioned pomp, the full supporting cast of machines, trap-doors, flying dragons, tumbling walls and inundations, survived for some time to come in the opera house. They were moreover the only means of paying tribute to the monarchic principle which were felt to be suitably lavish. It is significant that the

marriage of Louis XVI and Marie Antoinette in 1770 was celebrated with old favourites: *Persée* by Lully and Quinault, which had first been performed in 1682, Racine's *Athalie* (1691), Rameau's *Castor et Pollux* (1737) and Voltaire's *Tancrède* (1760) written when the author was already in his sixties. No more modern works offered the same opportunities for presentation in the grand style.

Stage sets in the high baroque period were strictly symmetrical, the vanishing point at which all the lines of perspective converged was dead centre and behind the actual backdrop, whether the scene was a landscaped park, the jaws of hell, a military encampment, a hall, a public square, a sylvan grotto, the clouded heights of Mount Olympus or a dungeon. In the early days the demands of symmetry were so strong that even the actors were grouped in symmetrical patterns. A seventeenth-century German setting for hell leads to the middle distance on precisely the same geometrical lines as Torelli's garden scene

pp. 120, 122–3, 126–7

p. 129

68

Les Festes de l'Amour et de Bacchus, Comedie en Musique
representeé dans le petit Parc de Versailles

II

Festum Cupidinis et Bacchi, Comœdia ad perpetuum vocum
et tibiarum cantum acta, In Hortis Versalianis.

Jean le Pautre *Carlo Vigarani's theatre in the park of Versailles, 1672*

designed for Venice in 1646, and whether the actors portray a pyramid of devils, elaborately casual strollers in the garden, or a royal procession, their grouping is always based on the same axis of symmetry as the scene itself.

pp. 138-9

This rigidity began to relax around the turn of the century. As in real life, the self-conscious, stiff splendour of the last decades of the seventeenth century gave way to supple elegance, graceful, lightfooted delicacy, spontaneity and naturalness, and in this process the symmetry of stage designs was abandoned too. Sets allowing more freedom to the imagination, act-drops painted in pastel colours, were more in sympathy with the age, with the new drama and the new opera. Pergolesi and Dittersdorf, Paesiello and Haydn, Beaumarchais and Marivaux required a different setting, a different production style from Monteverdi, Handel, Racine and Bidermann. In addition to the sliding flats which necessarily imposed a certain degree of symmetry, designers such as de Loutherbourg in London began to use free-standing pieces of scenery that could be placed anywhere on the

69, 70

stage. The aim now was a realistic representation and use of space. Idyllic, rustic landscapes were favoured instead of formal gardens, and a new source of inspiration in the theatre, as in other fields of design, was the Orient. Colonization and the expansion of trading companies in Africa and the Middle and Far East during the seventeenth and eighteenth centuries led to more than a thirst for tea. Every country house had its Chinese room, and Arabs and Turks abounded in the theatre and the opera house.

66

The realism of the eighteenth-century theatre was only relative and was still very stylized. Nature was represented by the idyllic pastures of Arcady, a painted, pacific backcloth for a life carefully composed of the elements pleasing to rococo man. It was only later, a generation or more after Rousseau, that the Romantics acknowledged the superior strength of the forces of Nature.

I have tried to give some idea above of the trends which were felt, at varying periods, in all European countries. Every nation added its own characteristics, which were carried abroad by its great artists. Men of genius had a wide sphere of influence, for they were called to many foreign courts. The invention of wings was not the only Italian gift to the theatre; throughout the two centuries following the Renaissance, Italy remained the chief source of new ideas, techniques and fashions, and her artists, travelling everywhere, were her missionaries.

Raphael is known to have worked in the theatre, and the great mannerists, Angelo Bronzino, Giorgio Vasari and his pupil Bernardo Buontalenti designed stage sets and fantastic festivals at court and in the theatre, but in their day their influence remained local. Even Giovanni Battista Aleotti (1546–1632), the inventor of the sliding wings, did not himself travel very far. He remained in the service of Duke Alfonso II d'Este and became city architect in Ferrara in

1598. At this time there was no distinction between the professions of architect and stage designer. Aleotti built a theatre for the Accademia degli Intrepidi in 1606 which was reputed to be among the finest in Italy; unfortunately it burnt down in 1679. His most important achievement was probably the Teatro Farnese in Parma (1618–19), one of the after p. 160, 105–7 greatest baroque theatres in Europe. Its stage was the prototype for all future stages furnished with wings, and its proscenium arch not only framed the stage but also hid the complex of grid and flies above it.

Aleotti's pupils improved his system and spread his ideas. Outstanding among them was Giacomo Torelli (1608 p. 120 to 1678). Theatres were rising all over Italy, and the princes of Florence, Bologna, Parma, Turin and Milan, as well as the citizens of Venice all wanted the most up-to-date designs

FERDINANDO AND GIUSEPPE GALLI-BIBIENA *Set for 'Angelica vincitrice di Alcina', Vienna 1716*

LUDOVICO OTTAVIO BURNACINI *Set for 'Il pomo d'oro', Vienna 1668*

and techniques. Aleotti's wings needed one man to move each separate flat; Torelli invented the system of wheels and rollers by which one man can change all the wings in one minute, and which is still in use at Drottningholm, Gripsholm and Český Krumlov. Torelli, a native of Fano, was first employed in Venice, designing for operas. His reputation spread, and he was summoned to the service of Ferdinand of Tuscany, and of Cardinal Antonio Barberini.[12] Then, in 1645, Cardinal Mazarin brought him to the court of Anne of Austria, who at that date was Regent of France for her son, Louis XIV. Torelli scored success after success until 1661, when he was eclipsed by Buffequin.[13] His years in Paris began the development of the *théâtre des machines* in France. His use of perspective was masterly, he invented new techniques, including a method of changing the back-drop, and his designs show an inexhaustible imagination. They never atrophy into pedantic exercises in spite of strict adherence to the rule of symmetry. Skilful use of lighting filled garden and grotto with mystery and magic, and no one before him had represented the heavens on stage as a cloud-drift or a bisected sphere with such great success. His famous sets for *Le Nozze di Peleo e Teti* (1654), *Ercole*

74–5, 78

amante (1662), *Cato in Utica* (1670), *Dario* (1671), *Divisione del mondo* (1675), and *Pastore del Anfiso* (1677) – to name only a few – made him the envy of his contemporaries and the model for his juniors.

Chronologically Niccolò Sabbattini (c. 1574–1654) stands between Aleotti and Torelli. He still used the fixed setting to great advantage, presenting squares and rows of streets with the utmost illusory effectiveness. His *Pratica di fabricar scene e machine ne' teatri* (Ravenna 1638) includes directions for perspective decorations with three vanishing points, that is, with three streets leading directly backwards from the stage, as we see them in Torelli's grove of laurel trees for *Venere gelosa*. He achieved an illusion of even greater depth by decreasing the rake of the stage, and supported this illusion by careful gradations of colour from dark in the front to pale at the rear. His book contains sketches of all the technical tricks available at the time: cylinders for dimming lights, lifts, traps, machinery for simulating celestial apparitions and earthly transformations, the bursting apart of rocks and the globe itself, the movement of water and clouds, thunderclaps, lightning flashes and the roaring of wind and water. He writes with all the experience gained in

p. 123

p. 120

p. 137

p. 130

the service of several masters: Francesco II of Urbino, Hieronimo Grimaldi, governor of Urbino and Parma, for whom he built the Teatro del Sol, and Lucretia d'Este, whom he followed to Mantua.

Alfonso Parigi (died 1656), was a pupil of Bernardo Buontalenti, the chief designer of the Medici festivals in Florence, in which capacity Parigi succeeded him. While his father Giulio Parigi (died 1635) was still working with *periaktoi* young Alfonso was already making skilful use of wings in a production of *La liberazione di Tireno*. He introduced the new baroque techniques from Venice to Florence, where audiences were transported and amazed by his scenery for the operas *La Flora*, *Il Giardino di Alcina* and *Le nozze degli dei*.

Giulio Troili (or Trogli, 1613–85) developed wings which were slanted away from the front of the stage, thus lessening the apparent gaps between them. This had the advantages of preventing spectators sitting at the sides of the auditorium from seeing behind the wings, and of increasing the illusion of depth by perspective painting on the flats. In 1672 Troili published the fruits of his experience in a theoretical work, *Paradossi per praticare la prospettiva senza saperla*. To this and to Sabbattini's work about stage machines must be added the *Prospettiva de' Pittori e Architetti* (Rome, 1693–1700) by the Jesuit Andrea Pozzo (1642–1709). Himself both painter and architect, he summarizes the state of knowledge of stage decoration and perspective painting, and develops it in the light of his own experience. He asks for wings to be made high and used so unobtrusively that the spectator is not aware of how they create the impression of space on the stage. Where the side-scene was composed of regularly spaced objects, as in a colonnaded hall, a camp with rows of tents, or a harbour with ships on either side, this had never presented any problems, especially where a separate flat was

p. 162

LUDOVICO OTTAVIO BURNACINI *Stage design, c. 1670*

used for each component of the scene. Pozzo wanted the same effect from scenes where each side of the stage was not the mirror-image of the other, and where a piece of scenery started on one flat and had to appear to continue without a break on the next. This had the advantage of disguising the outlines of the wings, and the whole was enhanced and unified by overall ornamentation.[14]

Pozzo was summoned to Vienna by Leopold I, where he carried out many other commissions besides his theatrical work. He painted ceilings in churches and town-houses, helped in the building of the Jesuitenkirche, and designed the high altar of the Franziskanerkirche.

The great age of baroque stage design in Viennese opera had begun with the arrival in the imperial capital of Giovanni Burnacini in 1651, at the invitation of Ferdinand III and his third wife, Eleanor of Mantua, whose enthusiasm for the theatre was matched by her knowledge and understanding of the arts. Burnacini, father of the more famous Ludovico Ottavio, had already scored notable successes in Italy including the Teatro dei SS. Apostoli in Venice and a number of brilliant stage sets in Mantua. In Vienna, in the p. 168 court theatre he had designed, he produced the opera *La gara*, with music by Antonio Bertoli and text by Alberto Vimina in 1652. This remarkable production was recorded in engravings, which show Jupiter descending on his eagle to arbitrate in the tournament spread out in the pit of the theatre. The stage was by no means small, but the spectacle was on such a grand scale that the body of the theatre had to be used as well to accommodate it all.[15] The function of the theatre, and particularly of the opera, was to arouse astonishment and admiration and above all to glorify the monarchy. Only the very best theatrical architects were good enough to shed lustre on the crown.

Giovanni Burnacini was commissioned to build a theatre on the occasion of a Diet of the German princes in Regensburg in 1653.[16] There was no specialization yet among the great theatrical artists: they designed the theatre buildings as well as the sets and costumes. Burnacini used the most up-to-date techniques in his production of the *dramma per musica, Inganno d'amore*: ballets, triumphal processions, sumptuous costumes and several transformation scenes. It was not yet the general practice to lower the house curtain between scenes, so the necessity of changing the scenery was made an opportunity to display the designer's ingenuity, the seemingly magic transformation being carried out by rapid movement of machinery above and below the stage. Burnacini's assistants were two Venetians and his son who succeeded him on his early death.

During the reign of Leopold I (1685–1705) the Viennese opera was unrivalled throughout Europe. It was still customary for each new work to be performed once only for a festive occasion, and every time the full mechanical resources of spectacle and surprise were employed to please the emperor and his court. The *crescendo* which began with Giovanni Burnacini reached *fortissimo maestoso* under Ludovico Ottavio Burnacini (1636–1707). It was his task, as architect and designer, to assert Vienna's superiority in the theatre as a counterpart to Austria's position in world politics, in spite of any rival claims on both scores from Versailles. From the age of fourteen, Burnacini lived in Vienna, the melting-pot of many nations, the capital, with Madrid, of an empire on which the sun still had not set.

The quantity of human and material resources involved in the 115 operas for which Ludovico Burnacini created the   after p. 8, decorations, machines and costumes is almost beyond imag-   pp. 11, 13 ination. We must also remember the part played by the courtiers in all this; they occupied a special position as actors of a different kind, as important to the success of the whole as the actors on the stage. The designer had to keep both sides of the footlights in mind. Burnacini's answer to his responsibilities consisted of some of the most magnificent *mises en scène* in the whole history of the baroque theatre,   p. 127 such as *Il pomo d'oro* (1667). The Greek myth of the dispute   p. 126 between Hera, Aphrodite and Pallas Athene as to which of them was the most beautiful, and of the judgment of Paris, gave Burnacini every opportunity to conjure with time and space, heaven and earth, water, air and fire. The audience was spellbound by the wealth of movement, colours and music. Hades and Olympus, the idyllic slopes of Mount Ida, the palace of Paris, a sea of ships, the fortress of Mars, the temple of Athene, the sky and the Milky Way were the scenes where the action was played out, constantly moving between heaven and earth. Discord flew on a dragon down into Hades and on a cloud to the summit of Mount Olympus in order to throw her famous golden apple among the goddesses. On the way to present themselves before Paris for his verdict Hera descended to the courtyard of his palace in a massive golden *galleria*, while Athene floated down on a triumphal arch, and Aphrodite transformed the courtyard into a garden. The gods made their entrances on eagles and in fiery chariots, the scenes changed as if by magic; gods and heroes, fates and furies, tritons and nereids, battles, rainstorms and pelting hail, animals of all sizes from salamanders to elephants, graces and monsters, all imaginable phenomena were included in the dispute over the apple, which, finally, as the goddesses continued to squabble even after Paris' judgment, Zeus commanded his eagle to carry to the Empress Margareta.

Burnacini usually divided the stage clearly into two   after p. 116 areas, a broad fore-stage and a shallower rear-stage. A per-

128

GASPARE AND DOMENICO MAURO *Set for 'Servio Tullio',
Munich, 1686*

ANON. *Design for Hell, Germany, seventeenth century*

ANON. *Design for a camp, Ansbach 1676*

spective back-scene carried the eye beyond the confined space of the stage. His costumes contributed in every detail to the effect created by the sets. His heroes were dressed with *23–4* the same painstaking attention, with the same regard to their attitudes, masks and assumed natures as the numerous weird and repulsive grotesques which the audiences of the time so *20–2* loved and believed to be talismans against evil spirits. Burnacini was perhaps one of the last of the great universal *87* geniuses in theatrical design. After he left Vienna the rise of the Galli-Bibiena family also marked the rise of specialization. Daniele Bertoli (1678–1743) was called to Vienna specifically as a costume designer, as was later Andrea Altomonte (1699–1780).

The Burnacinis' sphere was Austria and Italy. Giovanni's contemporary, Baccio del Bianco (1604–56/60), went to Spain to design sets for operas at Buen Retiro. At that date the technical and scenic resources at his disposal were ten years in advance of those enjoyed by Giovanni Burnacini in Italy. Francesco Mauro and his sons Domenico, Pietro and Gasparo took the festival traditions of Venice to Munich in the 1660s. In Venice they had staged fairytale serenades and operas on the Grand Canal, and in Munich their operatic scenes of palaces, gardens and the heavens led backwards *p. 129* apparently to infinity in perfect symmetry, their clouds suffused with rich light. Alessandro Mauro, Francesco's *p. 133* grandson, abandoned the heavy opulence of the high baroque for rococo delicacy of line and light.

Among the outstanding artists of the whole baroque age were the Galli-Bibiena family. Originally from Bologna, they founded in Vienna a reputation and influence which spread far and wide. For 150 years, from Giovanni Maria the Elder to his great-grandson Carlo, the Galli-Bibiena dynasty virtually determined the progress of European stage techniques.[17] Their work was seen everywhere: Barcelona, Potsdam, Prague, Bayreuth, Vienna, Lisbon, Siena, Bologna, Parma, Florence and London.

Ferdinando Galli-Bibiena departed from the customary central perspective, and by turning the wings arrived at an effect of a space lying on several axes. His flying machines *p. 132* were large enough to lower an entire palace on to the stage. He was in the service of the Hapsburg Archduke Charles, and became court architect in Vienna when the latter succeeded to the imperial throne as Charles VI in 1711. In the same year he published a theoretical work *Architettura civile preparata sulla geometria e ridotta alla prospettiva* which laid the foundations of spatial treatment in the eighteenth century. His predecessor in Vienna during the reign of Joseph I had been his younger brother Francesco. Francesco's work showed the last stages of the high baroque style. Foreground and background were no longer treated as separate compliment-

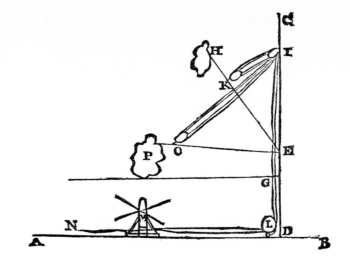

ary entities, but were continuous. The rule of symmetry was abandoned, so that distances could be brought near and, conversely, the whole stage could be filled by one, near-at-hand scene. Sometimes the brothers worked together, and it was not always easy to distinguish between their contributions.

p. 122

pp. 125, 138

p. 23

They had already perfected in theory the diagonal axes and asymmetry characteristic of their successors, above all of Giuseppe Galli-Bibiena, certainly the most notable member of this family. He collaborated with his father Ferdinando on the aquatic spectacle *Angelica vincitrice d'Alcina* held in 1716 in the park of the Favorita palace and on the opera *Costantino* performed in Vienna in the court theatre. For the coronation of Charles VI as king of Bohemia, Giuseppe designed the sets for the opera *Costanza e Fortezza* by Pietro Pariati and Johann Fux. A huge open-air theatre was erected in the garden of the Hradčany palace in Prague. The production was a glorious confection of artificial and natural elements skilfully intermingled: there were plays within the play, music and spoken dialogue, processions on the scale of Roman triumphs, in a setting where the permanent natural features of the garden were so blended with the decorations constructed for the occasion that they could not be distinguished. The spectators were overwhelmed and at the same time stimulated by the *maniera di veder le scene per angola*, the oblique perspective, to imagine the full extent of the space suggested by the scenery.

In 1747 Giuseppe left Vienna for Dresden. He was given leave to go to Bayreuth in the following year to design the interior of the Margravine Wilhelmina's opera house, returned to Dresden to supervise the building of a new opera house there, and spent the three years from 1754 to his death in Berlin.

His younger brother Antonio was deputy theatrical engineer in Vienna from 1727 to 1740, when he left to pursue his career in Italy, in Siena, Bologna, Mantua and Florence. Giuseppe's elder brother Alessandro became court architect and engineer to the Elector of Mannheim in 1719. He built the opera house in Mannheim, the Jesuit church and the right wing of the palace. His lighthearted, graceful stage sets are typically rococo. In the absence of by now old-fashioned symmetry the landscapes of his backgrounds are continued across the whole stage to the very front. The suggestion of depth is achieved not by straight lines but by a zigzag. The spectator's eye is drawn from the foreground to the centre right and from there to the back left-hand corner.

The course pursued by the successive generations of the Galli-Bibiena family is that of the development of all design for the stage from the high baroque to rococo, though baroque concepts always retained more significance in their work than in the French rococo. Carlo, in the fourth generation,

70

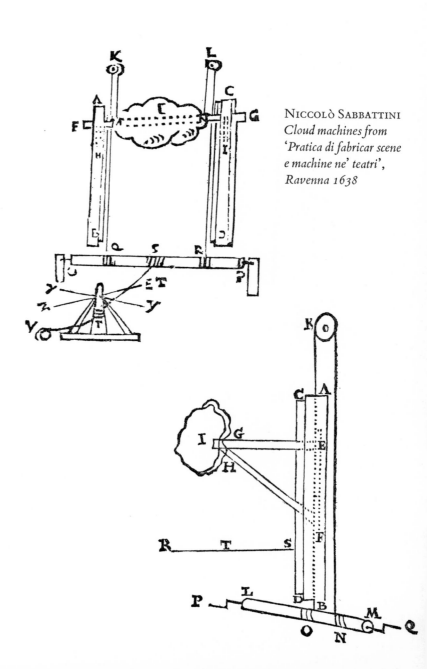

NICCOLÒ SABBATTINI
*Cloud machines from 'Pratica di fabricar scene e machine ne' teatri',
Ravenna 1638*

130

achieved the last flowering of Italian baroque in the Bayreuth opera house on which he worked with his father Giuseppe. Carlo designed for the stage in London and Berlin but his best work was done in Bayreuth for Margravine Wilhelmina. His sets were gossamer-fine, transcending space rather than creating it. Giovanni Carlo Galli-Bibiena designed sets for the opera house in Lisbon with Lourenço da Cumba and Inácio de Oliveira Bernardes.[18]

163, 165, 169–175

Aleotti, the Burnacinis, the Mauros and the Galli-Bibienas were the corner-stones and pillars of Italian theatrical art. Around them, like the pretty ornaments essential to their style, are grouped numerous minor artists who mostly derived and developed their ideas from those of the great geniuses. Pietro Righini (1683–1742) built a narrow forestage, creating variable depth by arching wings, moving balconies, stairways and domes. Vinzenzo dal Ré (died 1762) devised operas and balls at the court of Naples, at the time one of the most important in Europe, in which the stage continued into the auditorium and the auditorium became part of the stage. Bernardino Galliari (1707–94) designed costumes and decorations for ceremonies, betrothals and weddings, besides working at La Scala in Milan and the Teatro Regio in Turin. He was famous for his designs for curtains. He was summoned to Vienna by Joseph II, and to Berlin by Frederick the Great. He is regarded as the founder of the Piedmontese style of theatre decoration. His brother Fabrizio Galliari (1709–90) worked with him on charming, light-suffused stage sets and designed the necessary machines.

69

Filippo Juvarra (1676–1736) built the theatre in Genoa and the Teatro Regio in Turin, and renovated the Teatro Farnese in Parma. His designs for private theatres, such as the ones he built in the Palazzo della Cancelleria for Cardinal Ottoboni, and in the Palazzo Capranica, were reproduced in the published libretti of contemporary operas. His love for curves and asymmetry was equalled by Giambattista Piranesi (1720–1778).

p. 139

It is hardly possible to mention the names of all those Italians who fanned out across Europe like flocks of swallows in spring. As performances of opera became more popular and more frequent, Europe was inundated by the stream of architects and designers. Jacopo Fabris (1689–1761) had reached Copenhagen by 1747, prior to which he had been court painter to the Margrave of Baden-Durlach in Karlsruhe from 1719 to 1721, painted sets for the Opernhaus am Gänsemarkt in Hamburg in 1724, worked for Handel in London, and assisted Knobelsdorff in the building of a theatre in the palace of Frederick the Great in 1742.[19] Girolamo Bon, a native of Bologna, travelled to Russia in 1731, to Dresden in 1748, Berlin in 1750, then entered the service of Prince Thurn und Taxis, and by 1752 turned up in Amsterdam. The masters of this necessarily transient art were found everywhere from England to Russia; even a recital of their names – Bartolomeo Verona, Innocente Colomba, Vicenzo dal Buono, Lorenzo and Carlo Quaglio, Canaletto – does something to reveal their century's passion for the theatre.

When the native Spanish plays, the *autos sacramentales*, were banned in the eighteenth century, a great tradition of stage design was cut off short. The court theatres were soon overrun by Italian inventions and machinery, and of course Italian stage artists also entered Spain, such as Cosimo Lotti, an architect and designer who also invented machines.

On the one hand there was the baroque theatre of machines, and on the other advances were being made by the 'classical' French drama in which the unity of place robbed designers of the opportunity to display their imagination and skill in constant transformation scenes. The court theatre declined for a time after the death of Philip IV, reviving to new splendour in the court theatre at Buen Retiro under Philip V and Ferdinand VI. The Alcazar in Madrid, including its theatre, was destroyed by fire. Charles II created new centres for the theatre in his palaces at Aranjuez and San Ildefonso. Meanwhile public theatres continued to flourish.

Assisted by native artists, Giovanni Carlo Galli-Bibiena, Giovanni Bernardi, Niccolo Servandoni and others prepared magnificent spectacles for the court; and Spaniards themselves never attained the European eminence in the field of stage design that they had held in the drama.

The layout of the Shakespearean stage continued to influence productions in the public theatres in England throughout the seventeenth century. Important scenes were played on the apron-stage which projected into the pit and prohibited the use of wings as scenery.

In 1605 Inigo Jones (1573–1652) was called to the English court to design for spectacles and masques. There was no permanent theatre at his disposal; he built his stages and their complex machinery when and where they were needed. He had studied in Italy and during his career went through the stages from the single permanent set, to *periaktoi* and finally to the use of wings, being thereby far in advance of the public theatres. In front of the stage, with its proscenium arch, he arranged the auditorium to rise like an amphitheatre with a canopied seat for the king placed centrally, and in the space between the stage and the audience he had a floor for dancing. From an early date he used curtains to conceal the stage before and between the acts, but even so scenes were frequently changed in full view of the audience. After the Puritan interregnum the trend was away from pure spectacle and magical effects and towards emphasis on the meaning of words, gestures and music. This put opera in an unusual position, for throughout the rest of Europe this was the genre which made most use of spectacle. English audiences, however, differed in their expectations from Italians, Austrians and French and were primarily interested in the music and quality of singing, though scenery and costumes still had to be considerably more lavish than for plays. In the early eighteenth century Italian artists were employed: Marco Rizzi, Roberto Clerici, Jacopo Amiconi and Niccolo Servandoni who, with Joseph Goupy and Peter Tillemans (French and Flemish respectively, but both spent most of their lives in England), created delicate pastel sets, more delicate perhaps than any in use at that time on the continent.

Even during the great age when David Garrick dominated the English theatre there was no English stage designer of any great distinction. It was a native of Alsace, Philippe de Loutherbourg, who best fulfilled Garrick's wishes with transparencies and free-standing flats which he placed beside, or even in the place of the permanent wings.

In France the theatre of the religious orders had a primarily educational purpose and less energy was expended on creating spectacle for its own sake. In his *Perspective pratique* (1636–49) the Jesuit Jean Dubreuil gives an outline of the system of decoration used in religious theatres. He did not yet use sliding wings at a time when Torelli was already designing for operas in Paris. With a series of arches or borders to frame the stage in front of a perspective back-scene,

FERDINANDO AND FRANCESCO GALLI-BIBIENA *Set for 'L'Età dell'oro', Parma 1690*

IX LUDWIGSBURG *Curtain in the palace theatre, mid-eighteenth century*

ALESSANDRO MAURO *Set for 'Teofane', Dresden 1719*

changes of scene were executed by means of *periaktoi* and movable flats, possibly of the kind used today in the peasant theatre at Kiefersfelden. Simultaneous stages like the ones at Valenciennes mentioned at the beginning of this chapter remained in use until the eighteenth century, and Jacques François Blondel designed impressive and spectacular sets for them. They were used for passion plays, tragedies and ballets.

p. 118

The contrast between the settings used for operas and those used for plays was particularly marked in France. In the straight theatre the three unities prescribed by the Académie inhibited lavish fantasies: the words were all-important. Designers only came to be mentioned by name at quite a late date. One of the earliest was Georges Buffequin who worked for the company of the Hôtel de Bourgogne, after creating an all-purpose set for the production of *Mirame* with which Richelieu opened the theatre in his own palace. His son Denis Buffequin, a rival to Torelli, turned the Théâtre du Marais into a very successful *théâtre des machines*. In the years when Corneille was at the peak of his success, the

1630s and 1640s, the various companies of actors did not employ anyone as a full-time designer; usually there would be one actor of sufficient diversity of talent to act as producer, painter, engineer and treasurer as well. They would have a certain store of stock sets: caves, landscapes, trees, rocks, fences and gates for pastorals, the hall, courtyard or façade of a palace for tragedies. There were pieces of movable scenery and the machines necessary for lowering celestial chariots, frequently needed in plays which depended on the *deus ex machina*. Laurent Mahelot, active for many years at the Hôtel de Bourgogne, gives a reliable account of a leading theatre of the time in the *Mémoire de Mahelot*.[20] Gradually the opera came to wield more and more influence in the theatre, the sets and costumes for plays became more elaborate, particularly after the remarkable success scored in Paris by the 'Wizard of the Stage', Torelli, with *La finta pazza* in 1645.

p. 135

From this time onwards French designers began to appear in the courts of Europe, challenging the Italian supremacy, spreading French notions and fashions. Among

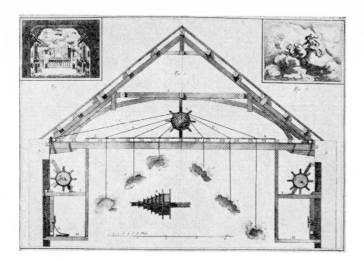
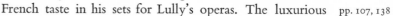

Cloud machine from Diderot's 'Encyclopedie'

D'HERMAND *Flying apparatus, early eighteenth century*

MACHINE INVENTEE PAR D'HERMAND

them was Jean Bérain, who adapted Torelli's ideas to suit French taste in his sets for Lully's operas. The luxurious pomp of the high baroque was modified to a more refined elegance of shape and line, foreshadowing the airy grace of the rococo.[21]
pp. 107, 138

It is hardly possible to treat costumes and sets separately. If one is played down the other is thrown into greater prominence, the balance varying with the fashion of the time. Stage costumes were never more magnificent than in France in the second part of the seventeenth century, inspired to a large extent by the luxury of court dress. But however rich, they are distinguished by the delicacy and grace which ensured France's pre-eminence in matters of style.

The theatre of machines had a long run in Paris. In the middle of the eighteenth century, Louis Alexandre Girault could still arrange for the stage to be flooded by a river, for gods to descend, for walls to tumble and for clouds to drift by laden with any number of passengers. The Florentine Giovanni Niccolo Servandoni (1695–1766), who took French citizenship as Jean Nicholas, lived in Paris from 1724 to 1746 and assimilated Italian styles to French tastes. His use of perspective gave the illusion of space without falling back on the obvious geometry of the high baroque. Gabriel Pierre Martin Dumont made similar tactful use of the rules of architecture.

The painter François Boucher (1700–70) conjured up an enchanted world of sunlit landscapes, idyllic cottages and smiling hamlets. He was as successful in creating this innocent, fragile, pastoral scene as the elegant intimacy of the boudoir and the mysterious shades of a more exotic, distant world.

Jean Louis Desprez (1743–1804) grew up in Paris, learnt his craft in Rome, and in 1784 entered the service of Gustav III of Sweden as architect, sculptor, painter and producer in the royal theatres at Drottningholm and Gripsholm, and for court ceremonies. Philippe de Loutherbourg (1740–1818) took the *Louis-Seize* style to Switzerland, Germany, England and Italy, and used three-dimensional scenery instead of flats. François Bélanger (1744–1818) designed the Roman scenery for Gluck's *Alceste*, and Pierre Adrien Paris (1745 to 1819), *architecte des menus plaisirs*, combined classical traditions with modern elegance. X, 71–2

The first German stage designer of note was Josef Furttenbach (1591–1667) from Leutkirch in Württemberg. He studied under Alfonso Parigi, but still advocated the use of *periaktoi* in his published writing on stage decoration. The Thirty Years War caused Germany to lag behind other countries in the development of theatrical techniques as in so many other ways. Although Ulm was able to build the first civic theatre in Germany during the war years and to keep p. 121

134

Furttenbach himself employed, and although the academic theatre continued in the religious colleges, a general blossoming of the theatre could only start later. Germany took many years to recover from the long and brutal war.

The first post-war designer of importance was Johann Oswald Harms (1643–1708) from Hamburg. He studied in Rome under Salvator Rosa and in Venice before being appointed 'Court Theatrical Painter-in-chief' in Dresden. He began his successful career with the *Musikalische Opera und Ballett von der Zusammenkunft und Wirkung der sieben Planeten* in Dresden in 1678, one of the most magnificent operatic productions ever seen in the German theatre.

It is difficult to avoid continuous use of superlatives when writing about theatrical occasions of this kind, if one is to give the faintest idea of the spectacle, the lavish splendour of these programmes which called into service all the arts. Harms was influenced to a certain extent by Burnacini in Vienna, but while Italian designers concentrated more and more on the architectural elements of stagecraft, the Germans emphasized colour and movement. Harms' work survives in a large number of sketches for sets. Like all the artists of his age, he did not stay in one place but was employed at other German courts, Cassel, Celle, Hanover and Brunswick.

In Germany as elsewhere, the most spectacular operatic settings were by Italians, but some pleasing work was accomplished by minor native talents such as Josef Ignaz Platzer (1751–1806) who, at the end of the eighteenth century, was still producing orthodox seventeenth-century baroque sets, with central perspective, symmetry and all, for the private theatres of the Liechtenstein family, for theatres in Prague, and for the Nationaltheater in Vienna. Johan Wetschel (1724–1773) and Leo Merkel followed the same principles when they painted the sets for the theatre in Český Krumlov and decorated the auditorium in *trompe-l'œil*. None of these men approached the stature of the great Frenchmen and Italians.

As the indigenous German drama and opera began to establish themselves towards the end of the eighteenth century, the day of the virtuoso baroque scenic designer, in Germany and elsewhere, was over.

In the middle ages, gospel stories and the lives of the saints were brought home as real to the congregations by being presented in the form of plays in the churches and outside the church doors. As late as 1677 a new stage was built for the Jesuit theatre inside the Michaelskirche in Lucerne. Conversely, methods derived from the theatre were used to present scenes from the lives of Christ and the saints in the decoration of eighteenth-century Bavarian churches. The high altar became a backcloth, the drama was contained in the legend acted out in stone or plaster by the saint who

JEAN BÉRAIN *Phaeton's chariot, Paris 1685*

JEAN BÉRAIN *Cloud apparatus with billowing action, Paris 1685*

lived it. Pozzo, the painter, architect and theorist, designed theatres and churches, Cuvilliés built churches and one of the very finest rococo theatres. The Asam brothers of Munich are not known to have built a theatre, but the altars in their churches are theatrical, the last expressions of the greatest baroque passion. The Mother of God rises to 83 heaven above the high altar in Rohr (1723) in the very attitude of a stage goddess. The apostles are transfixed in attitudes of awe and amazement. Double pillars frame the scene like a proscenium arch, and a curtain supplies the background. St George appears upon the high altar in Welten- 84 burg (1716–23) like a *deus ex machina* in the dark frame of pillars and walls, while the altar stretches away behind him like a stage, the illusion of depth and space being due to perspective painting.

in specially built theatres, with room for a large audience and protected against the vagaries of the weather. However, court society wanted open-air theatres as well. The greatest theatrical festivals of the baroque age took place out of doors, for they were conceived on so large a scale that no hall could possibly have accommodated them. In 1572, Ercole II of Ferrara had an island built for a production of Tasso's *Aminta*, and when the Emperor Charles VI was crowned king of Bohemia, the garden of the Hradčany palace became the set for Giuseppe Galli-Bibiena's production of *Costanza e fortezza*. Louis XIV of France used the P. 23 park of Versailles as the setting for his theatrical extravaganzas. These great occasions required temporary stages; but for other occasions court society also required smaller, permanent open-air theatres. Some of the most delightful

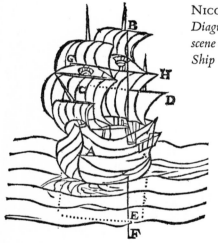

Niccolò Sabbattini
Diagrams from 'Pratica di fabricar scene e machine ne' teatri'
Ship

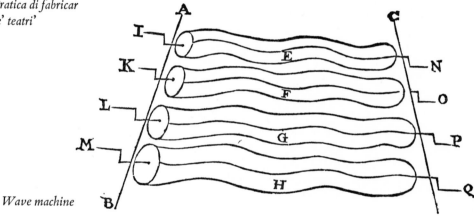

Wave machine

These groups in Rohr and Weltenburg are permanent fixtures, but in the church of the former community of 79–82 Augustine canons in Diessen am Ammersee, the high altar was designed by François de Cuvilliés like a real stage. The panel above the altar can be lowered out of sight, and behind it there are three pairs of wings which can form a setting for the Nativity, the Crucifixion or the Resurrection. Whether consciously or unconsciously, naive piety and delight in the theatre combine even at this late hour to create a baroque stage.

In the seventeenth and eighteenth centuries the mediaeval carts and simultaneous stages survived only in the market places and for the least sophisticated audiences. The majority of baroque stages were indoors, inside the halls of palaces, or

and imaginative theatres of the age were erected in response to this need.

The scene of the first opera performance north of Italy, in 1618, was the rock theatre in the park of Schloss Hell- 85 brunn near Salzburg. This is the oldest open-air theatre in Northern Europe, and one of the oldest garden theatres anywhere in the world. In 1616 the Archbishop of Salzburg, Marcus Sitticus von Hohenems, had a rocky cave in the side of a long, wooded hill hollowed out to a semi-circular apse; in the baroque age it was out of the question to leave nature alone. Parts of the rock were cut away to allow entrances, and provision was made for hangings and drapes to hide the naked stone from the eyes of the audience. On either side smaller caves were prepared to hold the musicians and to serve as dressing rooms. The theatre has excellent acoustics and would have been perfect for the performance of chamber operas before the Archbishop and his guests. There is room for one hundred spectators under an arch of rock, which would also provide shelter from sudden showers. Another hundred people could watch from the top of the arch. This charming theatre with its unusual formation is quite unique.

4   The gardens of Schloss Hellbrunn boast yet another theatre, the 'Roman theatre', but it is unlikely that this was much used for performances of plays or operas. It probably owes its name to the curving rows of stone seats which rise like a small amphitheatre. The 'stage' is occupied by the prince's table with its unkind trick fountains.

The rock theatre at Hellbrunn was designed for the per-

ances mounted with no thought of the cost, were the reserve of the most wealthy princes; but more modest shows, particularly those of the eighteenth century, could be staged on any flight of stone steps leading down into a garden. Seats of some sort could easily be improvized for the spectators, and royalty and distinguished guests could be seated on thrones beneath a canopy. A stage based on this scheme was built inside the Redoutensaal in Vienna for intimate plays in which the action could spread out from the steps into the space towards the audience.

Compared with these theatres built of stone, other kinds of open-air theatres had a short existence. The first garden theatres that we know of were in Spain, a country with hot summers and a predictable climate. One of the most famous was in the garden of the summer palace at Aranjuez, in which

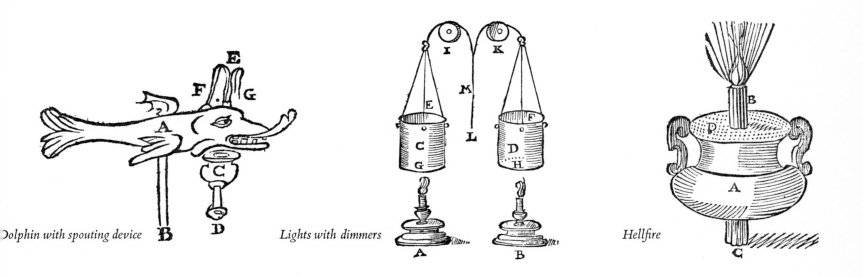

Dolphin with spouting device   *Lights with dimmers*   *Hellfire*

formance of intimate baroque operas; but the theatre in the
88 Boboli Gardens in Florence, built around the same time, continues the tradition of Renaissance spectacle on the most lavish scale. The stone seats for the audience sweep away from the Palazzo Pitti towards the slope, forming a broad arena where large numbers of men and horses could assemble for tournaments, processions and dramatic presentations.

Grander and more sumptuous still was the Zwinger in Dresden, built for Augustus the Strong of Saxony by Daniel Pöppelmann in 1719 to accommodate any kind of festivity; a complex of pavilions, colonnades and low buildings built of stone and adorned with elaborate reliefs and statues.

Large theatres, arenas and parks, for open-air perform-

performances were given from 1622. At about the same date, the king had several different theatres built in the garden of his palace of Buen Retiro, one on a lake, and the 'great theatre' in a vast open space encircled by trees, which even had balconies for the spectators. In such a warm climate it was far pleasanter to sit in the open than in a crowded room. Leading stage architects, like Cesare Fontana, were employed to design sets for productions in these theatres.

The Spanish garden theatres were probably similar to those in the parks of the imperial palaces in and around Vienna. In the garden of La Favorita there was a fairly large after p. 8, p. 11 lake, on and in which aquatic spectacles were performed. Ferdinand and Giuseppe Galli-Bibiena created enormous palaces and seascapes in the gardens of La Favorita, in which armies could march to and fro and naval battles were fought out, all for a single performance. The gardens of the Hofburg and Schönbrunn were also the scenes of lavish open-air spectacles, where all the splendour was spent after one showing.

The garden theatres built by the Margravine Wilhelmina of Bayreuth, inspired by romantic yearning, and by intimations of decline and death, are quite unique. The time for pomp and display was past by the mid-eighteenth century, and the broad expanses covered in Renaissance and baroque festivals would have been too vast for audiences in the rococo age, making them too much aware of each man's isolation. The Margravine had two theatres built for amateur performances by the court, by the French architect Joseph Saint Pierre, one in the park of the Eremitage near Bayreuth in 1743, and the other, between 1745 and 1748, in the Sans Pareil rock garden of her castle at Zwernitz. In them the architectural elements are enhanced by their natural surroundings. Shallow arches over the stage are supported by pillars, but the grass and plants that grow from the cracks and on the uneven, neglected stages are not the result of neglect: they were planted there. The theatres were conceived and built as ruins. The walls were partly covered with shells and pebbles, a style of decoration popular everywhere at that time, but which has survived only in the Sans Pareil theatre. Decorative ruins, a *memento mori*, were found in nearly all the great gardens of the late baroque, but these are the only ruin theatres known.

In baroque gardens there were few flowers, except in the *parterres*, where they were packed together in beds arranged in ornate geometrical patterns. The green of trees and hedges, cut in the forms of pyramids, cones, spirals and other bizarre shapes, was the perfect background for the colours of the rich costumes, and the immobility of the setting set off the movement of the noble guests. The only inanimate movement was that of the fountains. At the end of the eighteenth century the fashion for the 'English' garden swept away the formal 'French' garden of the seventeenth and eighteenth centuries and with it the 'hedge theatre', an arrangement of hedges of clipped box, lime, beech and yew planted in parallel lines to form wings. A popular setting, where the court demanded certain standards of comfort, took the form of a rising amphitheatre for the spectators, often semi-circular and enclosed by a sheltering hedge, as at Herrenhausen and in Warsaw. In front of this was a rectangular or semi-circular space for the orchestra, usually sunken, and beyond that the acting area, on either side of which were aligned the hedges which formed the permanent set. It was, of course, possible to vary the natural colour of this setting by adding normal painted scenery as well.

89

90–1

GIUSEPPE GALLI-BIBIENA
Design for a garden with fountain

Island for 'Angelo vincitrice', Vienna 1716

JEAN BÉRAIN *Harbour scene*

138

The first hedge theatre of this kind is thought to have been that of Count Garzoni in Collodi near Lucca (1652). North of the Alps in the eighteenth century, the one great model for all the others was probably that in the Tuileries gardens in Paris. No trace of it remains today, nor of the countless others that must have existed; it is reasonable to suppose that, as the passion for the theatre persisted, every country house, great or small, had its own open-air theatre, especially as it would be cheaper than one built on to the house.

86 One of the oldest and best-known hedge theatres in Germany is the one in the park of Herrenhausen, on the outskirts of Hanover, dating from 1692. There are eleven pairs of 'flats', planted progressively closer as they recede to enhance the perspective, giving a larger acting area than usual, and one that is open at the rear, so that the perspective backcloth is replaced by the natural expanse of the surrounding park. The idea of an inner avenue formed by statues is also
87 found in a late seventeenth-century sketch for a garden theatre by Ludovico Ottavio Burnacini.

The survival of the theatre at Herrenhausen is probably due to the fact that when Elector George Louis became George I of England the palace was left unoccupied and unchanged, like the castle of Sleeping Beauty, for over a hundred years, and so its gardens escaped the shifts of fashion which destroyed so many of the great formal baroque gardens. The Herrenhausen gardens have been restored almost to their earlier glory during the twentieth century.

The baroque garden was laid out in a geometrical pattern, divided by walks and hedges into smaller gardens, shaped according to the demands of the pattern as rondels, circles, ovals, squares, oblongs, trapeziums and triangles. The hedge theatre would be contained in one of these sections. When one was added to the pleasure garden at Veits-
92–3 höchheim at some date after 1760, it had to be fitted into a rectangular division which had already been part of the pattern of the garden for decades.[22] Similar circumstances prevailed at Drottningholm, Erlangen, Dresden (1719), the Nymphenburg outside Munich (1719),[23] Rheinsberg, Cassel,
97 Schwetzingen, in the garden of Schloss Mirabell in Salzburg and elsewhere. None of these have been preserved exactly as they were.

The theatre in the park at Schwetzingen (1775) has lost its wings and retains only the outline of the stage, orchestra and auditorium. The musicians would have occupied the sunken space surrounded by the sphinxes. Its designer, Nicolas de Pigage, did not give it a view across the park but backed the stage with a flight of steps culminating in the temple of Apollo built by Peter Anton Verschaffelt.

94–6 An unusual theatre that has been preserved in good condition is in the park of the Lazienki palace in Warsaw (1792).

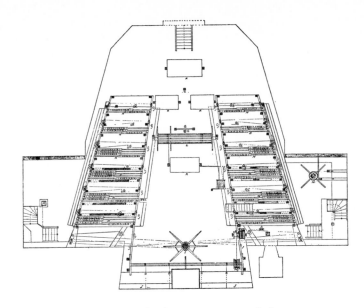

Diagram of the wings in the theatre at Drottningholm, near Stockholm 1766

GIOVANNI BATTISTA PIRANESI *Set with staircase, Rome 1743*

CHARLES COYPEL *Theatre in the Palais Royal in Molière's day, Paris, late seventeenth century*

The stage is on an island, like one at Buen Retiro in Spain. Pillars, a small house and other stonework set among the green trees and bushes furnish a permanent set, resistant to the weather and suitable for all kinds of plays. A stretch of water before the stage forms a proscenium and can also be used as an extension of the stage. A rising semi-circle of seats completes the theatre, with a good view for every member of the audience. The park has been remodelled, and the amphitheatre itself has been renovated, but we can still gain a good impression of what a garden theatre was like in this transitional period between the late baroque and the revival of classicism. The position of the theatre is strictly aligned to that of the palace, but the amphitheatre is reminiscent of a Greek theatre. The semi-circular auditorium does not abut on the stage as in Vicenza. There is a suggestion of a ruin, as in the Eremitage and Sans Pareil theatres, but it is executed on classical lines, while the artificiality of the geometrically arranged trees and the sets of parallel hedges have been abandoned for the romanticism of the 'English' garden.

X DROTTNINGHOLM *Set by J. L. Desprez*

67   VICENZA *Teatro Olimpico, permanent set, 1584*

69   BERNARDINO AND FABRIZIO GALLIARI *Set for 'La Vittoria d'Imeneo' with carriage of Venus, Turin 1750*

71   DROTTNINGHOLM *Stage set attributed to Jean Louis Desprez, late eighteenth century*

72   DROTTNINGHOLM *Detail of set shown on previous page*

73   ČESKY KRUMLOV *Wings for park and hall scenes, late eighteenth century*

74 GRIPSHOLM *Stage cellar*

75 ČESKY KRUMLOV *Undercarriage of the wings*

76 VICENZA *Teatro Olimpico, back view of the permanent set*

77
DROTTNING–
HOLM
Grid

78
ČESKY
KRUMLOV
Stage cellar

79–82   DIESSEN AM AMMERSEE
Klosterkirche, high altar showing:
Christ in the Sepulchre
Nativity
Crucifixion
Resurrection

83   ROHR *Stiftskirche, high altar*

84 WELTENBURG AN DER DONAU
Klosterkirche, high altar
1721

86 HANOVER *'Hedge theatre' in park of Herrenhausen*
c. 1690

87 LUDOVICO OTTAVIO BURNACINI
Design for garden theatre
with avenue of statues

88 FLORENCE *Amphitheatre in the Boboli gardens,*
seventeenth century

90 BURG ZWERNITZ *Sans Pareil,*
Ruin theatre, 1746–47

91 JOHANN GOTTFRID KOEPPEL
Sans Pareil ruin theatre, c. 1790

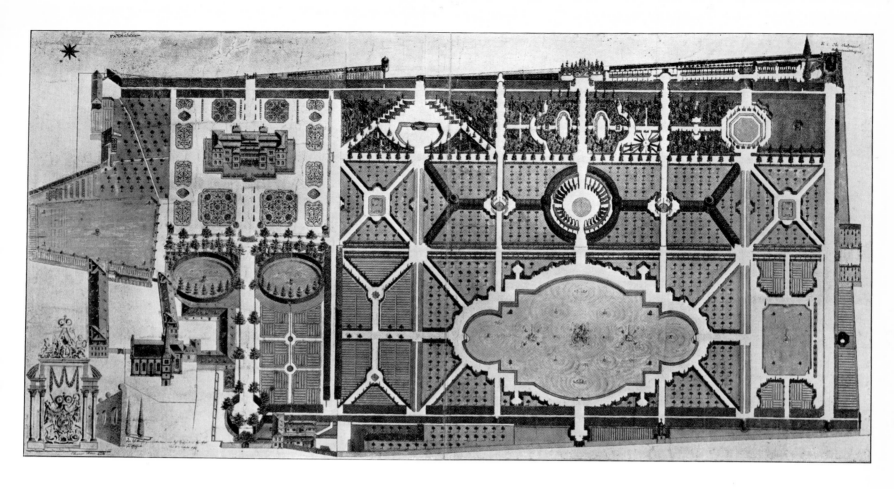

92   J. A. OTH *Plan of the gardens at Veitshöchheim,
near Würzburg c. 1770*

93   VEITSHÖCHHEIM 'Hedge theatre'

WARSAW *Open-air theatre in the Lazienki park*

94   *Corner of the stage*

95   *Amphitheatre*

96   *View of theatre and palace*

97
SCHWETZINGEN
*Open-air theatre
in palace park,
1775–77*

PARMA *Proscenium of the Teatro Farnese, 1618–19*

VI The Theatres

The essential steps in the development of theatre architecture from the Renaissance to the end of the eighteenth century can today be traced only in Italy. It was here that modern theatre building had its origins, and until the rise of nationalism it was Italians who not only equipped and decorated but built the majority of theatres from Portugal to Russia, from Italy to Sweden.

At the very start of modern theatre architecture stands the figure of Andrea Palladio (1508–80), who directed a festival production of Trissino's *Sofonisba* in 1562 in the Basilica in Vicenza, which he had himself built. Eighteen years later it was Palladio who began the construction of the *98–101* Teatro Olimpico in Vicenza, the oldest surviving theatre of modern times. It was begun only a short time before his death and was completed in 1584 by Vicenzo Scamozzi (1552 to 1616). The theatre owes its being to the spirit of the Renaissance, but already it bears the marks of the incipient baroque age. It is obviously modelled on Greek theatres, with the rising semi-circle of spectators' seats, and the permanent architectural set with its niches and statues. But an innovation, and one that was to be characteristic of the baroque theatre, is the continguity of stage and auditorium. In the Greek theatre, as can be seen at Epidauros or the theatre of Dionysos in Athens, the stage and the audience are separated by the open proscenium; in Vicenza the forestage and the proscenium are compressed into a single architectural unit, a narrow acting area immediately adjoining the auditorium.[1]

The semi-circular amphitheatre is enclosed in a rectangular hall, but the clouds painted on the ceiling make it appear open to the sky. The room is lit by its windows, but extra light could have come from candles and torches. Performances would usually have been given in the daytime.

XI, 102 The Teatro Olimpico (1588) in Sabbioneta, also built by Scamozzi, has a very similar layout. Daylight falling through the windows on to the auditorium and stage alike throws natural shadows, and in such a theatre one can see at least one purpose of Aristotle's unities of time, place and action. As in Vicenza, this theatre is built within a rectangular hall. The long sides are linked visually by a colonnade, surmounted by statues, which sweeps in an arc across the room, enclosing the lower part of the theatre, but making space for more spectators above. This intimate little theatre, built by the Gonzagas at a short distance from their capital of Mantua, is an intermediate architectural stage between the Teatro Olimpico in Vicenza and the Teatro Farnese in Parma. A space is left between the stage and the auditorium. Visual emphasis is given to the proscenium, which can be entered through a door at its side, as well as through the set. Another feature is the *trompe-l'œil* painting, showing pano-

FLORENCE *Theatre in the Uffizi 1616*

ramic views of Rome, with the Forum and the Castel *104* S'Angelo, through huge arches; there is also a *trompe-l'œil* painted gallery, with a balustrade exactly like that of the real gallery, immediately under the roof. Busts and statues are *103* reproduced in *grisaille* behind the pillars on the gallery.

In Vicenza all the themes of the statuary and reliefs are drawn from classical mythology and show a marked mascu- *98* line bias: generals, heroes, philosophers, the deeds of Hercules, trials of strength, abductions, combats with centaurs, lions and bulls. A few feminine figures are shown, but only as decoration, crowning an arch or presenting a laurel wreath, not as subjects in their own right. Sabbioneta shows the encroachment of women on the theatre, not only as actresses but as spectators. They appear in the false gallery *103* playing musical instruments, and on the set itself, girdled by walls, as the guardian spirits of cities, or as allegorical figures. The panoramic views in the Sabbioneta theatre are ascribed to Michelangelo Veronese and the figures in the gallery to the school of Paolo Veronese.

Giovanni Battista Aleotti's plans for the Teatro Farnese *after p. 160* in Parma (1618–9) are based on the same principle as the

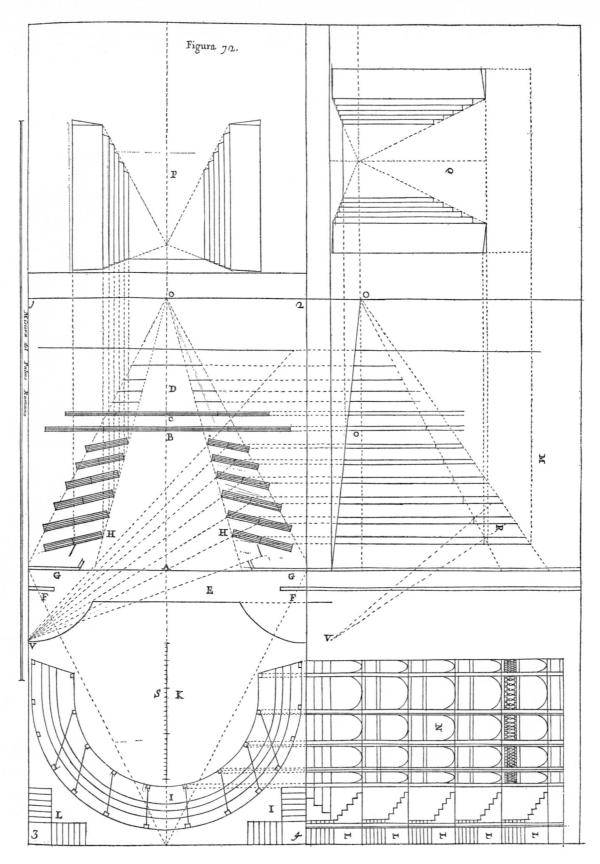

Figura. 72.

ANDREA POZZO
*Diagram for a theatre
with five tiers from
'Prospettiva de' pittori
e architetti', 1693–1700*

Teatro Olimpico in Sabbioneta. Ranuccio I Farnese had this enormous wooden building constructed in a wing of his p. 164 palace. The tripartite division into auditorium, proscenium and stage is as in Sabbioneta, but as in Vicenza there is no 105–7 orchestra. The proscenium arch is decorated with statues set into niches, and with paintings, and has no side openings. Immediately in front of it stretches a broad *parterre*, capable of fulfilling all the many functions expected of a theatre in the baroque era, with plenty of space for ballets, processions, triumphal royal entrances, and glittering balls. The important innovations in this theatre are the positioning of the proscenium arch at the very front of the stage and the shape of the *parterre*, a horseshoe, with the seats beyond it. This is still basically a theatre in a hall, but the two tiers of arches point towards the development of galleries for the spectators.[2]

p. 161 The theatre which Giulio Parigi built in the Palazzo degli Uffizi in Florence in 1616 is very similar to the Teatro Farnese, but now there is actually a gallery behind the rows of seats, as there is in the theatre in the Palais Richelieu in Paris.

Every *palazzo* had to have its theatre now. The Italians were swept off their feet by the new genre of opera, and the new theatres had to be big enough to accommodate large audiences. In 1633 the Barberini family opened a theatre with room for more than three thousand spectators in their Roman palace. In this they showed themselves to be true patrons of the arts, and also upholders of the ancient Roman tradition of *circenses*, public entertainments paid for by politicians.[3]

Besides all the private theatres in Venice, Rome, Bologna and the other princely capital cities, true public theatres now appeared. It is a commonly held opinion that the introduction of galleries in theatres was entirely due to the rigid social stratification of the seventeenth and eighteenth centuries, that they were designed to uphold the class distinctions whose immutability was an essential factor of the age of Absolutism. But this is not necessarily the only explanation. Ever greater numbers of people wanting to go to the theatres had to be accommodated in buildings on the limited sites available in the centre of old cities. The only possible direction of expansion was upwards, which necessarily meant building tiers of galleries. Another factor is acoustic: the horseshoe shape of theatre is the most favourable to the clarity of musical sounds, particularly the human voice singing *pianissimo*. Theatres with galleries could never have evolved before opera was established as a favourite entertainment, and as late as the 1690s Pozzo's plan for one p. 162 still bears a close resemblance to an amphitheatre.

It is not surprising that Venice, one of the most important

centres of opera, was also a leader in the field of theatrical building. During the seventeenth century it had no less than sixteen theatres. Many of these theatres burned down or were later put to other uses. We still know their names, which were those of the parishes in which they stood, in some cases we know the dates of construction or destruction, and playbills, manuscripts, libretti, and first editions give us a wealth of information about the programmes.[4]

Anno Secundo Pacis MDCXII, four years before the Uffizi theatre, the inhabitants of the tiny island of Hvar (then called Lesina) in the Adriatic built themselves a small 109 theatre above the old Arsenal. Hvar was an entrepôt for the trade of Venice and saw a lively traffic not only in merchandise but in culture also. The architect of this theatre is unknown but he is quite likely to have been a Venetian. There are two tiers of boxes around the horseshoe-shaped *parterre*. The walls and ceiling are smooth, and the original decoration probably consisted of paintwork, as it does today. We can imagine that the first theatres in Venice itself were equally modest, for probably no one parish would have had to cater for a larger number of theatregoers than did the theatre of Lesina.[5]

The basic layout of the Hvar theatre corresponds to a formula which in one form or another is almost universal in pp. 161, 167, 170 baroque theatre architecture. In seventeenth-century France, and in court theatres everywhere, the auditorium tended to be a rectangular room. In Sabbioneta and Lambach, the pp. 172, 104 rectangular shape both serves a practical purpose and adds to the visual effect; the gallery sweeps forward with its arms abutting on the stage itself. In theatres where the galleries were enclosed or divided into boxes, the tiers were arranged immediately above each other, or so that the edge of each was slightly behind that of the one below. With the corners of the rectangle cut off, the plan of the auditorium was now a curve: an oval, a semi-circle, a horseshoe or a bell, allow- pp. 162, 164, 173 ing a better view of the stage from all positions.

In the Hvar theatre the seats for special visitors are those in the very front row of the stalls, immediately in front of the stage, and not in one of the boxes. Sabbattini gives precise instructions for the positioning of seats for royalty in his *Pratica di fabricar scene e machine ne' teatri* of 1638. The first true royal box was built in the Zwinger in Dresden between 1664 and 1667; it was copied in subsequent p. 180 theatres in Potsdam, Drottningholm and Versailles, and soon became the rule rather than the exception. The idea of dividing galleries into private boxes is attributed to Benedetto Ferrari, who is believed to have done so in the Teatro San Cassiano in Venice, completed in 1637.[6]

Boxes were introduced in Rome later than in Venice. Carlo Fontana (1634–1714) built the Teatro Tordinona in

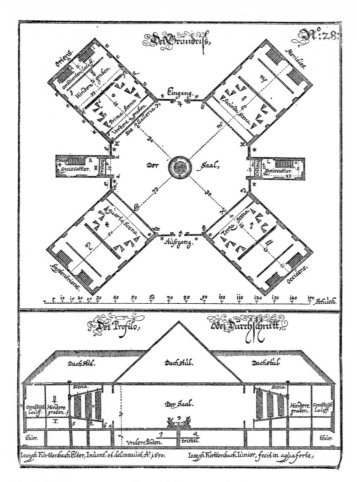

JOSEF FURTTENBACH *Plan and elevation of a theatre
with four stages, 1650*

1671 with six horseshoe-shaped tiers, and with a stage equal
in depth to the auditorium. A second building on the same
site was completed in 1696.[7] None of Naples' seventeenth-
century theatres has survived. An opera house was opened
in 1651 with a performance of Monteverdi's *Incoronazione di
Poppea*; and the Teatro San Bartolomeo was equipped with
wings as early as 1620. In Bologna both the Teatro For-
maglia, built in 1636 by Andrea Sighizzi, and the Teatro

PARMA *Teatro Farnese, ground plan, 1618–19*

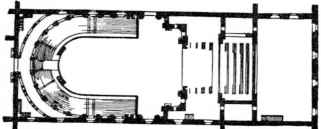

Malvezzi, opened in 1653, were destroyed by fire. Innumerable theatres, built at one time or another in Italy, have long
since disappeared.[8] We can guess what the larger ones looked
like from the pictures that have survived of the first two
opera houses in Vienna; and the theatre in Hvar is probably
typical of the smaller ones.

The eighteenth century did not bring any great changes
in the design of theatre buildings in Italy, comparable to the
changes the rococo brought to other fields of design. The
graceful bell shape became a favoured outline for balconies
to follow, and of course the style of decoration changed with
the times. The Venetians preferred to decorate the walls and
balustrades by painting them; in central Italy they were
covered with plaster mouldings.

There is a small theatre in one of the greatest buildings of
Italy, the 'Versailles of Naples', the Palazzo Reale di Caserta, *108*
built in the 1750s by Charles III of Bourbon. The auditorium
sweeps back in a semi-circle from the stage to the royal box.
The lowest tier of boxes forms the base for the powerful
vertical lines of engaged pillars set into pilasters which form
the visual link between the next three tiers. The moulded
entablature continues the vertical line to yet another row of
boxes set between the ribs of the ceiling vault. The effect is
one of vigour and movement, the balustrades of the boxes
thrust forward between the pilasters. The architect of this
theatre was probably Luigi Vanvitelli (1700–73) who designed the palace itself. The plans must have been made around
1750, at the same time as the theatres at Schwetzingen, and
Versailles and the Altes Residenztheater in Munich.

In Naples the theatre had to display the power and
wealth of the ruling house. The Teatro San Carlo dates *p. 168*
from 1737,[9] a few years earlier than the Caserta theatre. The
architectonic shape of the room itself and the complex
symmetry of the walls almost disappear under the festive
decoration of drapes, hangings, mirrors and candles designed by Vinzenzo del Ré, but no ornamental exuberance
can disguise the linking of the tiers by the continuous line
of the pillars, nor the triple rhythm of the lower boxes and
the horizontal bands along the upper tiers. The steps on
either side of the royal box allowed the king and his suite
immediate access to the *parterre* when the theatre was being
used as a ballroom. There is the same arrangement in the
Markgräfliches Opernhaus in Bayreuth.

The principle of Absolutism is really more forcefully
illustrated in a theatre with this kind of seating arrangement
than in one with tiers and boxes: a good view of the stage
from every seat is less important than that every seat should
be turned towards the prince. Even as a member of a
theatre audience he holds court, and no back may be turned
on him.

This point is underlined by the Teatro Filarmonico in Verona, built for the Accademia by Francesco Galli-Bibiena between 1717 and 1720. Here there is no need for a royal box, and the tiers sweep round in an unbroken, perfect bell.

Antonio Galli-Bibiena chose the same shape for the Teatro Communale in Bologna, built between 1756 and 1763 to hold twelve to fifteen hundred spectators. In the blind spot between the proscenium arch and the start of the boxes there is a stack of false boxes, a pause before the great sweep of the tiers, a curve in no way interrupted by the entrance to the stalls or by the slightly wider boxes above it. This is a public, 'community' theatre, with no need for an ostentatious royal box. Above the narrow proscenium, heavy brackets support the elaborate coffered ceiling, which holds a further row of boxes in the vault itself. The box in the second tier, over the main entrance, is furnished like a small *salon*. A visit to the theatre was not just a cultural, but also – even primarily – a social occasion. Mirrors gave the impression of more space and a greater company. You could receive visitors, and not only in the intervals; you might move to the front of the box once in a while to watch the performance, but you did not take it very seriously. This was one of the few built at this time to stand on an independent site. While its interior is baroque, its façade already shows the onset of neoclassicism in the gallery that runs right across it, in the way the upper story is set back, and in the regularity of the arcades. The Grand Théâtre in Bordeaux, built twenty years later, between 1773 and 1780, shows the same trend.

Altogether, about a hundred large theatres were built in Italy during the eighteenth century. The few which still stand today were all built around 1750, and of those only a very small number have not been substantially altered during the nineteenth or twentieth centuries. In some only the basic shape of the auditorium is left to show that it was built in the eighteenth century, as in the Teatro Grande in Padua.[10] With others it is the theatre records alone which prove the early date of its construction, as with the Teatro della Pergola in Florence[11] or the Teatro alla Scala in Milan, whose history is typical of many other theatres, in Turin, Padua, Brescia, Modena, Naples, Florence and Rome. The original Teatro alla Scala, an enormous building with six tiers, was begun by Giuseppe Piermarini (1734–1808)[12] in 1776, having been commissioned by the Empress Maria Theresa. It was ceremoniously opened in 1778 with the opera *Europa riconosciuta* by Antonio Salieri. It was renovated in 1830, burnt to the ground in 1943 and rebuilt in 1946. Giovanni Paolo Pannini shows a theatre of this kind in his *Concert donné en l'honneur de la naissance du Dauphin*:[13]

above five highly decorated tiers of boxes there is a high dome with painted sculpture and mouldings. The descriptions of the Teatro Ducale in Milan make it appear to have been very similar.[14]

The Teatro San Benedetto in Venice was built in 1755. The illustration I have reproduced shows a staircase built over the orchestra pit to lead from the stage to the auditorium, because a ball is taking place. The proscenium arch is hidden by the festive decorations, and everything has been arranged for the special entertainment.

The typical Venetian style of decorating walls and balustrades with paintings rather than stucco modellings is also seen in the Teatro La Fenice in Venice, which has been painstakingly and sympathetically restored to its original state. Designed by Giovanni Antonio Selva (1753–1819), and built between 1790 and 1792, it holds about three thousand people. On a difficult site, which had to be accessible both to gondolas and pedestrians, it has a horse-shoe-shaped auditorium. The balustrades run round in smooth curves, uninterrupted by vertical lines. The decoration emphasizes the richness of colour and gilded stucco. Only the central box is accentuated by a more elaborate decoration on its balustrade and by its frame of caryatids, trophies and armorial bearings. An engraving by Cagnoni[15] shows that at one time an intricate vault rose above the proscenium, but today the ceiling is flat. While the auditorium shows in its general outline that it is a product of the late baroque era, the foyer and the façade are in the neo-classical style, with Corinthian and Ionic pillars, straight lines, and statues in classical style in semi-circular niches, and are painted a cool white instead of being richly coloured.

As well as its permanent buildings, Italy also saw many temporary structures made in wood or some other material for single great occasions, sometimes showing extraordinary originality. In 1657 an amphitheatre in the shape of a ship was built on the Piazza Maggiore in Bologna for the traditional feast of the Porchetta da Insignia, a conception that fell halfway between a normal theatre and an open-air theatre.[16]

It seems to be the fate of theatres in large cities that they will not stand for long. If they are not destroyed by fire or war, the demands of fashion cause them to be modernized, altered or torn down altogether. Vienna and Paris, the two great metropolitan and theatrical centres of the seventeenth and eighteenth centuries, have retained none of their major baroque theatre buildings, although by a strange coincidence both have, in the palaces of Schönbrunn and Versailles, examples of the last phase of baroque theatre architecture on a smaller, though still regal, scale. Only the smaller cities and principalities, passed over by the nineteenth century, have kept their old buildings simply because they could no longer afford new, ostentatious ones.

The earliest theatres in Vienna, and indeed everywhere else in Europe, were built by Italians. The first Viennese opera house was started in 1651 by Giovanni Burnacini, and was opened in 1652 with a performance of *La Gara* by Antonio Bertali and Alberto Vimina. This theatre, the first milestone in Vienna's long and glorious operatic history, shows affinities with the courtyards of Italian Renaissance palaces in the two levels of its auditorium, framed by a double arcade of rounded arches. Italian influences were bound to be strong, since Italians played an important part in every aspect of theatrical activities at the imperial court in the early years. This first theatre had machinery to move the throne-dais backwards and forwards in accordance with the space needed by any individual production. The gallery for the other spectators reached forwards as far as the pillars of the proscenium arch.

p. 168

Ludovico Ottavio Burnacini was commissioned to build a much larger opera house, the Opernhaus auf der Cortina, for lavish, large-scale theatrical entertainments such as Cesti's *Il pomo d'oro*.[17] Only the foundations and the cellar under the stage were built of stone; the rest was of wood. It measured 212 by 88 feet and was nearly 50 feet high.[18] Three galleries with balustrades supported by pillars ran along the sides of the rectangular auditorium, which was made to appear higher than it was by the *trompe-l'œil* painting on the ceiling. The clustered pillars on either side of the proscenium were extended by more pillars painted on the walls. The seats for the imperial family were at this date still placed at the very front of the *parterre*, on a special dais. The galleries were not divided into boxes, for an operatic performance was still primarily an occasion for the audience to display itself publicly. The theatre was destroyed during the Turkish siege of Vienna in 1683. The summer palace, La Favorita, suffered the same fate, with its theatre, but its gardens continued to provide the setting for open-air performances.

p. 170

A Diet, a conference of the German princes, was an obvious opportunity for the emperor to display his theatrical pre-eminence, and so in 1653 the Burnacinis were commanded by Leopold I to construct a wooden theatre in Regensburg. It held several thousand people. After the Diet it was taken down, transported to Vienna and re-erected in the city centre, on what is today the Josefsplatz.

None of the theatres built during this great epoch of Vienna's theatrical history have survived to the present day. Their splendour lives on only in the music and libretti of the works performed in them, and in the engravings which depict scenes in their original settings. The title page of a published edition of *Il pomo d'oro* is framed by the pro-

p. 171

scenium arch of the theatre on the Cortina. Only the Redoutensäle, which Maria Theresa had built in the Hofburg for more intimate productions and balls, are used today for performances of chamber operas by the State Opera. Antonio Galli-Bibiena completed the larger Redoutensaal in 1752. A balcony runs across the back of the room, and at the other end the stage was built in the form of a flight of steps, as if it were an improvised open-air theatre. This suggestion is repeated in the tapestries, which show pastoral scenes of rustic idylls and smiling peasantry. The room has been re-decorated several times since it was first opened.

122
123

The decline of the once popular game of royal (or real) tennis left the roofed courts to stand unused. One, which had been used by courtiers and stood conveniently against the Hofburg, was converted into a theatre in 1741 by Josef Carl Selliers, the '*Entrepreneur* for Court Operas, Serenades, Comedies, Oratorios and the Holy Tombs'.[19] (There could be no better summing-up of theatrical concepts of the time than that title.) In 1776 it was reopened as a national theatre, the Theater an der Burg. No trace remains of the original building on the Michaelerplatz today, but the modern Burgtheater has kept the old name on its new site.

Between 1700 and 1744 all the more lavish productions of operas were staged in the Grosser Komödisaal in the Hofburg, which was pulled down to make room for the Redoutensaal. Like its successor it was built and decorated by members of the Galli-Bibiena family.

These two larger theatres were opened to the public before the middle of the eighteenth century, but private performances were given for the court alone in smaller rooms in the Hofburg or in the Zeremoniensaal in Schönbrunn.

12

In addition to the court theatres, Vienna boasted the first permanent theatre in the German-speaking countries built for the entertainment of the common people as opposed to the educated bourgeoisie. The Kärntnertortheater was built in 1710 by the theatrical designer Antonio Berduzzi at the command of the Emperor Joseph I.[20] Other theatres founded in the eighteenth century, in the suburbs of Josefstadt and Leopoldstadt, have been completely rebuilt since.

Only the Schlosstheater in the palace of Schönbrunn survives, and that not without some alterations.[21] The building of the palace was begun in 1694 to plans by Johann Bernard Fischer von Erlach. It was greatly altered and enlarged between 1744 and 1749 by Nicolaus Pacassi, and the theatre, designed by Friedrich von Hohenberg,[22] was added in 1766–67. The age of the great Italian architects was past. The opulent sensuality of Italian baroque is hardly hinted at, and in its place is classical calm, bearing witness to the German architect's French training. It is true that the general outline of the room is oval, but the shallow galleries and the

124

NAPLES *Theatre in the Palazzo Reale, c. 1750*

little balconies are pressed back against the sides as if to revive memories of the early rectangular theatres. The wheel has turned full circle. In the Teatro Farnese in Parma, for example, the seating was so arranged as to give the impression of a curve in a rectangular room. Here, the main tier runs back almost in a straight line, uninterrupted by any boxes, and adorned by the little balconies above. The upper gallery gracefully crowns the imperial box above which it appears to float, and the imperial box itself is no longer overhung by coats of arms, crowns, *putti* or plaster drapes.[23]

125–8

Vienna was, of course, the centre of all activities, theatrical and otherwise, in the Austro-Hungarian empire, but a great deal went on too in the provinces. A charmingly individual little theatre has been preserved in the Benedictine monastery at Lambach in Upper Austria, built like so many others for the performances of the pupils at the monastery school. The back third of the plain, oblong room is filled by a gallery decorated by painted drapes. A simple wooden partition in front of the stage separates the musicians from the audience. The apparently three-dimensional decorations on either side of the stage are painted in *trompe-l'œil*. Two female figures in *grisaille* who bear a mask and a scroll symbolize the theatre in general, and the teacher on a balcony and the boy peeping out from behind the curtain remind us that this was a school theatre.[24]

130

The small civic theatre in Grein on the Danube was built in 1791, during the French Revolution, but the rococo style lingered on in small, out of the way places and we may take this as typical of the many other little theatres which have long since disappeared. The rectangular room in the Rathaus (town hall) was originally the Corn Exchange, and with the addition of a balcony was able to seat about 160 people. There is only one box, placed at the side, for the notables of the little town. The most remarkable feature in

129

167

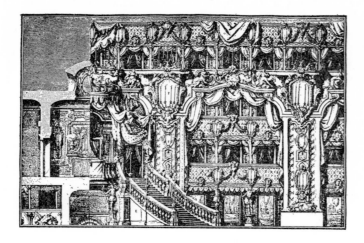

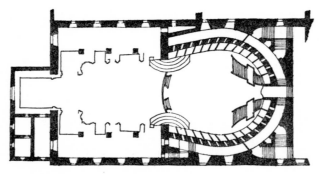

NAPLES *Teatro San Carlo, 1737*
Section
Plan

VIENNA *The first opera house, 1652*

the theatre is the original seating, which has been preserved. The citizens actually owned their places in the theatre; they could raise the seats and padlock them, as people in larger towns could lock their boxes.

Salzburg had the good fortune to be ruled by a succession of prince-archbishops who were also theatre enthusiasts. The Schönborn family, who gave Franconia so many of its finest buildings, were said to be possessed by the *Bauwurmb*, the 'building bug'; one might say that the archbishops of Salzburg were possessed by the '*Theaterwurmb*'. As well as the three delightful open-air theatres which still exist, the city possessed in the eighteenth century at least eight other theatres. Besides the rock theatre of Hellbrunn, Archbishop Marcus Sitticus had an indoor theatre equipped with all the latest technical resources. In 1775, Archbishop Hieronymus converted his tennis court into a theatre, and the theatre run by the Benedictines in the university flourished throughout the century. Plays were also performed in the Lodron Marianisches Kolleg and in the municipal wine parlour, the Stadttrinkstube.[25]

Innsbruck had a court theatre as early as 1654, built for Archduke Ferdinand Charles by Christoph Gumpp the younger (1600–72) in the Italian style.[26] Several private theatres were maintained in Linz by noblemen in their own houses, while Graz, which since the 1600s had received regular visits from travelling companies on their way north from Italy, only got its first permanent building in 1736, which held about four hundred people. A larger building, with a capacity of about eleven hundred, the Landesständisches Theater, was opened in 1776. In Klagenfurt a tennis court was converted to a theatre in 1737.

In Prague, in 1617, 'a noble theatre was erected at court, in the Provincial Chambers',[27] and by the eighteenth century Prague, like every other city of importance, had several theatres; none of these has survived. An opera house was built in 1725 at the behest of Count Sporck, and the magistrates of the Old City built the Kotzentheater beside the Galli monastery in 1737. Other theatres included the Hibernertheater, and theatres in the Palais Thun and the riding school of the Palais Wallenstein. The Nationaltheater, founded by Count Nostitz, was designed by Count Kunigl and built between 1781 and 1783 by Anton Haffenecker (1720–89),[28] and there was a 'Patriotic Theatre' on the Rossmarkt for Bohemian-German plays. The only sign that remains of all these is the façade of the Ständetheater, and even that has seen some alterations.

Outside Prague, Czechoslovakia has one veritable jewel: the theatre in the Schwarzenberg palace in Český Krumlov. Prince Josef Adam Schwarzenberg had an older theatre torn down in 1761, and the new Comödiehaus rose in its place five years later. The auditorium is small, even intimate, as so many others must have been at that date. The architect (the Prince's son, Prince Johannes Schwarzenberg) placed a single gallery to follow the curve of the wall back to the one, central box. The floor is level, although a steady rise in the height of the benches makes it appear to slope. Shallow pilaster strips are the only three-dimensional decoration. Everything else is *trompe-l'œil*: the cornice, the vaulting around the flat ceiling, the arch framing the box on which only the urns and flowers could be taken hold of, and the elaborately 'moulded' surround of the stage, except for the plump cherubs which hold the lights.

V, *63*   The Maskensaal in the same palace has two separate claims to a place in theatrical history. It was (and is) used for performances, and in 1748 Josef Lederer painted a permanent memorial to players and audiences in frescos that are alive with brilliant colour and movement. *Commedia dell'arte* characters make merry with masked, aristocratic guests, while peasants look on and wide-eyed children press around, and on the walls above hang masks and musical instruments.

The first opera house in Warsaw (1724–25) was a large theatre in which the nobility sat in the *parterre* and the *bourgeoisie* in the galleries.[29] A second one was designed in 1748 by Daniel Pöppelmann on the same lines as his opera house in the Zwinger in Dresden, but on a smaller scale. The stage, fitted out by Alessandro Mauro, had one innovation in that the back drop was semi-elliptical and set some way behind the last pair of wings, so that crowd entries could be made from the back of the stage. This theatre was pulled down in 1772. No trace remains either of Saxon Augustus II's Komödienhaus in Warsaw castle or of the Teatr Narodowy, the National Theatre, built in 1779 to designs by Bonaventuri Solari.[30] Another loss is the theatre in the Radziwil palace, in which, in 1748, Princess Ursula Franziska Radziwil began single-handed to create a Polish drama. Some of the great noblemen of Poland, such as Count Telckany, bankrupted themselves by their enthusiastic patronage of opera. Michael Kasimierz Oginski began by having concert halls built in his several houses for performances of plays and operas; in 1770 he advanced to having a stage erected on a ship, and finally in 1780 he had an opera house built in Slonim to hold a thousand people. The court architect and stage designer, Innocenzo Maraino,[31] placed this theatre in such skilful proximity to the river that real ships could float across the back of the stage. Every box in the two tiers had its own fireplace, a luxury that was a necessity in the cruel Polish winters if people were to visit the theatre.

The most famous theatres in Hungary were those in the fabulous 'Kingdom' of the Esterhazy family. When Prince Nicholas the Magnificent became head of the family in 1762,

there were already a new theatre, an old theatre and a theatre in the 'Pariser Mühle'.[32] Theatres sprang up all over Hungary in the second half of the eighteenth century, in towns which had previously housed touring companies in inns and wooden booths. The first permanent, brick-built theatre in Hungary was opened in Sopron (Ödenburg) in 1769, and other, larger towns were quick to follow suit: Bratislava (Pressburg, now in Czechoslovakia) in 1776, Buda in 1787, Sibiu (Hermannstadt, now in Rumania) in 1788 and Košice (Kaschau, now in Czechoslovakia) in 1789.

A similar development was followed in what is today Yugoslavia: the pioneers were Prince Auersperg, in Ljubljana (Laibach) in 1765, and Duke Madé in Zagreb, and then came public theatres in Split (Spalato), Zadar (Zara) and Rijeka (Fiume). We have already discussed the earliest

GERMANY *Public theatre, c. 1785*

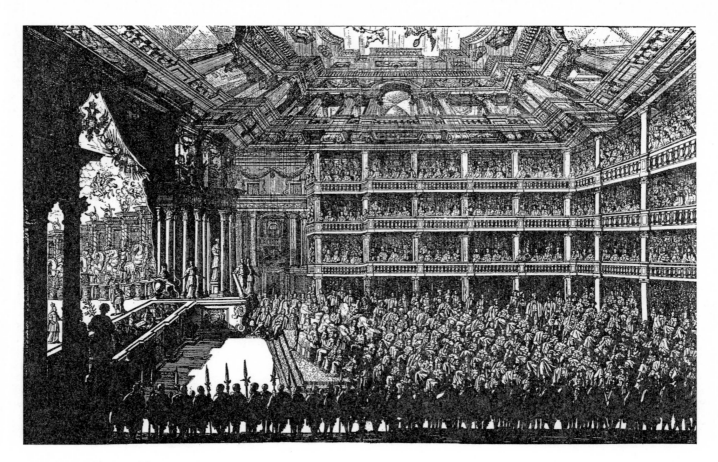

VIENNA *Opernhaus auf der Cortina, Vienna 1666–8*

theatre of all in this region, on the island of Hvar, in connection with early theatres in Venice. These later theatres would have resembled the palace theatre in Český Krumlov, or the theatre in Litomyšl (formerly Leitomischl) in Czechoslovakia, a later building in the neoclassical style of the 1790s, a high narrow room with boxes encircling the *parterre* and a single gallery above.[33]

In Russia, too, the building of permanent theatres began relatively late. It was customary to put up temporary theatres for a few performances only, as and when they were needed, as Peter the Great's niece Anna Ivanovna did with her transportable one. The first court theatre in St. Petersburg burnt down in 1749, and a new opera house was built in 1750, designed by Giuseppe Valeriani (died 1781), who also designed and equipped the interior of the theatre in the Winter Palace in 1755.

In 1779 Catherine the Great summoned Ludwig Philipp Tischbein (1744–1806) to St. Petersburg to decorate the imperial court theatre and to design sets for the stage thereafter. In 1783 he was commissioned to build the Bolshoi Theatre, also in St. Petersburg, which was completed in 1784.

This 'Great Theatre' had a capacious *parterre* with raked seating, three tiers of boxes and above them a gallery which ran round all four sides of the theatre, even over the stage.[34] The theatre was open to the general public, in accordance with Catherine's desire to educate her subjects. The private, court theatre was the Hermitage theatre, built in the Winter Palace between 1783 and 1786 by Giacomo Quarenghi,[35] which was chiefly used for the production of French plays. Moscow did not get an imperial theatre until 1800, and the façades of the theatre are the only things that remain of the pleasance in the Kremlin. *136–7*

Already before the erection of the big public theatres, the Russian nobility had started to build themselves small private theatres in their country houses. The theatres at Ostankino and Sailo Konskova near Moscow are charming *135, 138* examples, showing strong French influence.

Theatrical architecture in Spain followed a more individual line of which very few traces remain. One can reconstruct the theatre for which Lope de Rueda, Lope de Vega, Miguel de Cervantes and Tirso de Molina wrote only approximately. This theatre was in a courtyard, enclosed on two

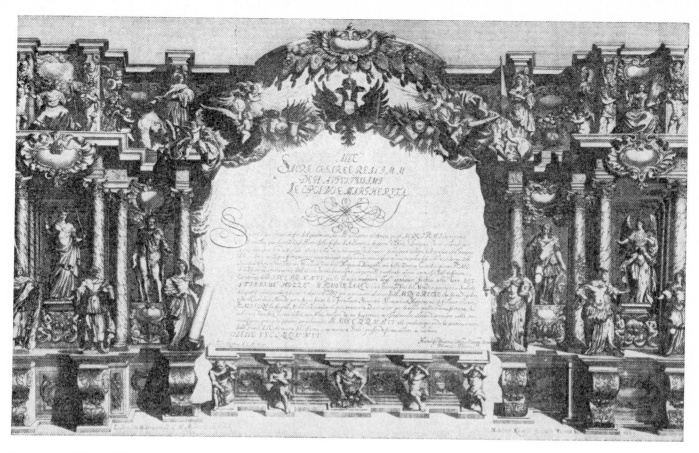

MELCHIOR KÜSEL *Title page of Cesti's 'Il pomo d'oro', showing the proscenium of the Opernhaus auf der Cortina, Vienna 1667*

or three sides by houses. The stage was erected along one of the narrower sides of this *corral*, and an awning was stretched over the spectators to provide shade. Nearest to the stage were benches for the respectable citizens, behind whom stood the rowdy *mosqueteros*. Women were seated in a gallery at the back of the yard, and the more refined among them watched invisibly from the barred windows of surrounding houses.

Such *corrales* were found throughout the land. The chief theatrical centre after Madrid was Seville, where plays were given in the Corral de Doña Elvira from 1579 onwards, in the Coliseo from 1607 and in four other theatres as well. There were theatres of this kind in Cordova from 1602, in Valencia from 1583 and in Zamora from 1606. The *corrales* continued in use until the middle of the eighteenth century, receiving some improvements over the years, such as upholstery on the seats and a roof over the whole theatre. The Corral de Santa Cruz in Barcelona was built as late as 1790, and was still in use in the nineteenth century. To begin with the *corrales* were built by the religious orders and hired to the touring companies, the profits being given over to charitable uses. The kings of Spain recognized the value of these pop-

ular theatres and even had one built in a courtyard of their palace in Madrid in 1607; they already had an indoor theatre, the Salon de Comedias. They wanted to enjoy the same tragedies and comedies as their people, but it was obviously out of the question for royalty to go to a public theatre.

The various royal palaces all had their own theatres. There was a particularly magnificent one at Buen Retiro, designed by Cosimo Lotti, in which the back wall of the stage could be removed altogether, so that the park itself became the setting.

The great age of the theatre in Spain was the first half of the seventeenth century, after which the court theatre fell into an uneasy state of neglect alternating with revival, according to the interests of the reigning king. In 1734 the Madrid palace obtained a second theatre, next to the queen's apartments, and the ruined theatres in the parks of Aranjuez and Buen Retiro were restored more richly than ever before only to be allowed to fall into ruins once more. Nothing is left of them today.

Manuel Salvador Carmona's engraving of the Coliseo del Principe in Madrid shows a highly individual style of 139

PARIS *Theatre in the Palais Royal, 1641*

PARIS *Plan of the Salle de l'Opéra in the Palais Royal, 1770*
PARIS *Plan of the Théâtre de l'Odéon, 1779–82*

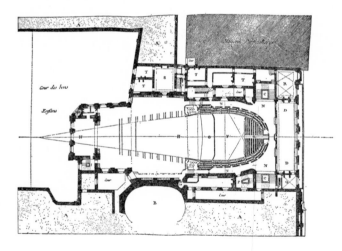

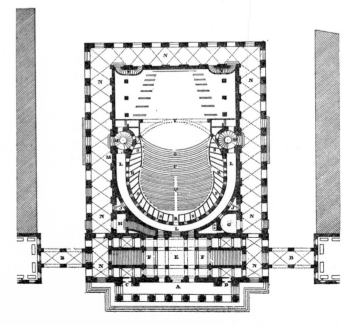

theatrical architecture, with swirling lines, lush, weighty scrolls, and tiers kept in a state of continuous movement by their forward-thrusting balconies.

The old theatres of Lisbon, the Teatro da Trinidade and the Opera do Tiejo, were victims of the 1755 earthquake, but new ones were built before the end of the century.

The only challenge to Italian pre-eminence in the field of theatrical architecture came from France. Cardinal Richelieu had a theatre in his palace in 1640, which he entrusted to Jacques le Mercier (*c.* 1585–1654). This theatre in the Palais Cardinal (re-named Palais Royal after being presented to the king) was a rectangular room. It retained an open arcade round the upper part of the room, like the early Italian theatres, and had two galleries below that. Seats were provided only for the royal family and the Cardinal. p. 172

When Molière was the tenant he had a number of alterations made. The rectangular shape was lost by cutting off the corners at the back, two tiers of boxes were installed, and the back half of the *parterre* was raked and filled with seats. The front half was reserved for distinguished visitors.

When Louis XIV came to the throne Paris had three proper theatres: those in the Palais Royal and the Hôtel de Bourgogne and the Théâtre du Marais. When the Académie Royale de Musique (the Opéra) was founded in 1671 it was assigned the Palais Royal theatre. The Théâtre Français, which included the former company of the Théâtre du Marais, exercised its monopoly over all French comedies and tragedies in the Hôtel Guénégaud, and the Théâtre Italien took over the Hôtel de Bourgogne.

The Théâtre de la Salle des Machines des Tuileries was yet another rectangular building. Two galleries ran round three sides and the stalls rose at the back to the level of the first tier of boxes. The pillars supporting the first tier were so high that there was room to suspend balconies between them, halfway up.[36] This vast theatre, built in the left wing of the Tuileries between 1662 and 1664 by Gaspare Vigarani (*c.* 1586 – 1663), his two sons Carlo and Ludovico, and Amandini, was equipped with such elaborate machinery that the singers could not make themselves heard above the thunderous rumbles and groans of the 'magic' transformations.

Carlo Vigarani designed a theatre for the park of Versailles in 1665, and was active as a theatrical architect until at least 1674. He built a number of smaller theatres, including one in the Rue de Vauginard.

We can make only approximate reconstructions of the Théâtre du Marais (1623), the Théâtre du Faubourg Saint Germain (1635), the Théâtre de la Croix Blanche, the Théâtre de Mademoiselle [de Montpensier] (1661) and the Hôtel Guénégaud (1673). All were pulled down to make way for newer buildings, rebuilt, or destroyed by fire.

In the Jeu de Paume de l'Etoile, a former tennis court, the proscenium boxes were reserved for the king and queen. Towards the end of the seventeenth century, however, Paris finally abandoned the old-fashioned rectangular shape, and from then on theatres were semi-circular, elliptical, oval p. 172 and bell-shaped, like the Nouvelle Salle de l'Opéra in the Palais Royal, designed by Moreau, Architecte du Roi et de la Ville.

The most famous Parisian theatre, the Comédie Française, has a long history of fires and re-construction. The first building, by François d'Orbay, was opened on 18 April 1689 with Racine's *Phèdre* and Molière's *Le Médecin malgré lui*. Moreau le jeune's engraving of Voltaire receiving his poet's crown shows the theatre in 1778.[37] There are three stacks of boxes on the stage itself, terminating the rows with their slightly curving balconies. The modern theatre still stands on the site it has occupied since 1786, on the corner of the Rue de Richelieu, where it was placed by Victor Louis (1731–1800), but the first alterations to Louis's building were

made in 1799; it was burnt to the ground in 1900, and has been restored several times since.

During Louis XIV's reign performances at Versailles were given on temporary stages, often erected for a single occasion.[38] Louis planned a permanent theatre with Carlo Vigarani, but nothing came of it, and Louis XV took nearly twenty years to make up his mind to instruct his architect Ange-Jacques Gabriel to proceed. When work finally started, it was completed in exactly twenty-one months, for the wedding of the Dauphin and Marie Antoinette in 1770. XII, *141–150*

Gabriel chose for the auditorium the shape of an oval, flattened at the proscenium. He wrote in the *Mercure de France* in August 1770[39] that this was the best shape because it involved the fewest angles and corners, which were the worst traps for voices, and because it permitted the best views of the stage.

This theatre completely avoids the uniformity and monotony of the great Italian theatres, with their four, five or six tiers rising at regular intervals and their gently, almost im-

PARIS *Théâtre de la Porte Saint-Martin, after 1781*

LONDON *Sadler's Wells Theatre (1765) as it was in 1792*

perceptibly sloping *parterres*. Here the body of the theatre is on two quite distinct levels, with a space in which spectators might stand in front and a large balcony for the court behind. This had immediate access to the foyer, the promenade which was a social necessity here as the boxes are shallow and have no partition walls. The two lower tiers sweep cleanly round the room; the lower with a smooth wall behind it, while the upper has each box set into a niche to give the necessary depth. The partitions between the niches thus become a row of solid supports for the fluted columns of the uppermost tier. This is twice the height of the other two, and in it the full glory of the theatre unfolds. Mirrors enlarge and multiply the space without the seats themselves obtruding, for the whole purpose of the room is to let the audience see and be seen. The columns support a coffered, painted ceiling, whose vault is broken by a semi-dome at the back. The shape and lines of the room are calm and classical, but its spirit is that of the preceding era: grandeur, illusion, surprise, conjuring with mirrors and space. The cool marble and the other semi-precious stones, lapis lazuli and porphyry, are a sham; for acoustical reasons the whole theatre is made of wood like the sound-box of a violin. The old-fashioned result may also in part be due to the fact that some of the plans had been made twenty years earlier.

The king would attend the theatre on state occasions with a large following, or if he wished to watch a performance privately he would use the middle one of the three screened boxes, and remain unobserved by the rest of the audience. For ceremonial balls, the open part of the *parterre* could be raised to the level of the stage. It was the scene of a few glittering festivals, and some magnificently staged operas, but already in the reign of Louis XVI productions

there had become too expensive. During the revolution it housed the Jacobin club, and afterwards was totally neglected. It was restored between 1952 and 1957, and the reliefs and mouldings of Augustin Pajou painstakingly renovated. The figures from classical mythology in the lower tier, the allegories, represented by children and symbols of the arts, in the upper tier, the branches, ribbons, wreaths and the geometrical devices can all be seen again in their former beauty. Louis Jacques Durameau's paintings have been restored and echo the blue, green and gold colour scheme of the whole room.

Schönbrunn and Versailles: two attitudes, two empires, two worlds are symbolized in the private theatres of these two palaces, completed within four years of each other. The Schönbrunn theatre is small, unpretentious, graceful, designed for private pleasure; the Versailles theatre is sumptuous, stately, intended to impress. And yet Marie Antoinette found, at the first productions of opera at Versailles, that the standards of performance were higher in Vienna.

Almost all the provincial theatres of France date from the second half of the eighteenth century, but even while the power and glory of the *ancien régime* was crumbling, Paris still attracted the most promising artistic talent. There are very few contemporary records of the original state of the theatres in Metz, begun in 1738 and re-built in 1751,[40] Nancy, built in 1755 by Emmanuel Héré de Corny, Lyon (1754–56), Amiens (1778–80), Besançon (1778, by Claude Nicolas Ledoux), or Nantes (1788, by Mathurin Crucy). The Grand Théâtre in Bordeaux is the only one that has remained unaltered to the present day. Built by Victor Louis between 1773 and 1780, it reversed the usual flow of ideas from Paris to the provinces by influencing Charles Garnier's designs for the Opéra in Paris in the nineteenth century. The basic form of the auditorium is circular, as is apparent from the ceiling, which rides above the balconies on flattened arches and pendentives. The distance between each tier grows less from floor to ceiling, emphasizing the elaborate ceiling itself.

p. 172 The Odéon in Paris was built between 1779 and 1782 by Charles de Wailly and J.W. Peyre on the same circular principle, although the auditorium itself is bell-shaped.

Theatrical life in England, as in France, was chiefly concentrated on the capital. Companies undertook provincial tours, but all the significant events and developments took place in London.

p. 119 In the reign of Elizabeth most theatres were circular wooden structures with tiered galleries, a few boxes formed by partitions, and a stage that projected well forward into the pit. At the time of her death there were altogether eleven theatres.[41] These round buildings were at this stage unroofed, and are perhaps directly comparable to the arena. They still showed their descent from the inn-yards in which the old mystery plays were staged, but their basic shape can be attributed to their original function, that of bear-pits. Even the Globe was used for bear-baiting, to help make ends meet. This kind of building, which was not found elsewhere in Europe, was gradually abandoned during the seventeenth century in favour of a rival type, a rectangular indoor hall, which had been used in the sixteenth century by the boy-players.

London's first public playhouse, the Theatre, was built in 1567 by James Burbage, a member of the Earl of Leicester's troupe, outside the City walls and thus outside the jurisdiction of the Puritan City authorities. It was replaced by a similar round wooden building, the Globe, the most famous theatre of the age, not least because Shakespeare was actor, director and sharer in it. The octagonal construction held three galleries around the open courtyard, into which the stage projected at about six feet from the ground, with a low

LONDON *Old Theatre Royal, Drury Lane, in 1792*

balustrade. The Globe was rebuilt after a fire in 1613 according to its original plan and stood until it was demolished in 1644, apparently unaffected by the Italian developments in theatrical architecture.[42]

The Fortune Theatre, built on a rectangular ground-plan in 1600 and rebuilt in 1623 after a fire,[43] marks the transition from the English open playhouse to the roofed-in theatre with its greater scope for scenery and stage illusion. The Blackfriars Theatre was roofed from the start; measuring 66 by 46 feet, it had originally been the refectory of a Dominican friary, and became the theatre of the Children of the Chapel Royal.

Even after the Restoration, Puritan influence continued to restrict theatrical development. Only two theatres of any importance were built in London between the Great Fire of 1666 and the end of the century. One was the Duke's Theatre in Dorset Garden, opened in 1671. The rows of seats, both in the pit and the galleries, rose in tiers as in an amphitheatre. There was still an apron stage. The Theatre Royal, Drury Lane (1674) was probably very similar; both were designed by Sir Christopher Wren (1632–1723).

An opera house with a similar stage layout was opened in the Haymarket in 1705, a sign of London's growing interest p. 175 in the theatre in the eighteenth century. The Drury Lane theatre, which under Garrick's direction became the first theatre in the land, has been rebuilt several times in the last two centuries, and the two modern opera houses, Covent Garden and Sadler's Wells, have only their names and sites p. 174 in common with their eighteenth-century predecessors. Section drawings by Sallay and Servandoni show us what p. 176-7 a London theatre of the time looked like, and also show the influence of Italian art and artists.

The difficult conditions of pioneering and the predominance of Puritans in colonial life made the theatre a late starter in North America. The first permanent buildings were the Southwark Theatre in Philadelphia in 1766 and the John Street Theatre in New York, a year later. Both were very simple structures, partly made of brick.

The Netherlands differed from almost every other country in that the theatre owed its development to the middle classes, not to the aristocracy. The overthrow of Spanish rule boosted the self-confidence of the Dutch middle classes, and while they may have been doctrinaire and materialistic, they were genuinely concerned to promote a national culture. In 1617 a wooden theatre was opened by Samuel Coster on the Kaizersgracht in Amsterdam with the *Treurspel van de Moordt begaan ann Wilhelm van Orangiën* by Gysbreght van Hoghendrop.

SALLAY and SERVANDONI *A theatre during a masked ball, cross-section, London, eighteenth century*

SALLAY and SERVANDONI *A theatre during a masked ball, longitudinal section*

The Schouwburg on the Kaizersgracht, built by Nikolas van Kampen in 1638, had an approximately horseshoe-shaped auditorium, with two tiers of boxes and above them yet another gallery, with a sloping floor and rows of seats. A barrel vault ran across the flat timber roof. When the Schouwburg was rebuilt in 1664–65 its stage was equipped with a comprehensive system of wings, traps, flies and machines. It retained its uppermost gallery, the 'gods', with steep rows of benches for the poorer theatregoers, and there were now benches in the pit as well.

Periodically the Netherlands, too, suffered Puritan campaigns against the theatre. Zealots managed to close the Schouwburg between 1747 and 1749, but when it burnt to the ground in 1772 a new one was built by J. E. Witte p. 174 near the city walls. The *parterre* had a tiled floor and was furnished with benches. The tiers swept round the room with French lightness and elegance, and the division into boxes avoided the solid walls of contemporary Italian theatres. A large bay in the centre gave more space to the 'gods'.

Amsterdam was one of the richest cities in Europe, and even in wartime its money market held firm. It was thus the first city to give uninterrupted support to a theatre. The theatres built in The Hague (1766), Rotterdam (1766–67) and Leiden were of less significance.

The first permanent theatre building in Scandinavia was opened in Slotsholm in Denmark as late as 1663. Until then, travelling companies, English to start with, later mostly German, had performed on makeshift stages. The first Danish opera house, by all reports a magnificent wooden building, built in the Amalienborg palace in Copenhagen in 1689, was destroyed in the same year by a fire which cost two hundred spectators their lives. Christian V had a similar theatre built of more enduring materials in 1703.[44]

In 1772, Copenhagen saw the opening, in the Lille Grönnegade, of Den Danske Skueplads, the first theatre devoted to plays in the Danish language.[45] It was a simple, galleried theatre, much like the one in Hvar, with wings and chandeliers on the stage. In 1748 a new theatre was built in Copenhagen on Kogens Nytrov, which became the Kon-

AMSTERDAM *Nieuwe Schouwburg, 1774*
Auditorium
Exterior
Stage, with a scene from 'Gysbreght van Amstel'

gelige Danske Skueplads in 1771.[46] The architect was Nicolai Eigtved (1701–54). N. J. Jardin was employed for the court theatre in Christiansborg palace in 1766.

The first permanent theatre in Sweden was opened in Stockholm in 1667. In 1699 the court architect converted a tennis court near the old palace for the use of a French company.[47] By 1737, there was a royal Swedish theatre, where Swedish was spoken, and which became the Swedish Opera in 1772, in the Slottbacken tennis court.

After the disasters brought by the wars of Charles XII in which the Baltic provinces were lost, and the wars with Russia, which resulted in the loss of part of Finland, Sweden had at last a chance to recuperate under King Adolf Frederick of the house of Holstein-Gottorp and his wife Louise Ulrike, a sister of Frederick II of Prussia. During this reign, from 1751 to 1771, there was an economic recovery, which in turn allowed the theatre to flourish again.[48]

Sweden's most important contribution to the history of the baroque theatre lies in the two surviving eighteenth-century theatres at Gripsholm and Drottningholm. The theatre that stands in Drottningholm today had a pre-decessor, which burnt down in 1762. The new building, by Carl Frederik Adelcrantz (1716–96), was completed in 1766. The simple, white-painted wooden exterior makes its effect by its lovely proportions; the two-storied façade is interrupted only by a central projection with windows from ground to roof level. In the auditorium the architect hit on an arrangement unique in theatrical building, in that the room is divided laterally into three distinct parts. The first division, boudoir-like with its smooth curves and supple elegance, is for the royal family. Behind that are two parts for the nobility, courtiers and servants. There is no royal box; the king sat in the front row, and if he wished to remain unobserved he used a small, screened box, like the one in Versailles. The three boxes on each side of the theatre are the only three-dimensional elements; the rest of the decoration is painted.

XIII, 160

The last and perhaps most exquisite of baroque theatre buildings is the little theatre in Slott Gripsholm, built by Gustav III, Adolf Frederik's successor. Its semi-circular shape, Ionic pillars, and plain, half-domed ceiling belong to the neo-classic revival, but the *trompe-l'œil* decoration, the use of mirrors to magnify and distort the space and the false proscenium pillars remain in the dying world of baroque illusion.[49]

158–9

The area covered by modern Germany was in the seventeenth and eighteenth centuries a collection of small sovereign states, owing only a very imprecisely defined fealty to the Holy Roman Emperor. Their political and economic rivalry was pursued with extraordinary ferocity, and they

BRUNSWICK *Festsaal in castle of Dankwarderode, 1642*

had also to defend themselves against invasion from beyond the empire's borders. Time and again the Turks advanced to the gates of Vienna itself. Saxony was involved in the Russo-Swedish wars from 1700 to 1721, the war of the Austrian Succession had Saxony, Bavaria and Austria at each other's throats from 1740 to 1748, Frederick the Great of Prussia went to war with Maria Theresa of Austria over Silesia in the Seven Years War from 1756 to 1763, and the disputed Bavarian succession brought more conflict in 1778. War and the resulting distress were constant factors in the lives of the German people, and yet the theatre prospered.

The principal motive for the German princes' patronage of the theatre was the desire to outshine each other, rather than to foster native talent, so their eyes were always on the foreign leaders of fashion, at first Italy, later France. It became essential to the prestige of every prince and duke to produce Italian operas and French plays in his own theatre,

MUNICH *Opernhaus am Salvatorplatz, 1654,*
Electoral box added 1685

and the result was a building boom comparable only to that of Italy. After the drastic regrouping and amalgamation of the German states by Napoleon, many a former capital became a sleepy provincial backwater, left to dream of its past splendours, while its theatre was spared further modernization. Of recent years, those theatres which did not actually fall into ruins have had a new lease of life, for we have come to appreciate the charm of a baroque theatre as a setting for the plays of the period.

To begin with, theatre building in Germany was slow and uncertain. When the Duchy of Brunswick-Wolfenbüttel dropped out of the Thirty Years War, the Festsaal in Dankwarderode castle was made the scene for the *Neu erfundenes Freudenspiel, genandt Friedenssieg* ('the triumph of peace'). A large room with a low, massive timbered ceiling was both auditorium and stage. The spectators sat round three sides, while the fourth side served as back-scene and provided the actors' entrances. p. 179

No descriptions exist of the first building in Germany intended solely for the presentation of plays, Maurice the Learned's Ottonium in Cassel (1611).[50] The only theatre building of any significance built during the Thirty Years War was that built by Josef Furttenbach in the free imperial city of Ulm in 1640–41. The city council commissioned him to build a civic theatre for the use of schools, guilds and touring companies. It was built on a plain rectangular groundplan with rows of seats in the pit. The stage was fitted with *periaktoi*, a feature hitherto unknown in Germany.[51]

The Salvatortheater in Munich was the first opera house in Germany to stand outside the walls of a palace. It was commissioned by the Munich court in 1654 from the Italian, Francesco Santurini, who built a theatre with galleries in the Italian style.[52] The royal box was not added until the theatre was renovated by Domenico and Gasparo Mauro in 1685, when the idea spread of this Saxon innovation with its opportunities for regal display. Before that the p. 179

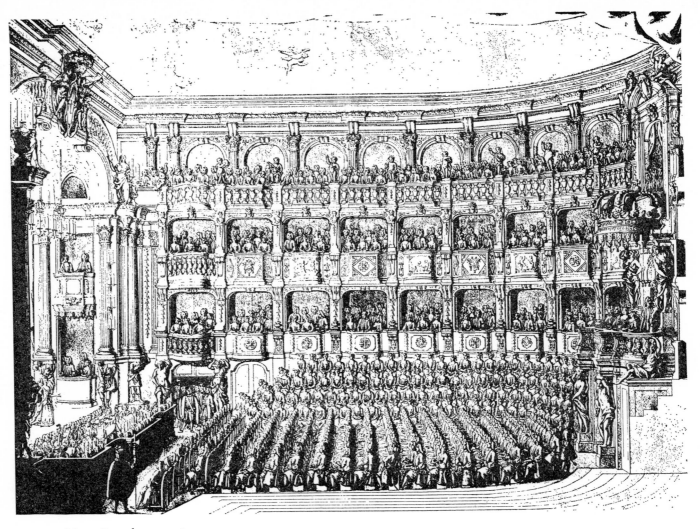

DRESDEN *Neues Opernhaus, 1718–9*

seats for the Bavarian Elector and his family had been in the middle of the *parterre*, as in every other theatre.

The first royal box in any theatre, with direct access from the palace, was built in the middle of the lowest tier in the Grosses Opernhaus in Dresden in 1664. However, it still remained the practice to erect a throne in the middle of the *parterre* on great occasions. Two galleries ran round the horseshoe-shaped auditorium which held two thousand spectators. In general layout it was very similar to the Salvatortheater in Munich, and had the very large stage that was essential in any opera house to accommodate the stage machinery; in some theatres the stage took up two-thirds of the entire area. The architect, Wolfgang von Klengel (1630 to 1691), had spent four years studying in Italy from 1651 and so was familiar with Italian theatres. Their influence was unmistakeable in the painted and plaster decorations.

What contemporary opinion held to be the finest theatre of the age, the opera house in Hanover, was built in 1690.[53] It had five tiers, each set slightly behind the one below, so that the room widened towards the roof. The galleries were divided into boxes, which the architect Tomaso Giusti, a pupil of Torelli, might have come across in the Teatro Tordinona in Rome. The theatre no longer exists, but from the plans it appears that there was no forestage or space between the front row of the stalls and the proscenium arch. A large chandelier could be raised or lowered in the auditorium by pulley, as in the theatre which still stands in Ludwigsburg near Stuttgart.

A permanent opera house was built in Hamburg in 1678 by Girolamo Sartorio,[54] and the opera house in Brunswick was thrown open to the public in 1690, the year which saw the opening of the opera house in nearby Hanover.

The large houses for the production of the typical lavish baroque operas were not the only ones to rise during these years; even before the beginning of the eighteenth century small theatres were sometimes built in the palaces of minor princes. An example is the theatre built for George William, the last Duke of Celle, in a wing of his palace by Giuseppe Arighini from Brescia (1674). This is believed to be the oldest surviving theatre of its kind in Germany.

All the different types of theatre were developed during the seventeenth century. With the possible exception of the ruin theatres at Bayreuth, no essentially new varieties evolved during the eighteenth.

If there were no other records, the theatres built in Dresden would be sufficient evidence of the vitality of the interest in the theatre there. As we have seen, the Grosses Opernhaus was built in 1664, but things really got under way under Augustus the Strong. The Kleines Komödien-haus was opened for the performance of French plays in 1697, a sign of the shift in the court's interest from Italy. The year 1719 saw the completion of the Zwinger, 'a festive garland turned to stone', which contained stages and sites for every kind of theatrical entertainment, and in the same year p. 180 Daniel Pöppelmann finished the Neues Opernhaus, which stood beside it. As in the Salvatortheater in Munich, seats rose round the sides of the stalls to the level of the lowest of the three tiers. Each box curved forward to form a little balcony, and rich paint and plaster work decorated the room. Stage boxes brought the spectators back on to the stage where they had once been in the past, but they were no longer in a position to hinder the actors. This theatre was twice altered by Giuseppe Galli-Bibiena, in 1738 and 1749, and acquired a bell-shaped auditorium; in 1772 it was turned into a ballroom. Dresden also had a much smaller wooden theatre by Pietro and Angelo Mingotti, which burnt down after three years.

Erlangen's first Markgrafentheater was almost exactly contemporary to the Dresden Neues Opernhaus, being started in 1715 and finished in 1719. On the occasion of a visit by her brother Frederick the Great, Margravine Wilhelmina of Bayreuth had alternations made by the Venetian, Giovanni Paolo, in 1743–4, which included the addition of a royal box, framed by two caryatids. At the same period 162–175 she had plans drawn up for an opera house in Bayreuth. The building was started in 1745 and completed in 1748. It is of incalculable interest and value, for of all the eighteenth-century theatres to have survived to the present day it is the one least touched by time. The rather cool classical façade can be ascribed to the French architect to the court of Bayreuth, Joseph Saint-Pierre, whose work we have already 166 seen in the Eremitage.[55] A central section, comprising three-

fifths of the total width, projects a little way forward, and pillars standing on a balcony with a dainty iron balustrade support a stone balustrade at roof level, crowned by statues. At first sight, the theatre appears to be part of a terrace of houses; that this is not so is clear at the back, where the massive, unadorned rear portion of the building stands isolated. The ramp still leads up to it by means of which carriages could be driven straight on to the stage, either for dramatic purposes or to carry pieces of scenery.

After the restrained façade and the sober, white staircase, 167 the auditorium glows with unexpected warmth and colour. Against a green background gleam golden ornaments and XIV white-gold figures, while a serene blue and a joyous red enliven coats of arms, curtains and ceiling. The auditorium is 165, XV an unemphatic bell in shape, and holds three boxes, each with a forward-curving balcony. The ends of the galleries

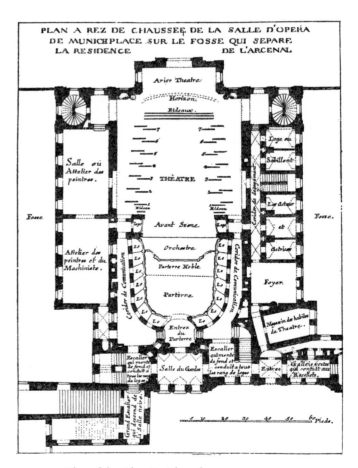

MUNICH *Plan of the Altes Residenztheater,* *designed by François de Cuvilliés, 1750–53*

do not abut immediately on the proscenium arch, but turn to the sides. The concave trumpeters' boxes which flank the stage complete the curve from royal box to proscenium arch. The effect of unity is enhanced by the flights of stairs leading to the *parterre* from both stage and royal box, and by the uniform balustrades.

162, 164   A design made by Francesco Galli- Bibiena in Vienna in 1704 inspired the architect, Giuseppe Galli-Bibiena, and the decorator, his son Carlo; but the change of style in the intervening forty years is clear. The shapes are less dynamic, the sensuous thrust of the balustrades is only hinted at, the
169   royal box does not rise through all the tiers to the ceiling, the pillars supporting the galleries are much less ornate, and the male heroes surmounting the royal box in Francesco's drawing have become graceful women.

    Not a single surface is free of painted decoration, and the walls and ceilings of the boxes are covered with golden-brown ornaments. From the walls behind the ornamental devices which top the trumpeters' boxes to the lozenge-patterned floor, every piece of wood is painted. The room was lit by candles in front of the boxes.

    Exactly two years after the completion of the Bayreuth opera house, in 1750, Elector Max III Joseph commissioned plans for a new 'Opera hauss' in Munich from François Cuvilliés the Elder (1695–1768). His assistants were Carl Albert von Lespilliez and François de Cuvilliés the Younger, while the technical side of stage equipment and machinery was referred to Paolo Gaspari, who may also have been involved with the Bayreuth theatre.

177–185   The Altes Residenztheater has the same bell-shaped auditorium as the Markgräfliches Opernhaus in Bayreuth, the same arrangement of galleries curving back to a central royal box, and yet the total effect is quite different. In Bayreuth the lights on the three upper tiers stand on a base, throwing the light up and outwards, away from the galleries, so that there appear to be layers of light and darkness, while in Munich the lines of the galleries are themselves less dramatic, and the light is spread more evenly over the
170–5   whole room. In Bayreuth details and individual components of the decoration on the boxes are moulded, but all the rest of the ornamentation is painted, giving only the illusion of plaster. In the Cuvilliés theatre in Munich all the decoration is three-dimensional. In no other surviving theatre of the same period are the details of the decoration executed with such care and skill as here.

    The building was required to be completed within two years. The court employed the best available craftsmen for the decoration. Adam Pichler, the *Hofkinstler* (court joiner), prepared the pinewood cartouches which were fixed to the ceiling, the proscenium arch and the panelling of the

boxes. This provided a basis for the work of the wood-carvers, Joachim Dietrich and Johann Baptist Straub, who made a strict division of labour. Straub, one of the greatest masters of south German rococo sculpture, carved the figures, the caryatids, Atlanteans and cherubs, the decorations over the proscenium boxes and the royal box and above the proscenium arch. The ornaments, capitals, draperies, emblems and garlands were by Dietrich, who worked with Cuvilliés on other projects. The work of the third artist employed, the painter Johann Baptist Zimmermann, has been lost.[56] The building, the stage, and the machinery for raising the *parterre* to the level of the stage, as in the Versailles theatre, were totally destroyed in 1944, but the irreplacable carvings that decorated the boxes and the galleries were saved. Between 1956 and 1958 the theatre was reconstructed in another wing of the Residenz, in the Apothekenstock, incorporating the carvings, and so one of the loveliest of all baroque theatres unfolds its ceremonial splendour once more in white, gold and red. Dietrich's carved draperies hang lightly, as if tossed down casually, the herms support the balconies and boxes with a graceful smile, as though the weight were no more oppressive than the garlands and wreaths around their heads, shoulders and arms. This theatre is full of light and joy. Everyone is smiling: the faun in his wreath of oak leaves, the seasons, the gods and goddesses, the continents who are spread with their attributes around the second tier. Exuberant cherubs dance and float around the crowns and heraldic devices. The royal box, like the original one, is panelled with mirrors to reflect the brilliance.

    The music composed and performed at the court of Mannheim under Charles Theodore (1743–77) was of an unusually high standard, even for that era. His predecessor Charles Philip had seen the completion in 1742 of the Kurfürstliche Oper, a large theatre built inside the Electoral palace by Alessandro Galli-Bibiena. The tiers were divided into boxes, the *parterre* was wholly given over to seats, instead of half of it being standing space. The nobility sat in a balcony below and in front of the royal box.[57] Another theatre, the Comödien- und Redoutenhaus, was built in Mannheim in 1767 by Lorenzo Quaglio (1730–1805); it held over a thousand people and was used for plays, routs and balls. It was in the Italian style, with tiers of boxes on a horseshoe-shaped ground-plan. Charles Theodore also wanted a theatre in his palace at Schwetzingen. Nicolas de
176   Pigage began work in 1752 and produced a theatre in the French style, in which the galleries are open, with boxes only at the back of the theatre. Pigage was a Frenchman, trained in Paris, and although none of the small private theatres built in France during the mid-eighteenth century

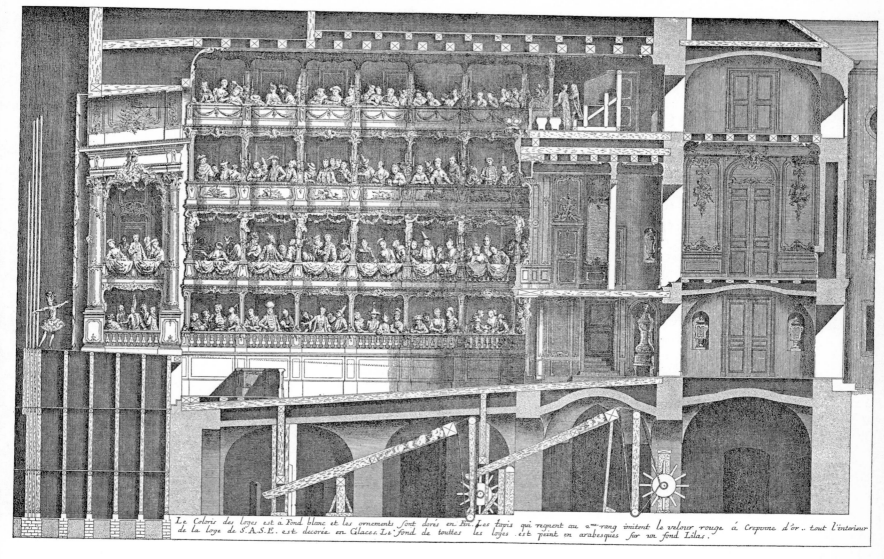

Le Coloris des loges est à Fond blanc et les ornements sont dorés en Fin. Les tapis qui regnent au 2me rang imitent le velour rouge à Crepone d'or. tout l'interieur de la loge de S.A.S.E. est decorée en Glaces. Le fond de toutes les loges est peint en arabesquies sur un fond Lilas.

MUNICH *Section drawing of the Altes Residenztheater 1750–53*

have survived, the Schwetzingen theatre gives a good indication of what they must have been like. One notable feature is that the stage can be opened at the back, so that the action of a play could extend into the park.

Like the other courts of southern Germany, the court of Württemberg at first preferred French drama to other forms of entertainment. When Charles Eugene began his reign in 1744 and married Friederike, the daughter of Margravine Wilhelmina of Bayreuth, the court maintained a private theatre for amateur performances; by 1750 the court of Stuttgart felt the need of an opera house with a capacity of three thousand. The Hofoper, in the Grosses Lusthaus, was designed by Leopold Retti from Ansbach and

Stefan Schenk of Mannheim, and had four tiers. It was altered by Philippe de la Guêpière in 1758–9.

Wherever the court went, the theatre had to follow. Interest in the theatre increased markedly in Ludwigsburg *188–190* when Charles Eugene made it his chief residence for several years. An opera house was built there at great speed in 1764–5, and was one of the biggest theatres of its day, with an unusually large stage. Instead of paintings, carvings or plaster decoration, the walls and pillars supporting the galleries were covered with mirrors, so that the court itself became the decoration, the space became endless and the glitter and sparkle, the lights and the colours stretched into infinity. The audience seated in the four galleries must have felt an exhilarating sense of self-realisation. Goethe mentions the theatre in his *Reise in die Schweiz* of 1797:

'The big opera house is a remarkable building, constructed of wood and planks, and testifying to the acumen of the architect, whose intention was to seat a large, well-born audience in comfort and with appropriate grandeur. The theatre is eighteen paces wide, also extremely high: the auditorium holds four tiers of boxes. Its overall length is perhaps seventy-six paces. The proscenium is very large, as is the orchestra, so that both together reach to the middle of the room; the *parterre* is in comparison very small. You can see very well from every seat, and probably hear well too. For the time being, during the visit of the Grand Duke, it has been converted into a ballroom.'

There were other theatres in the Electoral pleasance, Solitude, in Schloss Teinach, and in the hunting lodge, Schloss Grafeneck,[58] but the only one to have survived is at Ludwigsburg, originally built in 1730, but 'modernized' by Thouret in 1810. When Charles Eugene moved his residence back to Stuttgart, a small theatre with three galleries was built on the Planie by R. F. Fischer in 1780.

Hamburg, Brunswick, Leipzig and Dresden had all become important theatrical centres in the seventeenth century. But of the Opernhaus am Gänsemarkt, built in 1637 by Girolamo Sartorio, or of the Neues Schauspielhaus, built for Konrad Ackermann's company, or of the Theater auf der Ranstädter Bastion in Leipzig nothing remains.

Frederick the Great called Georg W. von Knobelsdorff to Berlin to build the Grosses Opernhaus. In 1745 Knobels-dorff built a theatre in the palace in Potsdam, and other *186–7* court theatres were built, in the Neues Palais in Potsdam, in Berlin and in the palace of Monbijou.[59] The Berlin court experienced a sudden surge of interest in the theatre. After 1750 private theatres were built on the Monbijouplatz, in the Behrenstrasse, and in the palaces of Schönhausen and Rheinsberg; and in the eighties Charlottenburg saw theatres built in the Orangerie and next door to the palace.

Of all the theatres erected after 1740 in or near the palaces in Berlin, Potsdam and Charlottenburg, only the intimate little theatre in the south wing of the Neues Palais in Potsdam has survived. The auditorium is in the form of an amphitheatre, seats for the king and the royal family being placed in front of the curving rows of benches. A bell-shaped gallery encloses the room, and caryatids support the domed ceiling. The theatre was probably designed by Büring and Manger at the same time as the rest of the Neues Palais, in 1755, but it was built in 1763–9. It is thus twenty years older than the theatre in Gripsholm, which it resembles in the seating arrangement; the decoration in the Potsdam theatre is entirely rococo.

We cannot mention all the little theatres built by the courts of spiritual and temporal princes. Some have special claims on our interest, like the first court theatre devoted to the performance of straight plays, in Gotha,[60] the little Komödienhaus in Rostock, built in 1750, the 1777 theatre in Schloss Ettersburg, the Redouten- und Komödienhaus in Weimar, built in 1779 and later used as a court theatre under the direction of Goethe, and the court theatre at Wolfen-büttel, which was for a long time believed to be the oldest theatre in Germany. They are all gone. A few of the smaller theatres have survived: a small, late rococo theatre is falling into ruins in the park of Schloss Öhringen, while the court theatre of the prince bishops of Passau, built in 1783 by Georg Hagenauer, with two tiers of boxes and a Louis XVI décor, has been lovingly restored.

The last theatre to be built in Germany before the French revolution is that in Coblenz, built by Grahé in 1787. Its *191* general design is in the French style of baroque theatres, with open galleries rather than boxes, but the decoration is classic and severe. There is no sign here of the cupids, rocaille, shells and ribbons which are scattered gaily over the galleries, balconies and boxes of earlier theatres; the charm, grace and enchantment of the rococo age were things of the past.

Overleaf:
98 VICENZA
Teatro Olimpico
1580–84

VICENZA
Teatro Olimpico
99 *Statue of*
Mucius Scaevola
on the stage set

186

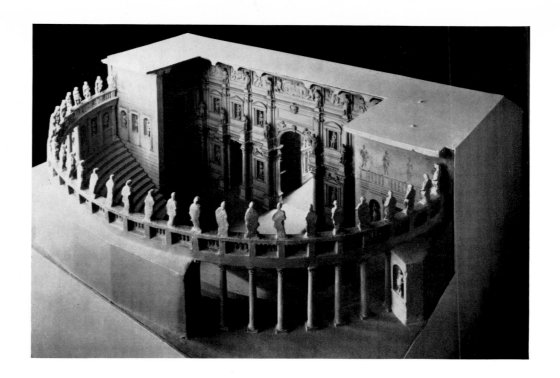

100 *Model*
101 *Proscenium*

108 CASERTA *near Naples, palace theatre, 1752–59*

109 HVAR, *Yugoslavia, civic theatre, 1612*

110 VENICE
*Teatro San Benedetto
(1755–56)
seen during a ball
in 1782*

193

111   VENICE *Teatro La Fenice, 1790–92, decoration of central box*

112   VENICE *Teatro La Fenice, foyer*

113   VENICE *Teatro La Fenice, auditorium*

195

115 VERONA *Teatro Filarmonico, 1717–20, exterior*

116 VERONA
Teatro Filarmonico, interior

117 BOLOGNA
*Teatro Communale, 1756–63,
exterior*

118 BOLOGNA
*Teatro Communale,
auditorium*

122 VIENNA *Grosser Redoutensaal, 1748–52, with stage*

124   VIENNA *Schlosstheater Schönbrunn, the imperial private theatre, 1766–67*

125 VIENNA *Schlosstheater Schönbrunn, imperial box*

126 VIENNA,
Schlosstheater Schönbrunn,
coat of arms above the stage

127 VIENNA, *Schlosstheater Schönbrunn,*
balcony adjoining proscenium arch

128 VIENNA *Schlosstheater Schönbrunn, part of the auditorium*

129   GREIN AN DER DONAU *Civic theatre, 1791*

130   LAMBACH *Theatre of the monastery school, c. 1770*

131   ČESKY KRUMLOV *Theatre in the Schwarzenberg palace, 1766*

132 ČESKY KRUMLOV *Stage of the palace theatre, with contemporary set*

133 PRAGUE
Ständetheater, 1781–83

134 PRAGUE
Former tennis court

135　MOSCOW *Ostankino palace theatre*

136 MOSCOW *West façade of the pleasance in the Kremlin, 1652–73*

137 MOSCOW *South façade of the pleasance in the Kremlin*

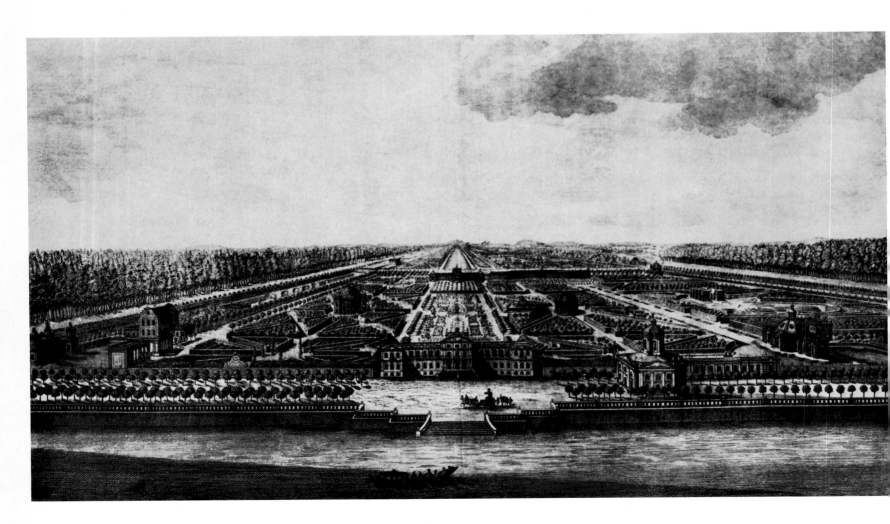

Primer bayle en Mascara que se dió en el Coliseo del Principe.

139   MADRID *Coliseo del Principe, 1766*

140   VERSAILLES *Madame de Pompadour in Lully's 'Acis et Galatée' in the small theatre, 1749*

141–2 VERSAILLES *Two muses in the Opera,*
1767–70

143–4 VERSAILLES
Opéra, 1767–70

145 VERSAILLES
*Opéra, court
balcony and boxes*

146 VERSAILLES
Opéra, ceiling

147 VERSAILLES *Opéra, one of the barred boxes*   149 *Royal box*

148 VERSAILLES *Opéra,*
Mars, relief on the balustrade

151 BORDEAUX
Grand Théâtre,
1773–80

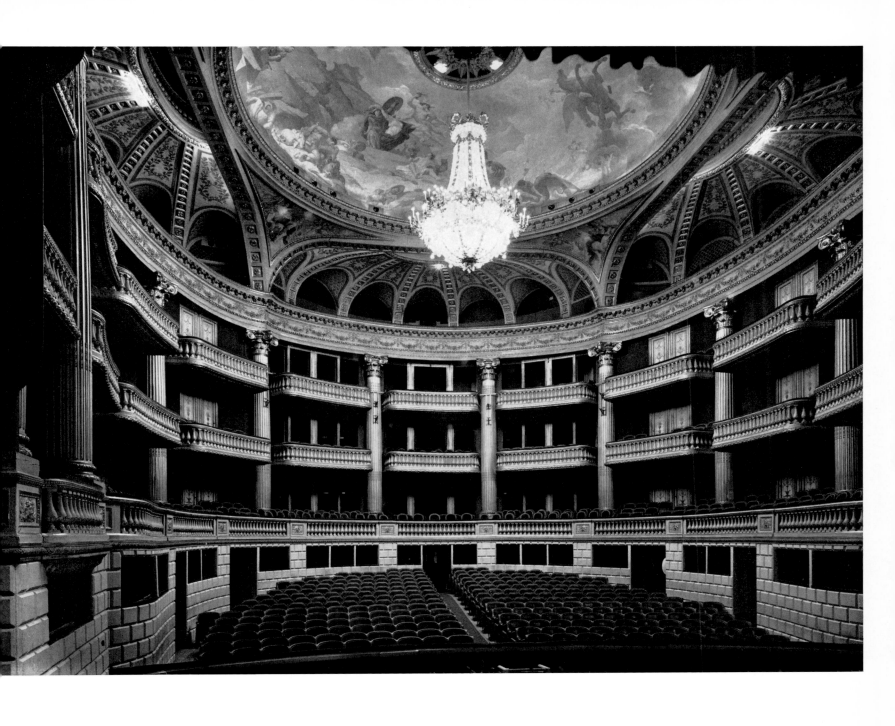

224

157 BORDEAUX
Grand Théâtre,
Stage boxes

160   DROTTNINGHOLM *Palace theatre, auditorium and stage with set, 1766*

XIII   DROTTNINGHOLM *Auditorium with royal seats*

161 OTTOBEUREN *Theatre in the Benedictine monastery, 1725*

162 FRANCESCO GALLI-BIBIENA
*Design for an opera house
with royal box, Vienna 1704*

163 BAYREUTH *Markgräfliches Opernhaus
with Margrave's box, 1744–48*

164 FRANCESCO GALLI-BIBIENA
*Design for an opera house
with trumpeters' boxes, Vienna 1704*

165 BAYREUTH *Markgräfliches Opernhaus
with trumpeters' boxes, 1744–48*

BAYREUTH *Markgräfliches Opernhaus*

166 *Façade*
167 *Staircase*
168 *Rear view with ramp*

169 BAYREUTH
Markgräfliches Opernhaus,
Margrave's box

234

BAYREUTH *Markgräfliches Opernhaus*
172   *Cartouche with commemorative
      inscription over Margrave's box*

175 *Decoration
over left-hand
trumpeters' box*

176 SCHWETZINGEN *Schlosstheater, 1752*

177–8 MUNICH *Altes Residenztheater, Caryatid and decoration over right-hand stage box, 1750–53*

179 MUNICH
Altes Residenztheater
Electoral box

180   MUNICH *Altes Residenztheater, Atlantean figure at the entrance*   181   *Faun over the entrance*

183   MUNICH *Altes Residenztheater, drapery on the first tier*

184   *Mirror in the royal box*

Overleaf:
182   MUNICH *Altes Residenztheater, auditorium*

185 *Caryatid*

187 *Amphitheatre*

186 POTSDAM *Theatre in the Neues Palais, Proscenium 1763–69*

188 LUDWIGSBURG *Palace theatre, façade, 1730*

189 *Royal box, decoration 1810*

190 *Proscenium, decoration 1810*

191   COBLENZ *Stadttheater, 1787*

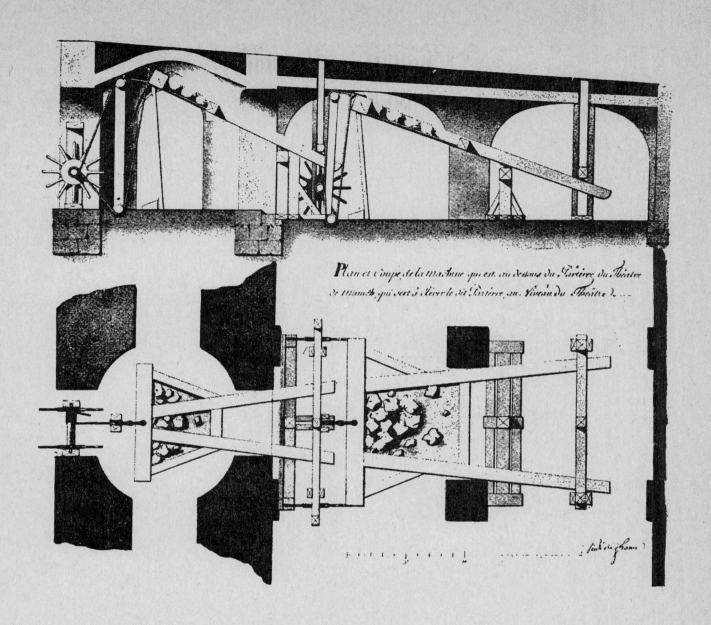

Plan et coupe de la machine qui est au dessous du Torière du Theatre
de Mambt, qui sert à élever le dit Torière, au Niveau du Theatre.

Chronological Tables

Chronological Tables

DRAMA AND OPERA

compiled by Veronika Baur

DRAMA

	SPAIN	ENGLAND	FRANCE
1530			**35 Robert Garnier ★ (1535-1590)** **Jean de La Taille ★ (1535-1611)**
40			
	47 Miguel de Cervantes Saavedra ★ (1547-1616) Rueda — La tierra de Jauja 48 — Las aceitunas	48 Bale — King John; Moses and Christ	
50		**54 John Lyly ★ (1554?-1606)** **58 Thomas Kyd ★ (1558-1594)** **George Peele ★ (1558?-1598)** **59 George Chapman ★ (1559-1634)**	
60	**62 Lope Félix de Vega Carpio ★ (1562-1635)**	**63 Bale †** **64 Christopher Marlowe ★ (1564-1593)** **William Shakespeare ★ (1564-1616)**	68 Garnier — Porcie, épouse de Brutus
70	**65 Lope de Rueda †** **71 Tirso de Molina (Fray Gabriel Téllez) ★** **(1571-1648)**	**73 Benjamin Jonson (1572/73?-1637)**	72 La Taille — Saül le furieux 73 — La famine ou les Gabéonites Garnier — Hippolyte, fils de Thésée 74 — Cornélie, épouse de Pompée **75 Antoine de Montchrestien, Sieur de Vasteville ★** **(1575-1621)** 78 Garnier — Marc-Antoine 79 — La Troade ou la destruction de Troie
		79 John Fletcher (1579-1625)	
80		**80 John Webster (1580?-1625?)** Peele — The Arraignment of Paris	80 — Antigone
	81 Juan Ruiz de Alarcón y Mendoza ★ (1581?-1639)	**83 Philip Massinger (1583-1640)** **84 Francis Beaumont (1584-1616)** Lyly — Alexander and Campaspe Sapho and Phao; Galathea	82 — Bradamante 83 — Sédicie ou les Juives
	84 Cervantes — La Numancia	**86 John Ford (1586-1640?)** Lyly — Love's Metamorphosis Marlowe — The Tragedy of Dido, Queen of Carthage 87 — Tamburlaine the Great 86/87? Kyd — The Spanish Tragedy 88 Marlowe — The Tragical History of Dr Faustus Shakespeare — King John; Richard III Peele — The Love of King David and Fair Bethsabe 88/89 — The Battle of Alcazar 89 Marlowe — The Famous Tragedy of the Rich Jew of Malta Lyly — Midas	
90		90 — Mother Bombie Shakespeare — Love's Labour's Lost 91 Peele — Edward I Lyly — Endymion 92 Shakespeare — King Henry VI (I–III) (90–92) Richard III (92?) Comedy of Errors (92?) Troilus and Cressida (92?) Marlowe — The Troublesome Reign and Lamentable Death of Edward II The Massacre of Paris Lyly — The Woman in the Moon **93 Marlowe †** Peele — The Old Wives' Tale Shakespeare — Titus Andronicus (93?) Kyd — Cornelia	**90 Garnier †**

ITALY	GERMANY	NETHERLANDS	DENMARK	RAGUSA
44 Torquato Tasso ★ (1544-1595)				
	78 Jakob Bidermann ★ (1578-1639)	**79 Samuel Coster ★ (1579-1665)**		
80 Tasso Aminta				
		81 Pieter Corneliszoon Hooft ★ (1581-1647)		
		85 Gerbrand Adriaenszoon Brederode ★ (1585-1618)		
87 Il Re Torrismondo		**87 Joost van den Vondel ★ (1587-1679)**		
				89 Ivan (Dzivo) Gundulic ★ (1589-1638)

DRAMA

	SPAIN		ENGLAND		FRANCE	
1590	94 Lope de Vega	El Maestro de danzar San Segundo del Avila Leal criado	94 Kyd **Kyd †** Shakespeare 94/95 95	Pompey the Great Romeo and Juliet The Two Gentlemen of Verona A Midsummer Night's Dream Richard II		
			96 Peele † (96?) Shakespeare 96/97 97 Chapman	 The Life and Death of King John (96?) The Merchant of Venice The Taming of the Shrew A Humorous Day's Mirth	96 Montchrestien	Sophonisbe
	98	La serrana de la Vera La fuerza latimosa La Francesilla	98 Shakespeare Jonson Chapman	King Henry IV (I–II) (97–98) Much Ado about Nothing The Merry Wives of Windsor Every Man in His Humour A Blind Beggar of Alexandria Bussy d'Ambois		
	99	El Rústico del cielo	99 Shakespeare Jonson	King Henry V; Julius Caesar As You Like It Every Man Out of His Humour		
1600	**00 Pedro Calderón de la Barca ★ (1600-1681)**		**00 Sir William Davenant ★ (1600-1668)** Chapman Shakespeare Jonson	 May Day Twelfth Night, or What You Will Cynthia's Revels		
	01 Lope de Vega	La hermosa Alfreda	01 Chapman Shakespeare	The Poetaster The Gentleman Usher; All Fools All's Well that Ends Well	01	L'Ecossaise ou le désastre Les Lacènes ou la constance de David Aman
	02	El Caballero de Illescas El Principe despeñado El cuerdo loco	02 Chapman Shakespeare	The Conspiracy and Tragedy of Charles Duke of Byron Hamlet, Prince of Danmark		
	03	El ingrato arrepentido Primer rey de Castilla	03 Jonson Shakespeare	Sejanus Measure for Measure		
			04	Othello	04	Hector
			05 Chapman, Marston and Jonson Jonson Fletcher Shakespeare	Eastward, Ho! The Masque of Blackness Volpone, the Fox The Woman's Prize King Lear; Macbeth		
	06	El Toledano vengado	**05/06? Lyly †** Beaumont 07 Shakespeare	 The Woman-Hater Antony and Cleopatra (06/07?)	**06 Pierre Corneille ★ (1606-1684)**	
	08	El divino Africano	08 Beaumont and Fletcher Jonson 09 Beaumont and Fletcher Shakespeare Webster	Coriolanus (07/08?) Timon of Athens (07/08?) Four Plays in One The Masque of Beauty The Masque of Queens Epicoene, or The Silent Woman The Knight of the Burning Pestle Cymbeline Appius and Virginia		
10	10	El caballero del Sacramento La creación del mundo y primera El robo de Dina Los trabajos de Jacob Historia de Tobias La hermosa Ester	10 Fletcher Jonson Shakespeare Beaumont and Fletcher	The Faithful Shepherdess The Alchemist The Winter's Tale The Scornful Lady	**10 Paul Scarron ★ (1610-1660)**	
			11 Beaumont and Fletcher	The Tempest King and No King Philaster Cupid's Revenge The Maid's Tragedy	**11 La Taille †**	

DRAMA

ITALY	GERMANY	NETHERLANDS	DENMARK	RAGUSA
	02 Bidermann Cenodoxus			
	07 Belisar			06 **Junije Palmotic★(1606-1657)**
	11 Nikolaus von Avancini ★ (1611-1686)	11 Brederode Roderick ende Alphonsus		

DRAMA

	SPAIN		ENGLAND		FRANCE	
1610	12 Lope de Vega	El bastardo Mudarra	12 Beaumont and Fletcher	The Captain		
			Fletcher	The Coxcomb		
			Webster	The White Devil or The Life and Death of Victoria Corombona		
			Shakespeare	King Henry VIII		
	13	Fuenteovejuna (13?)	13 Jonson	Bartholomew Fair		
		Villana de Getafe (13?)				
	14 Cervantes	Viaje del Parnaso	14 Webster	The Duchess of Malfi		
			Beaumont and Fletcher	Wits at Several Weapons		
				Bonduca		
			Fletcher	Wit without Money (14?)		
			15 Massinger	The Fatal Dowry		
	16 Cervantes †		**16 Beaumont †, Shakespeare †**			
	Lope de Vega	Proceles de Murcia	Jonson	The Devil is an Ass		
			Fletcher	Rollo, Duke of Normandy		
	18 Don Augustin de Moreto y Cabana *		18 Fletcher	Loyal Subjects		
	(1618-1669)		18/19	Valentinian; The Mad Lover		
	Lope de Vega	Las almenas de Toro		The Humorous Lieutenant		
		Lo fingido verdadero (–18)				
		El Hamete de Toledo (18)	19	Monsieur Thomas		
				The Knight of Malta		
				The Custom of the Country		
1620	20	Las grandezas de Alejandro	20 Massinger	The City Madam	**21 Montchrestien †**	
			Fletcher	The Chances; Woman Pleased (20?)		
			21	The Island Princess		
				The Wild Goose Chase		
				The Pilgrim		
			Beaumont and Fletcher	Thierry and Theodoret		
	22	La juventud de San Isidro	22 Massinger	The Virgin Martyr	**22 Jean Baptiste Molière (Jean Baptiste Poquelin) ***	
		El vellocino de oro			**(1622-1673)**	
	23–25 Calderón	Amor, honor y poder	23	The Duke of Milan		
				The Bondman		
			Webster	The Devil's Law-Case		
	24 Tirso de Molina	El vergonzoso en palaico	24	Monuments of Honour		
			Massinger	The Parliament of Love		
	Lope de Vega	Marqués de las Navas	Fletcher	Rule a Wife and Have a Wife		
				A Wife for a Month		
				The Two Noble Kinsmen (24?)		
			25 Fletcher †, Webster † 25?			
			Jonson	The Staple of News		
			Massinger	A New Way to Pay Old Debts		
			Chapman	The Tragedy of Chabot, Admiral of France (25?)		
	26	Pobreza no es vileza	26 Massinger	The Roman Actor		
	27 Tirso de Molina	La villana de Vallecas	27	The Great Duke of Florence		
	28 Mendoza	Ganar perdiendo	28	The Maid of Honour		
		Las paredes oyen				
		Mudarse por mejorarse				
		El semejante a sí mismo				
		El desdichado en fingir				
		La cueva de Salamanca				
	29 Calderón	El principe constante	29	The Picture	29 Corneille	Mélite ou les fausses lettres
		La dama duende (29?)	Davenant	The Tragedy of Albovine		
	Lope de Vega	La selva sin amor				
	30 Tirso de Molina	El Burlador de Sevilla y convidado de piedra	30 Massinger	Believe as You List		
				The Emperor of the East		
			Davenant	The Cruel Brother		
	31 Lope de Vega	La noche de San Juan	**31 John Dryden * (1631-1700)**			
		El castigo sin venganza (31?)	Jonson	Cloridia		
			Chapman	The Tragedy of Caesar and Pompey		

DRAMA

ITALY	GERMANY	NETHERLANDS	DENMARK	RAGUSA
		12 Brederode Griane Klucht van de koe Vondel Het Pascha oft de ver- lossinge Israels uit Egypten		
	13 Bidermann Macarius	13 Brederode Klucht van de molenaar Symen sonder soetig- heyt Hooft Geeraerdt van Velsen 14 Achilles ende Polyxena Ariadne		
	15 Josephus **16 Andreas Gryphius ★ (1616-1664)**	15 Granida;Ware-nar(15?) Brederode Het moortje 16 Lucelle 16/17 Hooft Baeto		
	18 Bidermann Jacobus Usurarius Johannes Calybita Philemon Martyr 19 Josaphatus	18 Brederode De Spaansche Brabander Stommen ridder **Brederode †** 19 Vondel Hierusalem verwoest		
	20 Stertinius Cosmarchia	21 Vondel De Amsteldamsche Hecuba		
		25 Palamedes		
		27 Coster De Boere-klucht van Teeuwis de boer en Juffer van Grevelinck- huysen 28 Vondel Hippolytus		27 Gundulic Dubravka 28 Arijadna Dijana Armida Prozerpina ugrabl- jena Posvetiliste ljuveno Galatea Kleopatra Adona Koraljka od Sira Cerera Palmotic Atalanta

DRAMA

	SPAIN		ENGLAND		FRANCE	
1630	32 Lope de Vega	Moza de cántaro	32 Jonson	The Magnetic Lady	32 Corneille	Clitandre ou l'innocence délivrée
						La veuve
	32–35	Las bizarrías de Belisa	33	The Tale of a Tub	33	La galerie du Palais
		El guante de Doña Blanca	Massinger	The Guardian		
		El desprecio agradecido	Ford	'Tis Pity She's a Whore		
		El Amor enamorado		The Broken Heart		
		El mejor alcalde el rey		Love's Sacrifice		
	34 Tirso de	La prudencia en la mujer	**34 Chapman †**		34	La suivante
	Molina	La mejor espigadera	Ford	Perkin Warbeck		La Place Royale
		La venganza de Tamar	Davenant	Love and Honour		
	Calderón	La gran Cenobia	Massinger	A Very Woman		
		La cena del rey Balthasar (34?)				
	Mendoza	Ganar amigos				
		La verdad sospechosa				
		El tejedor de Segovia				
		Examen de maridos				
		El Antichristo				
		Los favores del mundo				
		La prueba de las promesas				
		Los pechos privilegiados				
	35 Lope de Vega †				35	Médée
	Tirso de	El condendado por desconfiado				
	Molina	Don Gil de las calzas verdes				
		Deleitar aprovechando				
	Calderón	La devoción de la cruz				
		El medico de su honra				
		El mayor Enchanto Amor				
		La vida es sueño				
	36 Tirso de	Marta la piadosa	36	The Bashful Lover	36	L'illusion comique
	Molina		Davenant	The Platonic Lovers		Le Cid
				The Wits		
			37 Jonson †			
			38 Ford	Chaste and Noble		
				The Lady's Trial		
			Davenant	The Unfortunate Lovers		
			39 Massinger	The Unnatural Combat		
	39 Mendoza †				**39 Jean Baptiste Racine * (1639-1699)**	
40			**40 William Wycherley * (1640-1716)**		40 Corneille	Cinna ou la clémence d'Auguste
			Massinger †; Ford †			Horace
					42	Polyeucte
	43 Calderón	El alcalde de Zalamea (43?)	**42 Theatres closed by Parliament**		43	La mort de Pompée
						Le menteur
					44	La suite du menteur
						Rodogune
					45	Théodore vierge et martyre
					Scarron	Jodelet duelliste, ou le maître valet
					46 Corneille	Héraclius
	48 Tirso de Molina †					
50					50	Don Sanche d'Aragon
						Andromède
					51	Nicomède
	52	Perseus	**52 Thomas Otway * (1652-1685)**		52	Pertharite
	53	La hija del aire	**53 Nathaniel Lee * (1653-1692)**		53 Scarron	Don Japhet d'Arménie
	Mendoza	No hay mal que por bien no venga			54	L'écolier de Salamanque, ou
						Les généreux ennemis
					55 Jean-François Régnard * (1655-1709)	
					Scarron	Le marquis ridicule
					Molière	L'étourdi, ou les contre-temps
			56 Davenant	The Siege of Rhodes	56	Le dépit amoureux

DRAMA

ITALY	GERMANY	NETHERLANDS	DENMARK	RAGUSA
				32 Pavlimir
	34 Simon Rettenbacher ★ (1634-1706)			
	35 Daniel Caspar Lohenstein ★ (1635-1683)	35 Vondel Josef		
	36 Avancini Marius			
		37 Gysbreght van Aemstel		**38 Gundulic †**
	39 Bidermann †	39 Electra; De Maeghden		
	40 Johann Christian Hallman ★ (1640-1704) Avancini Franciscus Xaverius	40 Joseph in Dothan / Joseph in Egypten		
		41 Peter en Pauwels		
	42 Christian Weise ★ (1642-1708) Avancini Fiducia in Deum, sive Bethulia liberata			
				44 Palmotic Danica
	46 Gryphius Leo Armenius	46 Maria Stuart		
	47 Avancini Clodoaldus / Gryphius Cardenio und Celinde	**47 Hooft †** / 48 Vondel De Leeuwendalers / Salomon		47 Armida / Alcina
	49 Ermordete Majestät, oder Carolus Stuardus Beständige Mutter			
	50 Avancini Pax imperii, sive Josephus a fratribus recognitus			
	52 Lohenstein Ibrahim Bassa			52 Captislava
	54 Avancini Curae Caesarum pro Deo et pro populo, sive Theodosius Magnus	54 Lucifer / Salmoneus		

DRAMA

	SPAIN		ENGLAND		FRANCE	
1650	57 Calderón	El golfo de las sirenas				
	58 Moreto	El valiente justiciero	58 Davenant	The Cruelty of the Spaniards in Peru		
	59	El lindo don Diego	59	The History of Sir Francis Drake	59 Molière	La jalousie du barbouillé
						Le médecin volant
				The Playhouse to be let		Les précieuses ridicules
					Corneille	Oedipe
60			60 Dryden	Amphitryon	**60 Scarron †**	
					Corneille	La toison d'or
					Molière	Sganarelle, ou le cocu imaginaire
					61	Don Garcie de Navarre, ou
						le prince jaloux
						L'école des maris
						Les fâcheux
					62 Corneille	Sertorius
					Molière	L'école des femmes
					63	L'impromptu de Versailles
					Corneille	Sophonisbe
			64 Dryden	The Rival Ladies	64	Othon
			Howard and	The Indian Queen	Molière	Le mariage forcé; Le Tartuffe
			Dryden			Les plaisirs de l'île enchantée
						La princesse d'Élide
					Racine	La Thébaïde
					65	Alexandre le Grand
					Molière	Don Juan, ou le festin de Pierre
						L'Amour médecin
					Corneille	Agésilas
					66	Les trois discours
					Molière	Mélicerte; Le misanthrope
						Le médecin malgré lui
					67	Le Sicilien, ou l'amour peintre
					Racine	Andromaque
					Corneille	Attila
			68 Davenant †		**68 Alain-René Lesage * (1668-1747)**	
					Molière	Amphitryon; L'avare
						George Dandin, ou le mari confondu
					Racine	Les Plaideurs
			69 William Congreve * (1669-1729)		69	Britannicus
			Dryden	Tyrannic Love		Iphigénie en Aulide
					Molière	Monsieur de Pourceaugnac
70			70	The Conquest of Granada	70 Racine	Bérénice
					Corneille	Tite et Bérénice
					Molière	Le bourgeois gentilhomme
						Les amants magnifiques
			71 Wycherley	Love in a Wood	71	Les fourberies de Scapin
						La comtesse d'Escarbagnas
					Corneille &	Psyché
					Quinault	
	72 Moreto	El desdén con el desdén	72	The Gentleman Dancing Master	72 Corneille	Pulchérie
			Dryden	Marriage à la Mode	Racine	Bajazet
				Amboyna	Molière	Les femmes savantes
					73	Le malade imaginaire
					Molière †	
					Racine	Mithridate
			74 Wycherley	The Country Wife	74 Corneille	Suréna
			Lee	Nero		
	75 Calderón	El gran teatro del mundo	75	Sophonisba		
			Dryden	Aurengzebe		
			Otway	Alcibiades		
			76	Don Carlos, Prince of Spain		
			Lee	Gloriana, or the Court of Augustus		
			Wycherley	The Plain Dealer (76/77?)		
			77 Lee	The Rival Queens, or the Death of	77 Racine	Phèdre
				Alexander the Great		
			Otway	The Rival Queens		

DRAMA

ITALY	GERMANY		NETHERLANDS		DENMARK	RAGUSA
	57 Gryphius	Catharina von Georgien				**57 Palmotic †**
	58	Absurda Comica, oder Herr Peter Squentz				
	59	Großmütiger Rechtsgelehrter, oder sterbender Aemilius Paulus Papinianus	59 Vondel	Jephta		
	Avancini	Pietas victrix				
	60 Gryphius	Das verliebte Gespenst	60	Koning Edipus Koning David in Ballingschap Koning David herstelt Samson		
	61 Lohenstein	Kleopatra	61	Adonias		
	63 Gryphius	Horribilicribrifax Seug – Amme	63	Batavische Gebroeders Faëton Adam in Ballingschap		
	64 Gryphius †					
	65 Lohenstein	Agrippina; Epicharis	**65 Coster †**			
	Avancini	Connubium meriti et honoris, sive Evergetes et Endoxa				
	66	Dei bonitas de humana pertinacia victrix, sive Alphonsus X	66 Vondel	Iphigenie in Taurien		
	Hallmann	Theodoricus				
	67	Siegprangende Tugend	67	Noah		
	Avancini	Fides coniugalis, sive Ansberta sui coniugis Bertulfi e dura captivitate liberatrix				
			68	Feniciaensche of Gebroeders van Thebe Hercules in Trachin		
	70 Hallmann	Marianne				
	71 Hallmann	Sophia				
	72 Rettenbacher	Innocentia dolo circumventa seu Demetrius				
	73	Ineluctabilis vis fatorum seu Atys				
	Avancini	Cyrus				
	Lohenstein	Ibrahim Sultan				
	74 Rettenbacher	Perfidie punita seu Perseus				
75 Scipione Francesco Marchese Maffei ★ (1675-1755)						

DRAMA

	SPAIN		ENGLAND		FRANCE
1670			**78 George Farquhar ★ (1678-1707)**		
			Dryden	The Kind Keeper; All for Love, or the World Well Lost	
			Otway	Friendship in Fashion	
			Lee	Mithridates	
			79 Lee and Dryden	Oedipus	
80			80 Lee	Theodosius, or the Force of Love; Caesar Borgia	**80 Philippe Néricault Destouches ★ (1680-1754)**
			Otway	History and Fall of Caius Marius; The Orphan	
	81 Calderón †		81	Soldier's Fortune	
			Lee	The Princess of Cleves	
				Lucius Junius Brutus	
			82 Lee and Dryden	The Duke of Guise	
			Otway	Venice Preserved, or a Plot Discovered	
			83 Edward Young ★ (1683-1765)		
			84 Otway	The Atheist	**84 Corneille †**
			Lee	Constantine the Great	
			85 John Gay ★ (1685-1732)		
			Otway †		
			Dryden	Albion and Albianus	
			86 Otway	The History of the Triumvirates	
					88 Pierre Carlet de Chamblain de Marivaux ★ (1688-1763)
					Régnard	Le divorce
					89 Alexis Piron ★ (1689-1773)
					Racine	Esther
90			90 Lee	The Massacre of Paris	90 Régnard	Arlequin, homme à bonnes fortunes
					91	La coquette ou l'académie des dames
			92 Lee †		Racine	Athalie
			93 George Lillo ★ (1693-1739)		**92 Pierre Claude Nivelle de la Chaussée ★ (1692-1754)**
			Congreve	The Old Bachelor	
				The Double Dealer	
					94 Francois-Marie Voltaire (Arouet) ★ (1694-1778)
					Régnard	Attendez-moi sous l'orme
						Le bourgeois de Falaise
			95	Love for Love	95	La foire Saint-Germain
					96	Le joueur; Le bal
	99 Moreto †		97	The Mourning Bride	97	Le distrait
			99 Farquhar	Love and a Bottle	**99 Racine †**
1700			**00 Dryden †**		00 Régnard	Le retour imprévu
			Congreve	The Way of the World		Démocrite
			Farquhar	A Constant Couple or a Trip to the Jubilee	
			01	Sir Harry Wildair	
			Congreve	The Judgment of Paris	
			Steele	The Funeral or Grief-à-la-Mode	
			02 Farquhar	The Twin Rivals	
				The Inconstant	
			03 Steele	The Lying Lover (Corneille)	
			04 Farquhar	The Stage-Coach	04	Les folies amoureuses
			05 Steele	The Tender Husband (Molière)	05	Les Ménechmes
			06 Farquhar	The Recruiting Officer	
			07 Henry Fielding ★ (1707-1754)		07 Lesage	Crispin, rival de son maître
			Farquhar	The Beaux' Stratagem	
			Farquhar †		08 Régnard	Le légataire universel
					09 Régnard †
					Destouches	Le curieux impertinent
					Lesage	Turcaret
10					**10 Charles-Simon Favart ★ (1710-1792)**
					Destouches	L'ingrat

DRAMA

ITALY	GERMANY		NETHERLANDS	DENMARK	RAGUSA
	79 Weise	Der bäuerische Machiavellus	79 Vondel †		
	80 Rettenbacher Lohenstein	Prudentia victris seu Ulysses Sophonisbe			
	81 Masen †				
	82 Rettenbacher Weise	Frauen – Treu Abraham und Isaac Trauerspiel von dem Nea- politanischen Haupt- Rebellen Masaniello			
	83 Lohenstein † Weise	Von einer Zweyfachen Poeten–Zunfft			
	84	Neue Jugend Lust		**84 Ludvig Holberg ★** **(Ps. Hans Mikkelsen)** **(1684-1754)**	
	85	Der niederländische Bauer			
	86 Avancini †				
	93 Weise	Die böse Catherine			
98 Pietro Metastasio (Pietro **Antonio Domenico Bona-** **ventura Trapassi)** **★ (1698-1782)**	96	Der verfolgte Lateiner			
	00 Johann Christoph Gottsched ★ **(1700-1766)** Rettenbacher	Sacrum Connubium, sive Theandri et Leucothes sancti amores			
	03	Flamma divina amoris			
	04 Hallmann †				
	06 Rettenbacher †				
07 Carlo Goldoni ★ (1707-1793)	08 Weise	Ungleich und Gleich ge- paarte Liebes-Alliance			
	Weise †				

DRAMA

	SPAIN	ENGLAND		FRANCE	
1710				**13 Denis Diderot * (1713-1784)**	
				Destouches	L'irrésolu
		15 Gay	What D'ye Call it	15	Le médisant
		16 Wycherley †			
		17 Gay and Pope and Arbuthnot	Three Hours after Marriage	17 Marivaux	L'Iliade travestie
					Télémaque travestie
				18 Voltaire	Oedipe
		19 Young	Busiris, King of Egypt		
20				20 Marivaux	L'amour et la vérité; Annibal
				Voltaire	Artémise
		21 Young	The Revenge	22 Piron	Arlequin – Deucalion
		22 Steele	The Conscious Lovers	Marivaux	La surprise de l'amour
				23	La double inconstance
		24 Gay	The Captives	24	Le prince travesti
					La fausse suivante
					Le dénouement imprévu
		25 Young	The Love of Fame, the Universal Passion (25–28)	25	L'île des esclaves
					L'héritier de village
				Voltaire	Hérode et Marianne
				27 Marivaux	La séconde surprise de l'amour
				Destouches	Le philosophe marié
					L'envieux
		28 Oliver Goldsmith * (1728-1774)		28 Marivaux	L'indigent philosophe
		Gay	The Beggar's Opera		
		Fielding	Love in Several Masques		
		29 Congreve †; Steele †			
		Fielding	The Temple Beau		
		Gay	Polly		
30		30 Fielding	Rape upon Rape	30	Le jeu de l'amour et du hasard
			Tragedy of Tragedies, or The Life and Death of Tom Thumb the Great	Voltaire	Brutus
			The Intriguing Chambermaid		
		31	The Coffeehouse Politicians	31	La mort de César
		Lillo	The London Merchant, or The History of George Barnwell		
		32 Richard Cumberland * (1732-1811)		**32 Pierre Augustin Caron de Beaumarchais * (1732-1799)**	
		Gay †		Destouches	Le glorieux
		Fielding	The Mock Doctor (Molière)	Marivaux	Le triomphe de l'amour
			The Modern Husband		Les serments indiscrets
					L'école des mères
				Voltaire	Zaïre; Eryphile
		33	The Miser (Molière)	33 Marivaux	L'heureux stratagème
			Don Quixote in England		
				Nivelle de la Chaussée	La fausse antipathie
				Piron	Gustave Wasa
				34 Marivaux	La méprise
					Le petit maître corrigé
				Voltaire	Adélaïde Duguesclin
		35 Lillo	The Christian Hero	35 Niv. de la Chaussée	Le préjugé à la mode
				Marivaux	La mère confidente
		36 Fielding	Pasquin	36	Le legs
		Lillo	Fatal Curiosity	Destouches	Le dissipateur
					Le tambour nocturne
				Voltaire	Alzire
					L'enfant prodigue
		37 Fielding	Tumbledown Dick	37 Destouches	L'ambitieux
				Niv. de la Chaussée	L'école des amis
				Marivaux	Les fausses confidences
		38 Lillo	Marina	38	La joie imprévue
				Piron	La Métromanie
1740		**39 Lillo †**		39 Marivaux	Les sincères; L'épreuve

DRAMA

ITALY	GERMANY	NETHERLANDS	DENMARK	RUSSIA
13 Maffei Mérope	**13 Luise Adelgunde Gottsched ★ (1713-1762)**			
	15 Christian Fürchtegott Gellert ★ (1715-1769)			
	19 Johann Elias Schlegel ★ (1719-1749)			**18 Aleksandr Petrovich Sumarokov ★ (1718-1777)**
20 Carlo Gozzi ★ (1720-1806)				
21 Metastasio Gli Orti Esperidi Catone in Utica			22–23 Holberg Den politiske Kandestober	
23 Didone abbandonata	**24 Friedrich Gottlieb Klopstock ★ (1724-1803)**		Den Vaegelsindede Den Stundeslöse Jean de France Ulysses af Itaca Barselstuen Jakob af Tyboe Jeppe paa bjerget Erasmus Montanus	
			23–27 Det arabiske Pulver Julestuen Mascarade Henrik og Pernille Den pantsatte Bondedreng Den hotte Ambition	
	29 Gotthold Ephraim Lessing ★ (1729-1781)			
31 Adriano in Siria	**31 Philipp Hafner ★ (1731-1764)** J. C. Gottsched Sterbender Cato			
32 Goldoni Olimpiade Il gondoliere Vene-ziano				
	33 Christoph Martin Wieland ★ (1733-1813)			
34 Griselda Metastasio La clemenza di Tito				
36 Goldoni Don Giovanni Te-norio	36 L.A. Gottsched Die Pietisterey im Fisch-beinrocke			
37 Metastasio Temistocle				
38 Goldoni Momolo Cortesan				
39 Il prodigo				
40 Momolo sulla Brenta				

	SPAIN	ENGLAND		FRANCE	
1740				41 Marivaux	Le préjugé vaincu
				Favart	La chercheuse d'esprit
				Niv. de la Chaussée	Mélanide
				42 Voltaire	Mahomet
				43	Mérope
				Niv. de la Chaussée	Paméla
				44	L'école des mères
				Favart	Le coq du village
				47 Lesage †	
				Niv. de la Chaussée	La gouvernante
				48 Voltaire	Sémiramis
				49	Nanine ou le préjugé vaincu
50		**51 Richard Brinsley Sheridan ★ (1751-1816)**		50	Oreste
				52	Rome sauvée
		53 Young	The Brothers (printed)	53 Favart	Bastien et Bastienne
		54 Fielding †		**54 Destouches †; Nivelle de la Chaussée †**	
				Voltaire	La Princesse de Navarre
				55	L'orphelin de la Chine
				Favart	Ninette à la cour
				57 Diderot	Le fils naturel
				58	Le père de famille
60		61 Cumberland	The Banishment of Cicero	60	Tancrède
					L'Ecossaise
				61 Favart	Les trois Sultanes
				62	Annette et Lubin
				63 Marivaux †	
				Favart	Les Anglais à Bordeaux
		65 Young †		Voltaire	Olympie
		68 Goldsmith	The Good Natured Man	67 Beaumarchais	Eugénie
		69 Cumberland	The Brothers	68 Favart	Les moissonneurs
				69 Voltaire	Les Guèbres
70		71	The West Indian	70 Beaumarchais	Les deux amis
		73 Goldsmith	She Stoops to Conquer		
		74 Goldsmith †		**73 Piron †**	
		75 Sheridan	St Patrick's Day; The Rivals	Voltaire	Les lois de Minos
		76	The Duenna	Beaumarchais	Le barbier de Seville
		77	The School for Scandal		
			A Trip to Scarborough		
		78	The Stranger	**78 J.-J. Rousseau †**	
				Voltaire	Irène
		79	The Critic or a Tragedy Rehearsed	**Voltaire †**	
		Cumberland	The Battle of Hastings		
80				81 Diderot	Est-il bon? Est-il méchant?
				84 Diderot †	
				Beaumarchais	La folle journée ou le mariage de Figaro
90		94 Cumberland	The Jew	**92 Favart †**	
		95	The Wheel of Fortune	Beaumarchais	La mère coupable
1800		**11 Cumberland †**		**99 Beaumarchais †**	
10		**16 Sheridan †**			

DRAMA

ITALY	GERMANY	NETHERLANDS	DENMARK	RUSSIA
41 Goldoni — Mercanto fallito	41 J. C. Gottsched Atalanta			
43 — La Donna di Garbo	44 Gellert — Das Band			
— La Contessina	45 — Sylvia			**45 Denis Ivanovich Fonvizin * (1745-1792)**
45 — Il servitore di due patroni	— Die Betschwester			47 Sumaro-kov — Khorev
48 — Vedova scaltra	47 — Die zärtlichen Schwestern			
49 — Il cavaliere de la dama	— Das Loos in der Lotterie			
— Putta onorata	Lessing — Der junge Gelehrte			
	49 J. E. Schlegel †			
	Lessing — Der Freygeist			
50 — La bottega del caffè	— Die Juden			
— La famiglia dell'antiquario	— Die alte Jungfer			
— Pamela nubile				
— Il petteglozzi delle donne				
Metastasio Attilio regolo				
51 Goldoni — La Moglie saggia				51 — Sinav i Truvor
— Le donne gelose				Zemira
— La serva amorosa	55 Hafner — Der alte Odoardo und der lächerliche Hanswurst		**54 Holberg †**	
52 — La locandiera				
— Le donne curiose	Lessing — Miss Sara Sampson			
53 — Torquato Tasso	57 Klopstock — Der Tod Adams			
— La sposa persiana	58 Wieland — Lady Johanna Gray			
55 Maffei †	59 Lessing — Philotas			
59 Goldoni — Innamorata				
— Impresario delle Smirne				
60 — I Rusteghi	60 Wieland — Clementia von Porretta			
— La casa nova				
— Un curioso accidente				
61 — La buona madre	**62 L. A. Gottsched †**			
— Villa giatura	Lessing — Emilia Galotti			
— Buon compatrioto	63 Hafner — Die bürgerliche Dame			
Gozzi — L'amore delle tre melarance; Il corvo	64 Lessing — Der Schatz			
62 — Il re cervo	Klopstock — Salomo			
Goldoni — Le baruffe chiozotte	Hafner — Etwas zum Lachen oder Burlins und Hanswurst			
— Tòdero brontolon	— Megära die förchterliche Hexe oder das verzauberte Schloss des Herrn von Einhorn			
63 — Amori di Arlecchino e di Camilla	— Der Furchtsame			
Gozzi — La donna serpente	65 — Evakathel und Schnudi			
— Principessa Turandot	— Die in Freundschaft sich wandelnde Rache			
— La Zobeide				
64 — Il mostro turchino	**Hafner †**			
— I Pitocchi fortunati	**66 J. C. Gottsched †**			65 Sumaro-kov — Opekun
Goldoni — Zelinda e Lindoro	67 Lessing — Minna von Barnhelm			
65 — Amanti timidi	**69 Gellert †**			
Gozzi — Angellino belvedere	Klopstock — Hermanns Schlacht			66 Fonvizin Brigadir
— Zeim re dei geni				
71 Goldoni — Le bourru bienfaisant	72 — David			
73 — L'éventail	73 Wieland — Die Wahl des Hercules			71 Sumaro-kow — Dimitry Samotsvanets
74 — Avaro fastoso	— Alceste			
77 Gozzi — Droghe d'amore	74 Hafner — Die reisenden Comödianten			
	79 Lessing — Nathan der Weise			**77 Sumarokov †**
82 Metastasio †	**81 Lessing †**			
	84 Klopstock — Hermann und die Fürsten			
	87 — Hermanns Tod			82 Fonvizin Nedorosl'
93 Goldoni †				
				92 Fonvizin †
	03 Klopstock †			
06 Gozzi †				
	13 Wieland †			

265

	ITALY	GERMANY	FRANCE	ENGLAND
1550	**50 Giulio Caccini * (1550?-1618?)** **Orazio Vecchi* (1550-1605)**			
60	**61 Jacopo Peri * (1561-1633)** **67 Claudio Monteverdi * (1567-1643)** **Adriano Banchieri * (1567-1634)**			
80	**81 Francesca Caccini * (1581 [88?] -1640?)**			
90	**90 Steffano Landi * (1590?-1655?)** **92 Domenico Mazzocchi * (1592-1665)** 94 Banchieri Hora prima di recreazione Vecchi Amfiparnaso **95 Francesco Manelli * (1595?-1667)** 97 Peri Dafne **98 Luigi Rossi (Aloysius de Rubeis) *** **(1598-1653)** Banchieri La pazzia senile			

1600	**00 Michel Angelo Rossi * (1600?-1674?)**
	Francesco Paolo Sacrati * (1600?-1650)
	G. Caccini Euridice
	Peri Euridice
	02 Francesco Cavalli * (1602-1676)
	04 Banchieri Zabaione musicale
	05 Antonio Bertali * (1605-1669)
	Vecchi †
	Banchieri La barca di Venezia per Padova
	07 Monteverdi Orfeo
	08 Arianna
	           Il ballo dell'ingrate
	Peri Tetide
	Banchieri Il festino nella sera del Giovedi
	           grasso
		07 Sigmund Gottlieb Theophil Staden *
		(1607-1655)		

10	16 Peri La guerra d'amore **18 G. Caccini †** 19 Landi La morte d'Orfeo			

20	20 Peri Adone
	23 Marc'Antonio Cesti * (1623-1669)
	24 Monteverdi Il combattimento di Tancredi e
	           Clorinda
	25 F. Caccini La liberazione di Ruggiero
	          dell'isola d'Alcina
	26 Giovanni Legrenzi * (1626-1690)
	Mazzocchi La catena d'Adone
	28 Peri Flora
			28 Robert Cambert * (1628?-1677)	

30	30 Manelli La Delia 32 Landi Sant'Alessio **33 Peri †** M.A. Rossi Erminia sul Giordano **34 Banchieri †** **35 Antonio Draghi * (1635-1700)** 37 Manelli L'Andromeda 38 La maga fulminata M.A. Rossi Andromeda 39 Manelli L'Adone Sacrati Delia Cavalli Le nozze di Peleo e Teti		**32 Jean-Baptiste Lully * (1632-1687)**	
40	**40 F. Caccini † (40?)** Cavalli Gli amori di Apollo e di Dafne 41 Didone Mazzocchi L'innocenza difesa Sacrati La finta pazza Monteverdi Il ritorno d'Ulisse in patria			

	ITALY	GERMANY	FRANCE	ENGLAND
1640	42 Monteverdi **L'incoronazione di Poppea**			
	Cavalli La virtù degli strali d'amore			
	L. Rossi Il palazzo d'Atalante incantato			
	Sacrati Bellerofonte			
	43 Monteverdi †			
	Sacrati La Venere gelosa			
	Cavalli Egisto			
	44 L'Ormindo	44 Staden Das geistliche Waldgedicht oder Freudenspiel, genannt Seelewig		
	Sacrati Ulisse errante			
	Proserpina rapita			
	45 Cavalli La Doriclea			
	47 L. Rossi Orfeo			
	48 Sacrati La Semiramide in India			
	L'isola d'Alcina			
	49 Cavalli Giasone			
	Cesti L'Orontea			
50	**50 Sacrati †**			
	Cavalli L'Orimonte			
	51 Cesti Il Cesare amante			
	Cavalli L'Oristeo			
	Alessandro vincitor di se stesso			
	L'Armidoro			
	La Rosinda			
	La Calisto			
	52 L'Eritrea			
	Veramonda, l'amazzone di Aragona			
	Bertali Theti			
	53 L. Rossi †			
	Cavalli L'Orione			
	Bertali L'inganno d'amore			
	54 Agostino Steffani ★ (1654–1728)			
	Cavalli Serse; Ciro			
	Cesti Alessandro vincitor di se stesso			
	55 Landi † (c. 55)	**55 Staden †**		
	Cesti Argia			
	Cavalli Statira, principessa di Persia			56 Lawes and The Siege of Rhodes
	Erismena			others
	56 Artemisia		58 Cambert La muette ingrate	
	58 L'Ipermnestra		59 Lully Oedipe	**59 Henry Purcell ★ (1659–1695)**
	59 Elena			
60	**60 Pietro Alessandro Gaspare Scarlatti ★ (1660–1725)**	**60 Johann Joseph Fux ★ (1660–1741) Johann Sigismund Kusser ★ (1660–1727)**		
	Cavalli La pazzia in trono, ovvero Caligula delirante			
	Bertali La magia delusa		61 Cambert Ariane	
	61 Il ciro crescente			
	Cesti La Dori, ovvero La schiave fedele			
	62 La magnanimità d'Alessandro			
	Cavalli Ercole amante		63 Lully Impromptu de Versailles	
	64 Scipione Africano		64 Le mariage forcé	
	Legrenzi Achille in Sciro			
	Bertali Operetta (= Pazzo amor)			
	65 Mazzochi †			
	Legrenzi Zenobia e Radamisto			
	Cavalli Muzio Scevola			
	66 Pompeo Magno			
	Cesti Nettuno e Flora festeggianti			
	Il Tito		67 Lully Pastorale comique	**67 John Christopher Pepusch ★ (1667–1752)**
	67 Manelli †			
	Bertali La contesa dell'aria e dell'acqua			
	Cesti La Semiramide			
	Le disgrazie d'amore			
	Il pomo d'oro			

	ITALY	GERMANY	FRANCE	ENGLAND
1660			68 Lully La grotte de Versailles	
	69 Cesti †; Bertali †		69 Monsieur de Pourceaugnac (= Divertissements de Chambord)	
70	**70 Giovanni Battista Bononcini ★ (1670-1750?)**		70 Les amants magnifiques	
			71 La comtesse d'Escarbagnas	
			Cambert Pomone	
			72 Les peines et les plaisirs de l'amour	
			Lully Les festes de l'Amour et de Bacchus	
	74 M. A. Rossi † (74?)	**74 Reinhard Keiser ★ (1674-1739)**	73 Cadmus et Hermione	
	75 Legrenzi Eteocle e Polinice La divisione del mondo		74 Alceste ou Le triomphe d'Alcide	
	76 Cavalli †		75 Thesée	
	Legrenzi Germanico sul Reno		76 Atys	
	77 Totila			
			77 Cambert †	
			Lully Isis	
	79 Scarlatti Gli Equivoci nel sembiante (= Amor non vuole inganni)		78 Psyché	
			79 Bellérophon	
1680	80 L'onestà negli amori		80 Proserpine	
	81 Tutto il mal non vien per nuocere (= Dal male il bene)	**81 Georg Philipp Telemann ★ (1681-1767)**		
	Steffani Marco Aurelio			
			82 Persée	
	83 Scarlatti La Psiche, ovvero Amore innamorato; Pompeo		**83 Jean-Philippe Rameau ★ (1683-1764)**	
	Draghi La lira d'Orfeo		Lully Phaéton	
	Legrenzi I due Cesari; Giustino			
	84 Pertinace		84 Amadis de Gaule	
		85 Georg Friedrich Händel ★ (1685-1759)	85 Roland	
	86 Steffani Servio Tullio		86 Armide et Renaud Acis et Galatée	
	87 Alarcio il Baltho, cioè l'audace re dei Gothi		**87 Lully †**	
	88 Niobe, regina de Thebe			
	89 Enrico Leone La lotta d'Hercole con Achelao			89 Purcell Dido and Aeneas
90	**90 Leonardo Vinci ★ (1690-1730) Legrenzi †**	90 Kusser Julia		90 The Prophetess, or The History of Diocletian
	Steffani La superbia d'Alessandro (= Il zelo di Leonato)			
	Scarlatti Gli Equivoci in amore, ovvero La Rosaura Statira			
	91 L'umanità nelle fiere, o vero Il Lucullo	91 Cleopatra La grotta di Salzdahl		91 King Arthur, or The British Worthy
	Steffani Orlando generoso	92 Ariadne; Andromeda; Jason; Narcissus		92 The Fairy Queen
	93 La libertà contenta	93 Porus		
		Keiser Der königliche Schäfer, oder Basilius in Arkadien		
	94 Scarlatti Pirro e Demetrio	94 Kusser Erindo, oder die unsträfliche Liebe		
	Bononcini Tullo Ostilio; Serse	Scipio Africanus		
	95 Steffani Il trionfo del fato, o Le glorie d'Enea Baccanali	95 Keiser Die wiederaufgefundenen Verliebten (= Ismene 95)		95 The Tempest, or The Enchanted Island The Indian Queen
				Purcell †
	96 Briseide	97 Kusser Junia		
	97 Scarlatti La caduta dei Decemviri	98 Erminia; Der verliebte Wald		

	ITALY	GERMANY	FRANCE	ENGLAND
1690 **99**	Bononcini La fede publica Draghi Alceste	**99 Johann Adolf Hasse * (1699-1783)** Keiser Die wunderbar errettete Iphigenie		
1700 **00**	**00 Francesco Araja * (1700-1767?)** **Draghi †**	00 Keiser La forza della virtù		
01	01 Bononcini Gli affetti più grandi, vinti dal più giusto	01 Störtebecker und Jödge Michaels		
02	02 Polifemo	02 Orpheus Fux L'offendere per amare, overo La Telesilla La clemenza di Augusto		
03	03 Scarlatti Arminio	**03/04 Carl Heinrich Graun * (1703/4?-1759)**		
04	**04 Giovanni Battista Pescetti * (1704?-1766)** Scarlatti Turno Aricino Bononcini Gli amori di Cefalo e di Procri; Tomiri			
05	05 Scarlatti Lucio Manlio l'imperioso	05 Händel Almira Keiser Die römische Unruhe, oder Die edelmüthige Octavia		
06	06 Il gran Tamerlano Bononcini Endimione	06 Der durchlauchtige Secretarius, oder Almira		
07	07 Steffani Arminio Bononcini L'Etearco; Turno Aricino Scarlatti Il Mitridate eupatore Il trionfo della libertà			
08	08 Bononcini Mario fuggitivo	08 Fux Julo Ascanio, re d'Alba Pulcherva		
09	09 L'Abdolonimo Steffani Amor vien dal destino (09?) Tassilone (09?)	09 Gli ossequi della notte Il mese di marzo consecrato a Marte Händel Agrippina		
10 **10**	**10 Giovanni Battista Pergolesi * (1710-1736)** Bononcini Gaio Gracco Muzio Scevola	10 Keiser Der durch den Fall des grossen Pompeius erhöhete Julius Caesar Fux La decima fatica d'Ercole ovvero La sconfitta di Gerione in Spagna Keiser Der hochmüthige, gestürzte und wiedererhobene Croesus		
11		**11 Ignaz Jakob Holzbauer * (1711-1783)** **Händel (moves to London)**		11 Handel Rinaldo
12			**12 Jean Jacques Rousseau * (1712-1778)**	12 Il pastor fido
13				13 Teseo
14		**14 Christoph Willibald Ritter von Gluck * (1714-1787)** Fux Dafne in Lauro Keiser L'inganno fedele		
15		15 Fux Orfeo ed Euridice		15 Amadigi di Gaula
16		16 Angelica vincitrice di Alcina		
18	18 Scarlatti Il trionfo dell'onore			
19	19 Erminia Vinci Lo cecato fauzo	19 Elisa		
20 **20**	20 Bononcini Astarto			20 Il Radamisto
21	21 Ciro, ovvero odio et amore Crispo Scarlatti La virtù negli amori Griselda	21 Telemann Der geduldige Socrates		21 Il Floridante
22	22 Bononcini Griselda	22 Keiser Ulysses Fux Le nozze di Aurora		
23	23 Farnace Vinci Silla dittatore	23 Constanza e fortezza	23 Rameau L'endriague	23 Ottone; Flavio
24	24 La mogliera fedele Bononcini Calfurnia	24 Telemann Der neumodische Liebhaber Damon		24 Giulio Cesare; Tamerlano
25	**25 Ferdinando Giuseppe Bertoni * (1725-1813)** **Scarlatti †** Vinci Ifigenia in Tauride Astianatte	25 Pimpinone		25 Rodelinda
26	26 Ermelinda	26 Hasse Sesostre	26 L'enrôlement d'Arlequin La robe de dissention, ou Le faux prodigue	26 Scipione; Alessandro

	ITALY		GERMANY		FRANCE		ENGLAND	
1720	27 Vinci	La caduta dei Decemviri	**27 Kusser †**				27 Handel	Admeto; Riccardo I
	Bononcini	Astianatte	Graun	Sanico oder Die in ihrer Un-				
	28 Niccolò Piccinni ★ (1728-1800),			schuld siegende Sinilde			28	Siroe; Tolomeo
	Steffani †		28	Iphigenia in Aulis			Pepusch	The Beggar's Opera
	Pescetti	Gli odi delusi del sagne	Telemann	Emma und Eginhard				
			Hasse	Attalo, re di Bitinia				
	29 Araja	Dorinda					29	The Wedding
		Lo matremmonejo pè menetta						Polly
							Handel	Lotario
30	**30 Antonio Maria Gasparo Gioacchino**		30	Arminio			30	Partenope
	Sacchini ★ (1730-1786)							
	Vinci	Artaserse						
	Vinci †		31	Cleofide (= Alessandro			31	Poro
	31 Pergolesi	Salustia		nell'Indie)				
			Graun	Polidorus				
	32	Lo frate'nnamorato	**32 Franz Joseph Haydn ★ (1732-1809)**				32	Ezio
	Pescetti	Demetrio	Graun	Scipio Africanus				Sosarme
	33 Pergolesi	Il prigioniero superbo	33	Lo specchio della fedeltà	33 Rameau	Hippolyte et Aricie	33	Orlando
		La serva padrona		(= Timareta)		Samson		Arianna
	34	Livietta e Tracollo	34 Hasse	Artaserse	34	Les courses de Tempé	34	Ariodante
		(= La contadina astuta 44)						
		Adriano in Siria						
	35	L'Olimpiade	**35 Anton Schweitzer ★ (1735-1787)**		35	Les fêtes d'Hébé, ou	35	Alcina
		Flaminio	Graun	Pharao Tubaetes		Les talents lyriques		
						Les Indes galantes		
	36 Pergolesi †						36	Atalanta
	Bononcini	Alessandro in Sidone			37	Castor et Pollux	37	Arminio; Giustino
	37 Pescetti	Sabrina						Berenice
							38	Serse
	38 Araja	Berenice						Faramondo
	Pescetti	La conquista del vello d'oro	**39 Karl Ditters von Dittersdorf ★**		39	Dardanus	39	Giove in Argo
			(1739-1799); Keiser †					
40	**40 Giovanni Paisiello ★ (1740-1816)**				40	Prométhée	40	Imeneo
	Pescetti	Busiri	**41 Fux †**		**41 André Ernest Modeste Grétry ★**		41	Deidamia
			Graun	Rodelinda	**(1741-1813)**			
			42	Venere e Cupido				
				Cesare e Cleopatra				
			43	Artaserse				
	44 Pescetti	Tristomedo	44	La festa d'Imeneo	44 Rameau	Les fêtes de l'hymen ou La rose		
				Alessandro nell'Indie				
				Catone in Utica				
			45	Lucio Papirio	45	Les fêtes de Polyhymnie		
						La princesse de Navarre		
						Le temple de la gloire		
						Platée ou Junon jalouse		
			46	Demofoonte				
				Caio Fabrizio				
				Adriano in Siria				
			Gluck	La caduta dei giganti				
				Artamene				
			47 Graun	Le feste galanti	47	Les fêtes de l'hymen et de		
			Gluck	Le nozze d'Ercole e d'Ebe		l'amour		
			48	Semiramide riconosciuta	48	Les surprises de l'amour		
			Hasse	Demofoonte		Zaïs		
			Graun	Iphigenia in Aulide		Pigmalion		
				L'Europe galante				
	49 Domenico Cimarosa ★ (1749-1801)		49	Cinna; Angelica e Medoro	49	Naïs		
				Coriolano		Zoroastre		
			Gluck	La contesa de'Numi				
50	**50 Antonio Salieri ★ (1750-1825)**		50	Ezio				
	Bononcini † (50?)		Graun	Fetonte; Mitridate				
	51 Araja	La clemenza di Tito	51	Armida; Britannico	51	Acanthe et Céphise ou		
			51/52 Gluck	Issipile		La sympathie		
						La guirlande		

OPERA

	ITALY	GERMANY	FRANCE	ENGLAND
1750		52 Gluck La clemenza di Tito Graun Il giudizio di Paride Orfeo ed Euridice 53 Silla Hasse Eroe cinese; Solimano Holzbauer Il figlio delle selve 54 L'isola disabitata L'issipile Gluck Le cinesi Graun Semiramide 55 Montezuma; Ezio Holzbauer Don Chisciotte	52 Rousseau Le devin du village 53 Rameau Daphnis et Églé Les Sibarites 54 Zéphire La naissance d'Osiris	52 Pepusch †
	54 Piccinni Le donne dispettose			
	55 Araja Kephalos und Prokris			
	56 Piccinni Zenobia	**56 Wolfgang Amadeus Mozart ★ (1756-1791)** Holzbauer Le nozze d'Arianna e di Bacco I cinesi Graun I fratelli nemici Merope Gluck Antigono Il re pastore		
	57 Piccinni Nitetti Sacchini Il giocatore 58 Piccinni Alessandro nell'Indie	57 Holzbauer La clemenza di Tito Nitetti 58 L'isle de Merlin, ou Le monde renversé		
		59 Graun † Gluck Le diable à quatre Cythère assiégée L'arbre enchanté, ou Le tuteur dupé Holzbauer Alessandro nell'Indie Ippolito ed Arcia		59 Handel †
60	60 Piccinni La cecchina, ossia La buona figliuola 61 L'Olimpiade La buona figliuola maritata Sacchini Andromaca	60 Gluck L'ivrogne corrigé Tetide 61 Le festin de pierre (=Don Juan) Le cadi dupé Telemann Don Quichotte 62 Haydn Acide e Galatea Gluck Orfeo ed Euridice	60 Les paladins	
	63 Alessandro nell'Indie Piccinni Le donne vendicate 64 Sacchini Semiramide Paisiello I Francesi brillanti Il ciarlone 65 Demetrio	63 Il trionfo di Clelia 64 La rencontre imprévue 65 Telemacco, ossia l'isola di Circe Semiramis Il Parnasso confuso La corona	64 Abaris, ou Les Boréades **Rameau †**	
	66 Pescetti † Paisiello Le finte contesse Sacchini Isola d'amore (= La colonie) Piccinni La pescatrice, ovvero L'erede riconosciuta			
	67 Araja † (67?) Paisiello L'idolo cinese	**67 Telemann †** Mozart Apollo und Hyacinthus Dittersdorf Amore in musica Gluck Alessandro; Alceste Haydn La canterina 68 Lo speziale Hasse Piramo e Tisbe Mozart Bastien und Bastienne La finta semplice Holzbauer Adriano in Siria	68 Grétry Les mariages Samnites Le Huron	
	69 Sacchini Il Cidde (= Chimène 83)	69 Haydn Le pescatrici Gluck Le feste d'Apollo	69 Le tableau parlant Lucile	
70	70 Salieri Le donne letterate	70 Mozart Mitridate, rè di Ponto Schweitzer Walmir und Gertraud Apollo unter den Hirten Gluck Paride ed Elena Dittersdorf Il viaggiatore americano	70 L'amitié à l'épreuve Les deux avares; Silvain	

	ITALY		GERMANY		FRANCE	ENGLAND
1770	71 Salieri	Armida	71 Dittersdorf	L'amore disprezzato	71 Grétry	L'ami de la maison
			Hasse	Ruggiero, ovvero L'eroica gratitudine		Zémire et Azor
			Mozart	Ascanio in Alba		
	72	La fiera di Venezia	72	Il sogno di Scipione		
	Cimarosa	Le stravaganze del conte		Lucio Silla		
		Le magie di Merlina e Zoroastro	Schweitzer	Pygmalion		
	Sacchini	Renaud (= Rinaldo ed Armida 83)		Die Dorfgala		
			Gluck	Iphigénie en Aulide		
	73	Tamerlano	73 Schweitzer	Alceste	73	La rosière de Salency
		Perseo	Haydn	L'infedeltà delusa		Céphale et Procris, ou L'amour conjugal
				Philemon und Baucis		Le magnifique
			Dittersdorf	Il tutore e la pupilla		
	74 **Salieri**	**(moves to Vienna)**	74 Gluck	L'orfano della Cina		
	Paisiello	La Frascatana	Dittersdorf	Il tribunale di Giove		
		Il duello				
	Piccini	I viaggiatori				
	75 Paisiello	Socrate immaginario	75	Il finto pazzo per amore (75?)	75	La fausse magie
	Sacchini	Montezuma		Lo sposo burlato		
				Il maniscalco		
			Haydn	L'incontro improvviso		
			Mozart	La finta giardiniera		
				Il rè pastore		
	76 Bertoni	Orfeo	76 Dittersdorf	La contadina fedele		
				Il Barone di Rocca Antica (76?)		
				La moda, o sia gli scompigli domestici		
			Holzbauer	Günther von Schwarzburg		
	77 Paisiello	Lucindo ed Armidoro	77 Dittersdorf	L'Arcifanfano, re de'matti	77	Matroco
		Nitteti	Gluck	Armide		
			Haydn	Il mondo della luna		
	78	Achille in Scirio	78 Schweitzer	Rosamunde	78	Le jugement de Midas
	Piccinni	Roland				Les fausses apparences ou l'amant jaloux
	Cimarosa	L'Italiana a Londra				
	Salieri	Europa riconosciuta				
	79	La scuola dei gelosi	79 Mozart	Zaide	79	Les événements imprévus
		Il Talismano	Haydn	La vera constanza		Aucassin et Nicolette, ou Les moeurs du bon vieux temps
	Paisiello	Gli astrologi immaginari		L'isola disabitata		
		Il matrimonio inaspettato	Gluck	Iphigénie en Tauride		
				Echo et Narcisse		
80	80	Alcide al bivio			80	Andromaque
	Piccinni	Atys				
	81	Iphigénie en Tauride	81 Mozart	Idomeneo, rè di Creta	81	Émilie
	Cimarosa	Il pittore parigino				
		Il convito				
	Salieri	Der Rauchfangkehrer				
	Paisiello	La serva padrona				
	82	Il barbiere di Siviglia, ovvero La precauzione inutile	82	Die Entführung aus dem Serail	82	L'embarras des richesses
			Haydn	Orlando Paladino		La double épreuve, ou Colinette à la Cour
	Cimarosa	La ballerina amante				
	Sacchini	Rosina				
	Salieri	Semiramide				
	83		83 **Hasse †**		83	La caravane du Caire
	Piccinni	Didon	Holzbauer	Tancredi		
	Cimarosa	I due baroni di Rocca Azzurra	**Holzbauer †**			
	84	L'Olimpiade; Artaserse	84 Haydn	Armida	84	Théodore et Paulin (= L'épreuve villageoise)
	Paisiello	Il re Teodoro in Venezia				Richard Coeur-de-Lion
	Sacchini	Dardanus				
	Salieri	Les Danaides				
	85 Sacchini	Oedipe à Colonne			85	Panurge dans l'île des lanternes
	Cimarosa	Il marito disperato				
	Salieri	La grotta di Tronfonio				
	86 **Sacchini †**		86 Mozart	Der Schauspieldirektor	86	Le Comte d'Albert
	Cimarosa	L'impresario in angustie		Le nozze di Figaro		Les méprises par ressemblance
	Salieri	Les Horaces	Dittersdorf	Betrug durch Aberglauben		Amphitryon
				Doktor und Apotheker		

	ITALY		GERMANY		FRANCE		ENGLAND
1780	87 Salieri	Tarare	**87 Gluck †; Schweitzer †** Mozart Il Don Giovanni, ossia Il dissoluto punito Dittersdorf Liebe im Narrenhaus (= Orpheus der Zweyte) Hironimus Knicker Democritto corretto		87 Grétry	Le prisonnier anglais, ou Clarice et Belton	
	88 Paisiello	L'amor contrastato (La molinara)	88	Das rothe Kaeppchen	88	Le rival confident	
	89	Nina, ossia La pazza per amore I zingari in fiera	89	Der Schiffspatron oder Der neue Gutsherr	89	Raoul Barbe Bleue Aspasie	
	Cimarosa	La vergine del Sole Cleopatra					
	Salieri	Il pastor fido					
90			90 Dittersdorf Der Teufel ein Hydraulikus Hockus-Pockus	90	Pierre le Grand	
			Mozart Cosi fan tutte, ossia La scuola degli amanti			
			91 La clemenza di Tito Die Zauberflöte	91	Guillaume Tell	
			Mozart † Haydn L'anima del filosofo			
	92 Cimarosa	Il matrimonio segreto			92	Cécile et Ermancé ou Les deux couvents Basile	
	94	Le astuzie femminili	94 Dittersdorf Das Gespenst mit der Trommel	94	Denis le tyran, maître d'école à Corinthe La Rosière républicaine, ou La fête de la vertu Callias, ou Nature et patrie Joseph Barra	
			95 Don Quixote der Zweyte Der Schach von Schiras Die befreyten Gwelfen Gott Mars oder Der Hauptmann von Bärenzahn			
	96	Gli Orazi e i Curiazi	96 Der schöne Herbsttag Der Durchmarsch Die lustigen Weiber von Windsor Ugolino			
	Salieri	Il moro				
			97 Der Ternengewinnst (= Der gedemüthigte Stolz) Der Mädchenmarkt	97	Anacréon chez Polycrate Lisbeth	
			98 Die Opera Buffa (98?) Don Coribaldi, ossia L'usurpata prepotenza			
	99 Salieri	Falstaff, ossia le tre burle	99 Hochzeit des Figaro **Dittersdorf †**	99	Élisca, ou L'amour maternel	
1800	**00 Piccinni †**					
	01 Cimarosa	Artemisa				
	Cimarosa †					
	03 Paisiello	Proserpina				
	04 Salieri	Die Neger	**09 Haydn †**			
10	**13 Bertoni †**				**13 Grétry †**	
	16 Paisiello †					
20	**25 Salieri †**					

Notes to the Text

Introduction

1 Carl J. Burckhardt, *Richelieu, der Aufstieg zur Macht*, Munich 1961, p. 7.

I The Courts

1 At the banquet given by Philip the Good, Duke of Burgundy, in Lille in 1453, to gather support for a crusade, the table decorations included a church with four singers, a fountain in a field scattered with 'boulders' of sapphires and other jewels, and a pie containing twenty musicians. The wedding of Frances I of Tuscany and Bianca Capello in Florence in 1579 was celebrated with tilting, bullfights, hunting, jousting, a spectacular carousel and plays. To celebrate the christening of the eldest daughter of the Landgrave Maurice of Hesse-Cassel, Elizabeth I of England gave a feast which featured a romance of chivalry as the framework for the tournament and plays.

2 Numerous descriptions of festivals and dramatic entertainments throughout the sixteenth, seventeenth and eighteenth centuries are to be found in the diaries and other memoirs of travellers like Michel de Montaigne, Aulus Apronius, Richard Lassals and Lady Mary Wortley Montagu. Other sources include the memoirs of Catherine II of Russia, Wilhelmina of Bayreuth, Lucca Landucci, Karl Ludwig Freiherr von Pöllnitz and Oliver de la Marche, and the letters of Charlotte Elizabeth of the Palatinate and Mme de Sévigné.

3 A book of illustrations of every scene was published by the engraver, Melchior Küsell. There is a copy in the Staatsbibliothek, Munich. See also Günther Schöne, *Tausend Jahre Deutsches Theater*, Munich 1963, pp. 48–53.

4 *Les Plaisirs de l'Isle enchantée. Cours de Barque ... faites par le Roy à Versailles 1664*, Paris 1673. Other contemporary accounts in J. B. P. de Molière, *Théâtre*, Edition Hachette, vol. IV, pp. 89 to 268.

5 H. Prunières, *Le Ballet de Cour*, Paris 1914; H. Kindermann, *Theatergeschichte Europas*, vol. IV, p. 14 ff.

6 Johann Rist in *Das Aller Edelste Leben der gantzen Welt* (1663), quoted in Albrecht Schöne, ed., *Deutsche Literatur – Texte und Zeugnisse*, vol. III, *Das Zeitalter des Barock*, Munich 1963, p. 343 ff.: 'Moreover all manner of pleasurable and artistic firework displays are given at court, which, although very costly, sometimes consuming whole villages, yet cheap in relation to the delight they cause in the eyes and spirits of the beholders, are greatly to be praised. For you may see all kinds of excellent inventions, such as fine houses or castles, which give out many thousands of bursts of flame before they go up in smoke. The artists set up and show fire-breathing dragons, salamanders, hellhounds and crocodiles, and there are all sorts of grenades, water bombs, fire bombs, letters of fire, catherine wheels, prisms, squibs, and many kinds of rockets, some of incredible size ...'

7 Notably of *Les Fâcheux*, *Le Mariage forcé* and the first three acts of *Tartuffe*, which was subsequently banned.

8 A detailed description is given in Wolfgang Geiger's *Theatrum Europäum*, published by Merian 1677, and quoted in A. Schöne, *op. cit.*, p. 353, p. 1083.

9 After the mediaeval tournament had died with the Emperor Maximilian I, there were equestrian ballets also at other courts, e.g. *La guerra d'amore*, 1615, in honour of the Grand Duke of Tuscany. See also p. 10, *La guerra di bellezza*, Florence, Carnival 1616, in honour of the Duke of Urbino. But it is quite possible that these ballets were nowhere executed with such art as in Vienna, the city in which, even today, the traditions of the Spanish Riding School are upheld.

10 Wilhelmina, Margravine of Bayreuth, writes in her memoirs: 'On the 30 [May 1730] he travelled, at the invitation of the king of Poland, to a review of troops in Mühlberg. The whole of the Saxon army was assembled there and carried out the exercises and manoeuvres which have been described by the famous Chevalier Follard. The uniforms, liveries and the horses were quite magnificent and matched by the splendour with which the hundred tables were decked; everyone agreed that this far surpassed Louis XIV's "Field of the Cloth of Gold".' Quoted in Heinz Bien, *Feste und Feiern im alten Europa*, p. 49.

11 'The floor on which the table stands is covered with scarlet or velvet; sometimes, as at solemn feasts, it stands on a dais and the guests must climb on to the scaffold, as in a theatre.' From the *Einleitung zur Ceremonial-Wissenschaft grosser Herren*, 1729, Part 1, Chapter 8, quoted in Bien, *op. cit.*, p. 155.

12 Detailed descriptions of decorative confectionery are given in the anonymous *Trincir-Buch* published by Georg Philipp Harsdörfer in 1652. Quoted in A. Schöne, *op. cit.*, p. 345 ff.

13 Translator's note. The most frequent modern use of *Wirtschaft* is 'economics' but its basic meaning is 'housekeeping', and by extension 'household' and thus 'public house', which is normally *Gastwirtschaft* in modern usage. The word *Wirt* means 'host' or 'innkeeper'.

14 *Mémoires de l'Impératrice Catherine II, écrits par elle-même ...* London 1859, pp. 292–3.

15 Quoted in Marion, Countess Dönhoff, *Namen, die keiner mehr nennt*, Deutscher Taschenbuchverlag 247, p. 113.

16 Bien, *op. cit.*, p. 341 ff.

17 This passage, much abbreviated, is quoted from E. & J. Goncourt, *La femme au 18e siècle*. As well as this passage there are descriptions of the *journées de campagne* at the great houses of the eighteenth century, of the *salon* comedies of the coffee-houses, of actors, of the performances of *Proverbes*, embellished with arias and rhyming couplets.

18 Romain Rolland, *Les origines du théâtre lyrique moderne*, nouv. éd., Paris 1931, p. 149. The quotation within this quotation is from John Evelyn.

19 The *sacra rappresentazione* was a kind of acted oratorio on a religious subject, and a direct ancestor of opera.

20 Anton Ulrich of Brunswick-Wolfenbüttel wrote about ten opera libretti. He became acquainted with the Ballet de Cour at the court of Louis XIV and introduced an opera-ballet at his own court, of the kind that flourished at all the courts of central Germany at the end of the seventeenth century. In 1688 a large theatre with five tiers was opened in Wolfenbüttel, and in 1690 an opera house with four tiers, open to the general public, was opened in Brunswick. The summer palace at Salzdahlem was equipped with both an indoor theatre and an open-air theatre for pastorals. Stefani wrote grand operas for the Duke, Harms designed the sets for them and distinguished musicians were engaged such as Johann Sigismund Kusser (1660 to 1727).

II The Public

1 Karl Vossler, *Lope de Vega und sein Zeitalter*, Munich 1932, p. 190.

2 Vossler, *op. cit.*, p. 191.

3 Kindermann, *op. cit.*, vol. III, p. 211.

4 See *pl. 54*, *The entry of Harlequin*, from a tapestry in the Würzburg Residenz. – The custom was continued until well into the nineteenth century. See also Goethe's *Wilhelm Meister*.

5 Kindermann, *op. cit.*, vol. V, p. 437, and, for further references, p. 733, note 15.

6 Johann Beer, *Die teutschen Winter-Nächte und die kurzweiligen Sommer-Täge*, 1682. New ed., Frankfurt 1963, p. 390.

7 R. Prölss, *Geschichte des neueren Dramas*, Leipzig 1882, vol. III, p. 172 ff.

8 Kindermann, *op. cit.*, vol. IV, p. 87. Police censorship was instituted because the Duchess of Orléans was offended by the presentation of what she considered to be lesbian relationships in Bondin's *Le Bal d'Anteuil*.

9 Stamm, *Geschichte des englischen Theaters*, Berne 1951, p. 205.

10 Showing a scene from Holberg's *Jeppe paa Bjerget*, reproduced in Kindermann, *op. cit.*, vol. V, p. 474.

11 Niccolò Sabbattini, *Pratica di fabricar Scene e machine ne' Teatri*, Ravenna 1638, chap. 34.

12 Standing room in the *parterre* was a feature even of some of the large civic theatres, like that in Bordeaux, and even in the opera house in Versailles.

13 Johann Beer, *op. cit.*, p. 390, note 26.

14 In chapter 3 he describes a theatre erected in a barn. A factory owner had had it put up to entertain and edify his workers and thus keep them from playing cards.

15 Kindermann, *op. cit.*, vol. IV, p. 85. – M. Albert, *Les théâtres de la foire*, Paris 1900.

III The Players

1 F. de Dainville, 'Lieux de théâtre et salles d'action dans les collèges de Jésuites de l'ancienne France', *Revue d'Histoire du Théâtre*, 1950, p. 185.

2 Vossler, *Lope de Vega*, op. cit., p. 194 ff.

3 In a satirical *loa* addressed to The Public, quoted in Vossler, *op. cit.*, p. 195.

4 No woman appeared on a public stage in England until 1656, when on 23 May a Mrs Coleman appeared in Davenant's *Siege of Rhodes*: see Kindermann, *op. cit.*, vol. III, p. 159.

5 Gunther Schöne, *Tausend Jahre deutsches Theater*, Munich 1962, p. 34.

6 She was bold enough to demonstrate her determination to see Hans Wurst banned from the stage by publicly burning him in effigy in 1737. But even when Lessing's 'straight' literary comedy *Minna von Barnhelm* was performed in Hamburg thirty years later the programme included performances by acrobats in the intervals.

7 He gave Lessing's tragedy *Emilia Galotti* its first production in Berlin on 6 April 1772 and in his later years made great efforts on behalf of German opera.

8 Act 2, scene 2.

9 Act 3, scene 2.

10 Gerard de Lairesse (died 1711) was also an etcher and painter. His decorations for the Nieuwe Schouwburg in Amsterdam were famous.

11 Lessing, too, in the third and fourth articles in his *Hamburgische Dramaturgie*, dated 8 and 12 May 1767, gives analyses of dramatic technique and quotes Eckhof as an example for others to emulate. 'He used his hands more sparingly than they do in mime, but no less effectively … He made no gesture that did not add meaning or emphasis.' Hogarth told actors to learn to move their hands in all directions so beautifully that graceful movement would become natural to their arms. Diderot refers to Francesco Riccoboni's *L'Art du théâtre* (1750). Prior to that there were *Dell'arte rappresentativa* (1728) and *Pensées sur la déclamation* (1737) by his elder brother Ludovico Riccoboni. Among other works *Le comédien* (1747) by Rémond de Sainte-Albine should also be mentioned.

12 R. Krauss, *Das Stuttgarter Hoftheater und seine Zeit*, Stuttgart 1908, and *Herzog Karl Eugen von Württemberg und seine Zeit*, Esslingen 1907–9. There were 'artists' classes' in which were placed the children of court artists and of lower ranking offi-cials, sometimes against the will of their parents. An institute for music and mime was also founded.

13 G. H. Reese, *Studien und Beiträge zur Geschichte der eng-lischen Schauspielkunst im Zeitalter Shakespeares*, Diss., Jena 1911, p. 6 ff.

14 Charles Simon Favart (1710–52), *Mémoires et correspond-ence littéraire*, 3 vols, Paris 1808.

15 On the history of the puppet theatre see also Hans Netzle, *Das Süddeutsche Wandermarionettentheater*, Munich 1938.

IV The Plays

1 The Latin plays, modelled on Terence, of the nun Hrotsvita of Gandersheim (*c.* 935 to after 975), were an isolated pheno-menon.

2 There were also the *autos de nacimiento* to celebrate Christ-mas, and *autos* for other Christian feasts.

3 He started as an actor and became the leader of a *garnacha* (see p. 46). He became famous for his *pasos*, a form which developed into the *entremés*, realistic, down-to-earth scenes of ordinary life with lively, witty dialogue, relying on comic situations, rather than sustained plot.

4 Vossler, *Lope de Vega*, p. 2. His work is reckoned to consist of between 1500 and 1800 *comedias*, 400 Corpus Christi plays, as well as *entremeses* and *loas*. The titles of at least 770 are known; surviving texts number about 470.

5 There survive about 120 *comedias*, 80 *autos* and 20 smaller pieces by him.

6 Karl Vossler, 'Calderón', *Romania*, Leipzig 1950, p. 208.

7 *El desdén con el desdén* by Moreto y Cabaña (1618–1669), one of Calderón's circle, was the model for Molière's *Princesse d'Élide*; Roman de la Cruz Cano y Olmedilla (1731–1794) translated and adapted French and Italian comedies, but towards the end of his life reverted to the traditional Spanish forms, *sainetes*, *pasos* and *entremeses*.

8 *King Arthur* shows Dryden to be the chief exponent of the baroque drama in England.

9 In his treatise *De l'art de la tragédie* (1572). His neo-classical Renaissance dramas were strongly influenced by Seneca.

10 Philippe Quinault (1635–88) is known principally as Lully's librettist, but his plays, with their sensitive treatment of emotion, were not without influence on Racine.

11 In the *Hamburgische Dramaturgie* Lessing makes an attack on his views in detail. Voltaire's plays were frequently per-formed in his lifetime. From 1753 onwards he personally directed productions of French plays in Mannheim and Schwet-zingen.

12 The traditional Oberufer nativity play, for instance, owes its final form to the time of the early Reformation, but its roots are clearly much older. Some of its elements can only derive from classical Greek drama. The strict scansion of the *Knittelvers*, with four strong beats to a line, is late mediaeval, but much of the material is older and is found all over Europe. The devil is allowed to improvise, there are songs scattered throughout the action, costumes are changed on stage and the scenes are changed by the simplest methods. The devil performs a comic dance to provide light relief. The oral tradition persists in the southern and eastern areas of the old Holy Roman Empire, along the Slovakian and Hungarian marches, where the plays are still performed on primitive wooden platforms. The most famous of these plays, produced even today entirely by local efforts, are those of Oberammergau and Erl in the Inn valley.

13 Writers influenced by him include Jakob Balde (1604–68) and Jakob Mason (1606–81). Mason's dramatic theories were important for the development of the Jesuit drama in the seven-teenth and early eighteenth centuries.

14 His theoretical work *Von der deutschen Poeterey* (1624) was of greater importance for German drama.

15 See Lessing, *Hamburgische Dramaturgie*, article 20, 7 July 1767.

16 Recorded by the Deutsche Grammophon-Gesellschaft in their Archive series, Research period II, The central Middle Ages, Series A: Troubadours, trouvères and minnesingers.

17 The manuscript, from Artois, dating from the second half of the thirteenth century, is in the Bibliothèque Nationale in Paris.

18 In his *Annals of Opera*, Cambridge 1940, Loewenberg puts *Dafne* firmly under the heading 1597, but in his note on the performance he inclines towards January or February 1598 in the Gregorian calendar, which would have been 1597 in the Julian calendar, whose New Year came in March.

19 Performed for the marriage of Maria de' Medici and Henry IV of France in the Palazzo Pitti in Florence. Recorded on Amadeo, Arcophon series, no. 1, AVRS 5002/3.

20 It tells the story of the judgment of Paris and the dispute between Aphrodite, Hera and Pallas Athene. A description can be found in A. Schöne, *Deutsche Literatur in Texte und Zeugnisse*, vol. III, Barock, p. 73 ff. Antonio Draghi (1635–1700) composed numerous operas in the style of Cesti and, like him, went from Venice to the court of Leopold I in Vienna.

21 He came to the French court at the age of twelve. Both Mazarin and Louis XIV were his patrons. Made *Surintendant de la musique de la chambre du roi* in 1661 and *Maître de la musique de la famille royale* in 1662.

22 Lully was awarded *lettres patentes* by Louis XIV which gave him the license for opera and for the founding of an Académie Royale de musique. He thus had control of all performances of opera in both Paris and the provinces; none could be given without his permission. Lully had a librettist of literary merit in Philippe Quinault, who had the gift of reworking the material of classical tragedy in a style acceptable to contempo-rary French taste.

23 He began his career as a choirboy at the court of Landgrave Maurice the Learned of Hesse, worked as an organist while studying in Venice, then went to the court of John George I, Elector of Saxony.

24 See H. J. Moser, *Heinrich Schütz*, Cassel 1936, p. 342.

25 Theatres in Leipzig, Brunswick and Hanover all began to present German operas at this time.

26 Goethe in the *Italienische Reise*, Bericht aus Rom, 1787, says: 'Remember the age of innocence in German opera, when a simple intermezzo like Pergolesi's *Serva padrona* aroused interest and applause.'

27 Helmut Wirth, Introduction to *La Serva padrona* accompanying the Deutsche Grammophon Gesellschaft recording, Archive, Research period VIII, series B.

28 Rameau had opened a private school for composition in Paris. One of his pupils, Madame de la Popelinière, and her husband introduced his work to Louis XV in their private theatre. Louis appointed him *Compositeur de musique de la chambre*.

29 Translator's note: the word *Singspiel* was used in this sense from the middle of the eighteenth century. Before that it meant any kind of opera with a German text.

30 He directed all the productions on special occasions in the Favorita palace, in the Redoutensaal in Vienna, and later in Schönbrunn.

31 Hasse went to Naples in 1722, then spent thirty years in the service of the Saxon court. He visited Italy, London, Munich, Paris, Warsaw and Berlin for performances of his works. He finally settled in Venice.

32 Günther Schöne, *op. cit.*, p. 102.

33 His librettist was the indefatigable Giambattista Lorenzi (1719–1805), director of the court opera in Naples, who wrote nearly one hundred texts.

34 Goethe says on the subject of the *Singspiel* in his *Italienische Reise, Bericht aus Rom*, 1787, 'All our efforts to lose ourselves in unsophisticated simplicity went for nothing when Mozart came on the scene. *The Seraglio* took the theatre by storm and the piece at which we had worked so hard [*Scherz, List und Rache* with music by Keyser] sank without trace.'

V The Stages

1 Ludwig Pfandl, *Spanische Kultur und Sitte*, Munich 1924, p. 162.

2 Karl Vossler, *Lope de Vega*, p. 196, in a letter to Pablo Bonnet.

3 Woodcuts in the Lyons edition of Terence's works (1493) show an early stage in the development of scenery on the 'Terentian' stage. – Schöne, *Tausend Jahre deutsches Theater*, p. 29. A woodcut of a scene from a French farce of 1580, in *L'Ancien Théâtre en images* by Jean de Gourmont, shows an even simpler setting.

4 This can still be seen in the best-preserved Roman theatre, at Orange, in southern France.

5 H. Tintelnot, *Barocktheater und barocke Kunst*, Berlin 1939, p. 4.

6 The folk theatre in Kiefersfelden on the Inn still uses a rudimentary from of *periaktoi*, two-faced wooden frames, turned by hand.

7 In the opera house in Hanover, the forestage could by 1690 be divided from the rear part by a partition. There was a permanent set on the rear part of the stage, like the one in the Teatro Olimpico. The forestage had six sets of wings.

8 Furttenbach, *Architectura recreationis*.

9 Johann Beer, *Die kurzweiligen Sommertäge* (see Chapter 2, note 6) Chapter V, p. 577.

10 G. Schöne, *op. cit.*, p. 43.

11 Invented in 1646 by a Jesuit, Athanasius Kirchner.

12 First employed in the Teatro dei SS. Giovanni e Paolo in Venice. Designed sets for *La finta pazza* in the Teatro Novissimo. In 1642 his sets for Vincenzo Nolfi's *Bellerofonte*, for Ferdinand II of Tuscany, involved the first use of his system for changing the wings. In 1644 he did *Polissa e Niso* for Cardinal Barberini.

13 Shortly before his death he was again engaged by Louis XIV to build the theatre in Versailles.

14 He built 'astonishing' perspective models in churches for special feasts, for example a *Marriage at Cana*, packed with figures, in 1685. Other such models are illustrated in his *Perspectiva*.

15 *Theatrum Europäum* (see Chapter 1, note 8) gives a detailed account of the technical devices and the machinery for transformations.

16 A wooden construction was put up beside the Capuchin monastery, with two tiers and seating for 'several thousand' people.

17 Franz Hadamovsky, *Die Familie Galli-Bibiena in Wien*, Vienna, 1962.

18 He directed the festival performances in the Teatro da Ajuda and in the Opera do Tejo.

19 His *Instruction in der Teatralischen Architektur und Mechanique*, 1760, is also important. It expounds the fundamental principles of eighteenth century theatrical architecture. See also T. Krogh, *Danske Teaterbilleder fra det 18de Jarhundrede*, Copenhagen 1932.

20 H. C. Lancaster, *Mémoire sur Mahelot et autres décorateurs de l'Hôtel de Bourgogne*, Paris 1920.

21 His principal designs are collected in *L'Oeuvre de Jean Bérain, recueillie par les soins du sieur Thuret*.

22 Heinrich Kreisel, *Veitshöchheim*, Munich 1964, *Plan D-F*.

23 Luisa Hager, *Nymphenburg*, Munich n.d., ill. g, m.

VI The Theatres

1 Lionello Puppi, *Il Teatro Olimpico*, Vicenza 1963.

2 Renovated in 1716 by Filipo Juvarra. The paintings which have in part survived to the present day probably date from then. The theatre has been rebuilt after its destruction in the Second World War.

3 The first work performed there was *Alessio*, with music by Stefano Lando and libretto by Cardinal Giulio Rospigliosi.

4 The Teatro San Apollinare saw the production of eleven new works in the short period 1651–60. Forty-nine operas

received new productions at the Teatro dei SS. Giovanni e Paolo, opened in 1639, closed in 1715 and demolished in 1748. The Teatro San Moise, also opened in 1639, later became a puppet-theatre and is now a cinema. The wooden Teatro Novissimo, open for a very short period in the seventeenth century, was re-opened in the middle of the eighteenth century and remained active until the fall of the Republic. The theatres of San Salvatore (opened 1661), San Angelo (1677) and San Giovanni Crisostomo (1678) all saw intense operatic activity in the seventeenth century, but were later closed. In the eighteenth century, Venice had only seven theatres.

5 This theatre was restored on several occasions, in 1803, 1900 and 1955, but the basic structure can be regarded as the original.

6 A. E. Brinckmann, *Baukunst des 17. und 18. Jahrhunderts in den romanischen Ländern*, p. 147.

7 It was extensively altered in 1830.

8 *Cf.* the *Enciclopedia dello Spettacolo*, Rome 1954–.

9 Built under Charles III by G. A. Medrano. Restored by A. Niccolino after a fire in 1816.

10 A horseshoe in shape, its decoration was completely altered during the nineteenth century. The old division of the tiers into boxes was retained.

11 Renovated several times in the nineteenth and twentieth centuries.

12 He also built the theatre in Monza in 1782.

13 The illustration reproduces only a part of the original painting in the Louvre, and of the interior of the Teatro Constanza where the concert was given. See K. M. Komma, *Musikgeschichte in Bildern*, Stuttgart 1961, ill. 399.

14 See the *Enciclopedia dello Spectacolo* under Milan. An eighteenth century engraving by Marc Antonio Dal Ré shows the theatre during a celebration of the birth of Archduke Peter Leopold of Austria. Reproduced in Kindermann, *op. cit.*, vol. V, p. 411.

15 Reproduced in Kindermann, *op. cit.*, vol. V, p. 417.

16 See the *Enciclopedia dello Spectacolo* under Bologna.

17 Planned for the marriage in 1666 of Leopold I and the Spanish Infanta Margareta. Its enormous size prevented its completion in time.

18 Kindermann, *op. cit.*, vol. III, p. 496.

19 Kindermann, *op. cit.*, vol. V, p. 16.

20 Josef Anton Stranitzki (1676–1726) became director in 1711. It burnt down in 1761, was rebuilt in 1763, and altered several times after that.

21 Performances of opera had been given in the park since 1673 and continued during the eighteenth century. In 1742 performances were given in the park in a wooden theatre. Performances became more frequent after the building of the theatre in the palace.

22 Hohenberg also provided decorations for the smaller Redoutensäle and for the theatre in the Hofburg in Vienna for special occasions.

23 The seats are modern. According to a water-colour by Alt (reproduced in Kindermann, *op. cit.*, vol. V, p. 19) on some occasions benches were arranged in a similar manner to that seen in our illustration (*p. 167*) of the Palazzo Reale in Naples, or the *parterre* was used as part of the scene.

24 On the left-hand side there is a *bas-relief* of Pater Marcus Lindermayer (1723–83), whose plays in the Upper Austrian dialect made a large contribution to the reputation of this theatre.

25 Arthur Kutscher, *Vom Salzburger Barocktheater zu den Salzburger Festspielen*, Düsseldorf 1939.

26 He had been sent to study in Italy.

27 Kindermann, *op. cit.*, vol. III, p. 486.

28 Oskar Schürer, *Prag*, Munich 1935, pp. 271, 282–4.

29 Before the opera house was built there were already five public theatres. There is a plan of the second opera house in Kindermann, *op. cit.*, vol. V, p. 589.

30 Goethe, *Dichtung und Wahrheit*. See also M. Fürstenau, *Zur Geschichte der Musik und des Theaters am Hofe der Kurfürsten von Sachsen und Könige von Polen*, Dresden 1862.

31 Trained in Milan, active in Warsaw as a stage designer 1790–4, he built a new theatre in Lemberg in 1779.

32 A smaller theatre for four hundred people burnt down in 1779; a new one was designed by Michael Stöger and opened within ten months. M. Horányi, *Das Esterhazysche Feenreich, Beitrag zur ungarischen Theatergeschichte des achtzehnten Jahrhunderts*, Budapest 1959.

33 Illustrated on p. 58 of *Burgen und Schlösser in der Tschechoslowakei*, Prague 1962.

34 After training in Rome and Paris, Tischbein began his career as a theatrical painter in Wabern, Wilhelmstal and Weissenstein. The Bolshoi Theatre in St Petersburg burnt down in 1811. For an illustration see Kindermann, *op. cit.*, vol. V, p. 577.

35 It may have been a little earlier, 1782–5. Quarenghi was Catherine II's favourite architect. His style showed strong Palladian tendencies.

36 Illustrated in *Prestigieux théâtres de France, de l'Académie Royale à la Salle Garnier* by André Boll, Paris 1960. It was the fifth opera house in the Tuileries.

37 Olivier Perrin, *La Comédie Française 1680–1960*, Paris 1960. A. Schönberger & H. Söhner, *Die Welt des Rokoko*, Munich 1962, ill. 166; English translation by D. Woodward, *The Age of Rococo*.

38 See above, Chapters 1 and 5.

39 Rose-Marie Langlois, *L'Opéra de Versailles*, Paris 1958, p. 22ff.

40 It is not quite certain who the architect was when it was rebuilt. It may have been Charles François Rolland Leverloys (1716–1772) or Robert de Virelois, together with Oger, the 'architecte et inspecteur des bâtiments de la Ville de Metz'.

41 Including Whitefriars (1576), Newington (1580), the Rose (1585), the Hope (1585), the Paris Garden playhouse (after 1588), the Swan (1595) and the Fortune (1599).

42 Other London theatres of the same, or a very similar design were the Curtain, built in 1577, next door to The Theatre; the Rose, built by Philip Henslowe on Bankside in 1587; the Swan, which stood from c. 1595 to 1614 and was the largest of the four theatres built at about the same time, a twelve-sided construction with two exterior staircases and a roof to cover the three galleries; the Hope (1585) originally a bear-pit but used as a theatre from 1613 to 1619; and the Red Bull, from c. 1605, the first to re-open at the end of the Commonwealth, in 1659, but closed in 1660.

43 Again re-built in 1649, finally demolished in 1662.

44 T. Overskon, *Den Danske Skueplads*, Copenhagen 1854.

45 A very early portent of the rise of national theatres. The time was not yet ripe in Denmark; after several financial disasters it had to close in 1728.

46 Founded with the encouragement of Holberg and Count Rantzau.

47 It continued in use for a comparatively long time: as late as 1773 it was restored by J. E. Rehn. See also Agne Beijer, 'Le Théâtre en Suède jusqu'à la mort de Gustave III', *Revue d'Histoire du Théâtre*, 1956, p. 140ff.

48 At first the only permanent professional company in Sweden was a French troupe, performing the French classics in the theatres built by Adelcrantz in the Drottningholm and Ulriksdal palaces.

49 Gustav III was murdered at a masked ball in the Stockholm opera house in 1792. An earlier theatre at Gripsholm was built in the tower in 1773 and was altered and enlarged by Erik Palmstedt in 1782.

50 Hans Hartleb, *Deutschlands erster Theaterbau*, Berlin 1936.

51 Furttenbach published a series of theoretical works which exercised a considerable influence on German architects: *Newes Itinerarium Italiae*, Ulm 1626; *Architectura recreationis*, Ulm 1640; *Architectura civilis*, Ulm 1628; *Mannhaffter Kunstspiegel*, Augsburg 1663. See also M. Berthold, *Joseph Furttenbach*, Diss., Munich 1951.

52 Completed in 1657, with the assistance of Marx Schinnagl. H. Bolongaro-Crevenna, *L'Arpe festante, die Münchner Oper, 1651–1825*, Munich 1963.

53 Günther Schöne, *Tausend Jahre deutsches Theater*, Munich 1962, p. 45 and p. 84.

54 He also designed the opera houses in Amsterdam and Leipzig.

55 Luisa Hager, *Markgräfliches Opernhaus*, Bayreuth 1966.

56 Hildegard Steinmetz & Johann Lachner, *Das Alte Residenztheater zu München, Cuvilliéstheater*, Starnberg n. d.; Herbert Brunner, *Altes Residenztheater, Cuvilliéstheater in München*, Munich 1963.

57 Destroyed in the bombardment of the city in 1795.

58 Pulled down by King Frederick of Württemberg in 1809 and reconstructed in Schloss Monrepos near Ludwigsburg.

59 H. A. Frenzel, 'Brandenburg-preussische Schlosstheater', *Schriften der Gesellschaft für Theatergeschichte*, vol. 59, Berlin 1959.

60 In 1774 the court issued a contract to Eckhof to perform there, but it was withdrawn in 1779.

Notes on the Illustrations

Monochrome plates

1 FILIPPO GAGLIARDI. *Carnival in honour of Queen Christina, Rome, 1956. Oil on canvas. Musei di Roma, Rome.* A number of stands for the spectators were built in front of the Palazzo Barberini. The protagonists included knights, Amazons, Heracles and Phoebus. Over 200 models were made by Filippo Lauri. See: *Christina, Queen of Sweden*, catalogue of an exhibition held in the National Museum, Stockholm 1966, item 706.

2 LUDOVICO OTTAVIO BURNACINI *Carnival float, Vienna.* The animals and animal heads show this to be the float of the Butchers' Guild.

3 ANON. *Sketch for festival costume, Paris, seventeenth century. Bibliothèque Nationale, Paris.* This shows the sort of costume worn by horsemen in court festivities all over Europe.

4 *Roman theatre with trick fountains, Schloss Hellbrunn near Salzburg, 1613–19.* Hellbrunn was visited by many distinguished guests in the 17th century: the Emperors Ferdinand II and Leopold I, the electors of Bavaria and Cologne, the Grand Duke of Tuscany and others. The centre-piece of this horseshoe-shaped theatre is the so-called Princes' Table, with ten marble stools through which fine jets of water can be shot. The figure in the niche of the rear wall is a Roman emperor. The Roma Victrix above it was by the Salzburg court sculptor Johann Waldburger. Neptune sits at the entrance.

5 HYACINTHE RIGAUD. *Louis XV of France in his coronation robes. Musée du Château, Versailles.* Rigaud (1659–1743) was court painter to Louis XIV, the Regent Philippe d'Orléans and Louis XV, and portrayer *par excellence* of the grand official pose. Louis XV, son of Louis de France, duc de Bourgogne, and Marie-Adelaide of Savoy, great-grandson of Louis XIV, called *le Bien-Aimé*, was five years old when crowned in 1715.

6 GIOVANNI PAOLO PANNINI. *Aquatic festival on the Piazza Navona, Rome 1756. Niedersächsische Landesgalerie, Hannover.* The Piazza Navona was deliberately flooded for a *corso*, in order to offer a novel entertainment to an aristocratic audience. In this picture there are no gondolas but two rings of carriages driving round the square in contrary directions. On the left is the Palazzo Panfili; it was a member of the Panfili family, Innocent X, who had this square laid out and built the church of Sant' Agnese. Cardinal Benedetto Panfili was Handel's patron in Rome. Pannini (1696–1765) was famous not only for his realistic paintings of the court life of his age, but also for his designs for theatres and arenas for special occasions. His architectural drawings are extremely accurate.

7 JEAN MICHEL MOREAU LE JEUNE. *Festival with illuminations.* An open-air festival at night, with all the decorations picked out in lights was a favourite court entertainment.

8 GIOVANNI PAOLO PANNINI *Concert in honour of the birth of the Dauphin, Paris 1729, detail. Louvre, Paris.* The child in question was the son of Louis XV and the father of Louis XVI. This allegorical scene was built as a background for the cantata *La Contesa de Numi* by Metastasio and Leonardo Vinci, performed in the Teatro Constanza. The orchestra plays in the clouds, the singers are seated in the middle of the scene, and the *continuo* players are on either side of them.

9 *Sledge belonging to Frederick II of Prussia, eighteenth century. Neues Palais, Potsdam.* There is only one seat, for a lady; a gentleman would stand behind her.

10 *Sledging party on the Mehlmarkt, Vienna, eighteenth century. Theatermuseum, Munich.* Peepshow scene. Horses, in fine harness and led by footmen, pull the sledges in which the ladies are enthroned, showing themselves off to the best advantage. Peepshows were very popular at this time, and were frequently found in private houses. Theatrical scenes were a common subject.

11 *Sledge belonging to Maria Theresa of Austria. Wagenburg, Schönbrunn, Vienna.* Covered with intricate carving of shells, foliage and *rocaille*.

12 ANON. *Performance of Gluck's 'Il Parnasso Confuso' in the Zeremoniensaal, Schönbrunn, Vienna 1765. Leopoldinischer Trakt, Präsidentschaftskanzlei, Hofburg, Vienna.* The performance shown was given on the occasion of the marriage of Joseph II and Maria Josefa of Bavaria. The performers were courtiers. Italian was still the chief language for opera.

13 JEAN MICHEL MOREAU LE JEUNE. *At the door of the box, 1777.* From *Monument du costume physique et moral de la fin du dixhuitième siècle*, Neuwied sur le Rhin, Chez la Société Typographique, 1789. Engraved by De Launay le Jeune, 1777. This plate was included in the complete edition of Moreau le jeune's work with earlier series of engravings. After a year in St Petersburg, Moreau le jeune (1741–1814) returned to Paris in 1759, became court engraver in succession to Charles-Nicolas Cochin, and a member of the Académie Royale in 1789. Under the revolution he became a member of the fine art commission. His work numbers some 2000 pictures of social life and book illustrations.

14 *Group outside the Chinesisches Haus, Sanssouci, Potsdam 1755.* The so-called tea-house was built in 1755 by Johann Gottfried Büring, in the popular eighteenth-century style of *chinoiserie*. This group is in gilded stone.

15 *Peepshow picture showing Théâtre de la foire on the Place Vendôme, Paris eighteenth century. Coloured engraving.* A peepshow scene showing two booths with the *Jeu du Sieur Gaudon* and the *Jeu du Sieur Nicole* on the Place Vendôme during the Foire St-Ovide. The booths are made of wood, with galleries and balconies. On the right is a toy-stall.

16 *Theatre (Théâtre chez les Nicolet) at the Foire St Germain, Paris late eighteenth century.* Inscription: *Un Prince bienfaisant pour récréer Paris a rétabli ce lieu digne séjour des Ris.* ('For Paris' diversion, a benevolent Prince set up this place, worthy home of laughter.') This elegant building is in contrast to the temporary booths on the Place Vendôme in pl. 15.

17 ANON. *The Comedien-Haus, Nuremberg c. 1730. Coloured copper engraving.* From *Angenehme Bilderlust*, Nuremberg, c. 1730. A travelling company has set up a stage with proper scenery and wings in the courtyard of the fencing school. The inscription is part of the text of the play shown:

Die zwey Acteurs:
– *Ach liebster Printz! Wenn meine Schmertzen*
Euch gar nicht gehen mehr zu Hertzen,
so bin ich auch im Leben todt.
– *Prinzessin schweigt von eurer Liebe,*
Ihr setzet mich durch solche Triebe,
Und Euch zugleich in grosse Noth.
Die Vier Narren:
Wer uns nur sieht, der muss gleich lachen,
bloss weil wir das vorstellig machen,
wofür man uns doch selbst nicht hält.
Am Ende: Wenn man es betrachtet,
so ist dies Spiel, zwar ohnverachtet,
mit Narrheit meistentheil bestellt.

The two actors:
– Oh dearest Prince! But if your ear
My yearning sorrow will not hear,
Down will I fall and here expire!
– Princess, be silent with your plea.
Your passion places you and me
In dreadful need and peril dire.
The four fools:
You mock our antics, for you know
We are not what we seem in show;
We players do but act the play.
The end: you will in truth observe
Although your scorn we don't deserve
'Twas mostly folly all the way.'

18 ANON. *Popular theatre on the Anger, Munich, c. 1750. Theatermuseum, Munich.* This theatre on a common in Munich is much less sophisticated than the one in Nuremberg twenty years earlier.

19 DANIEL RABEL *Entrance of the esperlucattes. Water colour, early seventeenth century. Water colour. Louvre, Paris.* Masked dancers in a country dance.

20 LUDOVICO OTTAVIO BURNACINI *Grotesque masks and allegorical beasts, late seventeenth century.* There is a gruesome relish in these portrayals of the depths of human nature by deformities, bestial eyes, snouts and unrestrained outbursts of feelings.

21-22 LUDOVICO OTTAVIO BURNACINI *Male and female grotesques, late seventeenth century.* The comic, female grotesques, with their bawdy humour, were also played by men, who kept their moustaches for added comic effect. The squabbling couple, the scold and the clown with his cudgel are drawn in effective bold colours and simple lines.

23-24 LUDOVICO OTTAVIO BURNACINI *Spanish court costume. Male and female figures, late seventeenth century.* The lady and the nobleman stand in stiff, rich costumes, proudly conscious of their rank and dignity. The court of Vienna remained under the influence of Spain longer than other countries because of the Habsburg family ties. There are still some remnants of Spanish court dress in the traditional black wedding garments of Alpine regions and in the tall black hats worn by peasant women in the region of the Inn valley and the Chiemsee.

25 JEAN BÉRAIN (ATTRIB.) *Turkish costumes. End of seventeenth century.* Authenticity in costume became current only in the eighteenth century.

26-28 JEAN BÉRAIN *Ballet costumes: Neptune, Hymen, dancer.* Bérain (cf. note on ills on p. 48) developed further the trends started in France by Torelli, but showing greater independence of Italy. He designed sets and costumes for Lully's works. These elegant costumes allow the feet and legs greater freedom.

29 JEAN BÉRAIN (ATTRIB.) *Lady in court dress. End of seventeenth century.* The Spanish ruff has gone, the décolleté is very low. The stiffness of the horizontal bands is relieved by ornamental trimmings.

30-32 ANON. (SCHOOL OF BÉRAIN?) *French designs for Pan, or a faun, and dancers with castanets.* These costumes are at once more delicate and more elaborate. Female dancers, too, now wear tossing plumes.

Pls 26-32 *are all in the Bibliothèque Nationale, Paris.*

33 NICOLAS DE LARGILLIÈRE *Anna-Marie Chateauneuf-Duclos in the title role of Corneille's 'Ariane', 1714. Engraving by L. Desplaces, 1714.* The original painting is in the Foyer des Artistes in the Comédie Française, Paris. Artists in a particular role became a common form of portraiture, with a scene suggested in the background.

34 JEAN ANTOINE WATTEAU *Love in the Comédie française, c. 1720. Gemäldegalerie Berlin-Dahlem.* Watteau (1684-1721), a pupil of A. Gérin, was admitted to the Académie Royale as a *painter of fêtes galantes*. His pictures of theatrical life are masterpieces. In this picture, Bacchus is drinking with a huntsman, a shepherd and shepherdess are about to dance, with actors on one side and musicians on the other, playing flutes, fiddles and bagpipes.

35 JEAN RAOUX *Mlle Prévost as a Bacchante, c. 1723. Musée des Beaux-Arts, Tours.* Against a mythical landscape, the dancer portrays Philomèle in the opera of that name by Roy and Lacoste.

36 NICOLAS LANCRET *Scene from 'Le Glorieux' by P. N. Destouches, c. 1738. Engraving by N. Dupuis.* Lancret (1690-1745) became a member of the Académie Royale in 1719, like Watteau, for a painting of a *fête galante*. It is sometimes hard to distinguish between his scenes of the pleasure-loving society of the Regency and the early years of Louis XV's reign and those of Watteau. He also liked to paint theatrical scenes. *Le Glorieux* was first performed in 1732 and was performed in Germany as *Der Ruhmredige* in 1745. The painting shows Grandval as Valère, Quinault Dufresne as the Comte de Tufière and Mlle Grandval as Isabelle in Act III, scene 3.

37 ELIAS GOTTLOB HAUSMANN *Friederike Caroline Neuber, alias 'Die Neuberin'.* Engraving of a painting made in 1744 when the actress was forty-seven.

38 ANTON RAPHAEL MENGS *The singer Domenico Annibali, 1750. Pinacoteca di Brera, Milan.* Annibali (c. 1700-79) was a famous castrato who lived in Rome, Venice, Dresden and London. This portrait shows him not in any particular role but as himself. It is typical of the early portraits of Mengs, a famous artist and court painter in Dresden and Madrid.

39 JOHN JOSEPH ZOFFANY *Garrick, Aicken and Bransby in 'Lethe', 1760. City of Birmingham Museum and Art Gallery.* Pictures of scenes from stage productions were very popular in England, too, in the second half of the eighteenth century, and Zoffany (1734?-1810), a German by birth, was patronized by Garrick as a master of the theatrical scene. *Lethe* was a farce by Garrick and the picture shows Garrick, on the left, as Lord Chalkstone, Aicken as Bowman and Bransby as Aesop.

40 FERDINAND DIETZ *Minerva, Veitshöchheim, near Würzburg c. 1768. Sandstone.* Gods were represented in art in the same costumes that they had on stage.

41-42 *Costumes in the theatre museum at Drottningholm.* The jewels that covered court dress were reproduced in gold thread and spangled embroidery on stage costumes in the second half of the eighteenth century.

43 G. SHEMCHUGOV *Russian serf actress as Eliana in Grétry's 'Mariages Samnites', c. 1770.* Even a serf actress could be held in sufficiently high esteem to be painted in this stiff ostentatious costume with helmet and spear.

44 *Russian stage helmets.* These helmets are almost functional without the usual coloured ostrich feathers. Probably used in the eighteenth century serf theatre.

45 SEBASTIAN LE CLERC *Mlle Clairon as Idamé in 'L'Orphelin de Chine', 1779.* Costume by Sarrazin Costumier Ord're des Princes. Engraving by Dupin from *26e Suite d'Habillements à la mode en 1779*, Bibliothèque de l'Arsenal, Paris. Mlle Clairon was considered the greatest tragedienne in France. Her private life consisted of a sequence of affairs with rich and famous men; on stage she was, like Mme Favart, a pioneer of authenticity in costume.

46 LOUIS CARROGIS DE CARMONTELLE *Pas de deux from the opera 'Sylvie'.* Engraving by J. T. Tillard. Bibliothèque de l'Arsenal, Paris. The dancers are M. de Dauberval and Mlle Allard. There is an inscription to explain the scene:
Sur sa fierté la Nymphe se repose
Son amant perd déja l'espoir de l'attendrir
Mais elle le regarde en songeant à le fuir,
Nymphe qui rêve aux tourmens qu'elle cause
Touche au moment de les guérir.
('The nymph relents not in her proud disdain,
Her lover, downcast, fears his suit is vain.
She flees, but turns to look at him again.
The nymph who dreams of torments she inspires
Is almost ready to assuage the fires.')

47 *Commedia dell'arte: Three masks.* Bibliothèque de l'Arsenal, Paris. Fine leather masks were worn in the *commedia dell'arte* from its very beginning until the eighteenth century, during which they were gradually abandoned.

48 ANON. (FRENCH ARTIST, PERHAPS UNDER DUTCH INFLUENCE) *Commedia dell'arte: 'I Comici gelosi' with Isabella Andreini. c. 1580. Hôtel Carnavalet, Paris.* Isabella Andreini (1562-1604) was acclaimed by court society both as actress and writer, and *I Comici*

gelosi are heard was mentioned as early as 1575 in France and Vienna. In this scene Isabella and her maid are being closely watched by the jealous Pantalone. A lover in the background is trying to smuggle a message to her by his servant. A *zanni* stands behind Pantalone. Flaminio Scala, for many years principal of the Gelosi, published a collection of *canevas* (scenarios) in Venice in 1611 under the title *Il Teatro delle favole rappresentative overo la recreazione comica, boscareccia e tragica.*

49 ALESSANDRO SCALZI *Fools' Staircase in the castle of Trausnitz, near Landshut, Bavaria. Fresco.* See also p. 103.

50 FRANÇOIS BUNEL LE JEUNE *The Commedia dell'arte at the court of Henry of Navarre. c. 1578-1590. Musée de Béziers.* A classic *commedia dell'arte* situation. Vigilant old Pantalone, with his dagger at the ready, is distracted by having his beard pulled by the masked *zanni*, Brighella, while his mistress is passed a *billet doux* by her lover. One of her servants crowns Pantalone with a cuckold's horns.

51 JEAN ANTOINE WATTEAU *Love in the Théâtre Italien. c. 1720. Gemäldegalerie Berlin-Dahlem.* This shows a troupe of *commedia dell'arte* players in typical attitudes: coquettish Isabella with her pert maid Columbine, Pantalone, old and bent, Mezzetino with the guitar, Crispin with the torch, which is dazzling Arlecchino.

52 FRANZ ANTON BUSTELLI *Commedia dell'arte figurines: Ottavio, Isabella and Julia.* The moulds for these figures were made c. 1760; these are modern castings by the Staatliche Porzellanmanufaktur Nymphenburg. The original Octavio is in a private collection, the Isabella and Julia are in the Nationalmuseum, Munich. Bustelli (1723-63) was a model-maker at the Neudeck-Nymphenburg factory from 1754. The grace, refinement, elegance and colour of his work make it the highest achievement of rococo porcelain. (See also Plate VII.)

53 JOHANN JOACHIM KAENDLER *Harlequin and Columbine. 1744. Rijksmuseum, Amsterdam.* Kaendler (1706-75) was a model-maker at the Meissen factory from 1731, became master modeller in 1733 and Hofkommissar in 1749. He is regarded as the founder of porcelain modelling in Europe. These *commedia dell'arte* figures are characterized by boisterous *joie de vivre* and a sense of the comic.

54 ANDREAS PIRROT *Harlequin's entry into Venice,* tapestry in the *Residenz, Würzburg, c. 1745.* Wool and silk. The Fürstbischöfliche Manufaktur in Würzburg was founded in 1721 by Prince Bishop Johann Philip Franz von Schönborn. In its best period, from about 1730 to 1750, it produced grotesques, *chinoiserie* and several tapestries with scenes from the *commedia dell'arte* probably designed by the court painter Johann Rudolf Byss, and by Johann Joseph Scheubel, the elder, painter to the court of Bamberg. Harlequin and Columbine are being carried across the Piazza San Marco on a litter, while Pantalone, Crispin, Mezzetino, Capitano Spavente and the ladies are dancing round them, joking and singing.

55 *Marionettes: Brighella and Arlecchino. Venetian, 18th century. Collection Duchatre, Paris.* There are very few surviving marionettes of this age, and accurate dating is very difficult.

56 MARTIN ENGELBRECHT *Puppet theatre (Policinello). Augsburg c. 1730. Coloured copper engraving.* From the sequence *Nahrungsart von leichtem Sinn* ('Lighthearted refreshment'). The superscription *Des Policinello Abenteuerliche Reise* ('Policinello's adventurous journey') is the play's title. The puppeteer is peeping through the curtains from above the stage, so the puppets were manipulated by strings from above. There is painted scenery; Policinello, with mask and cudgel, is being threatened by the Turkish wizard. The musicians are life-sized and, indeed, human.

57 G. A. AND F. GUARDI *The Parlour of the Convent of San Zaccharia, Venice, 1745–50.* During Carnival, nuns were allowed to receive visitors in the 'Parlatorium' and to watch masked balls and puppet shows. Here, the puppets are manipulated from below, and are perhaps glove-puppets. The puppeteer himself is looking out between his puppets.

58 *Salzburg. Mechanical theatre in the park of Schloss Hellbrunn, near Salzburg, c. 1750.* Built by Andreas Jakob, Count Dietrichstein, Archbishop of Salzburg from 1747 to 1753. The figures are set in motion by water power transmitted by wires, wooden discs and metal rods. This is the only surviving example of its kind and can be studied in connection with Renaissance books on the techniques of building fountains. (See the official guide to Schloss Hellbrunn.)

59 ASAM BROTHERS *St Bruno and Xenodoxus, over a confessional in the Asamkirche, St Johannes Nepomuk, Munich 1733.* The Asam brothers took a literary theme for the decoration of the confessional on the right of the entrance of the church of St Johannes Nepomuk: Xenodoxus being damned by St Bruno, from the play by Jacob Bidermann first performed in Augsburg in 1602 and translated from Latin into Bavarian dialect in 1635.

60 C. FRUSOTTE *Scene from 'Les deux solitaires', Théâtre de l'Ambigu-comique, Paris.* Performed by the company of the Théâtre Italien.

61 ANON. *Voltaire receives a laurel wreath from Mlle Clairon, Paris 1778. Bibliothèque de l'Arsenal, Paris.* On 30 March 1778, after the sixth performance of his tragedy *Irène, Voltaire's* bust was crowned with a laurel wreath on the stage of the Comédie Française. In this engraving, the ancient playwright himself receives the wreath. Moreau le jeune's picture of the scene (reproduced in Schönberger and Söhner, *The Age of Rococo,* ill. 166) shows Voltaire watching from a box. Between 1770 and 1782 the Comédie Française occupied the Théâtre des Machines in the Tuileries, an excessively large, uncomfortable house.

62 ALESSANDRO LONGHI *Carlo Goldoni, c. 1757. Casa Goldoni, Venice.* Longhi (1733–1813), a member of the Accademia and much sought after by Venetian society as a portrait painter, shows the man who rescued the *commedia dell'arte* in a formal pose with the tools of his craft.

63 JOSEF LEDERER *The Maskensaal in the Schwarzenberg palace, Česky Krumlov.* Fresco. (See also Plate V.) Commedia dell'arte characters and masked spectators appear in all the rooms and in the park, represented by *trompe-l'oeil* painting. The whole illusion is repeated in mirrors round the room.

64 WILLIAM HOGARTH *Scene from Gay's 'Beggar's Opera', 1729.* Act III, scene 2. Polly and Lucy are pleading for Macheath's life. On the left of the scene are spectators, members of London society, and on the right the author, John Gay, the director of the theatre, John Rich, and the Duke of Bolton. The actors are also portraits of the actual performers, including the famous Lavinia Fenton as Polly Peachum. *The Beggar's Opera* was first performed in 1728, in Lincoln's Inn Fields. The text by John Gay (1685–1732) includes a large number of songs, set to melodies arranged from folksongs and popular songs of the day by Christopher Pepusch (1667–1752). It has been re-arranged by Benjamin Britten, and was the model for Brecht's *Threepenny Opera.*

65 PHILIPPE MERCIER *George Frideric Handel, c. 1730. Newnham House, Basingstoke.* Property of the Earl of Malmesbury. The composer, who had lived in London since 1711, is dressed informally, without a wig. Mercier (1689–1760) studied in Berlin under

Pesne, in Frankfurt and Italy. In 1723 he was summoned to England by the Prince of Wales and became court painter in 1728. This portrait was made soon after, at the beginning of his artistic maturity.

66 ANON. *Final scene from 'L'Incontro Improvviso' with Haydn at the harpsichord, Esterhaza, c. 1775. Gouache. Theatermuseum, Munich.* Haydn (1732–1809) lived at Esterhazy from 1761 to 1790, when he moved to Vienna and lived as a freelance composer. This picture shows the orchestra, composed of strings and woodwind. The singers' heads are painted on ivory.

67 VICENZA *Teatro Olimpico, permanent set, 1584.* Detail of proscenium wall, showing three 'streets'. Wood and plaster are painted to give the illusion of marble. See p. 202 and Pls 98–101.

68 VERSAILLES *Model of a stage set, reign of Louis XIV. Drottningholm palace museum.* Presented to the king of Sweden by Louis XIV. Typical high baroque scene, involving many technical resources.

69 BERNARDINO AND FABRIZIO GALLIARI *Set for 'La Vittoria d'Imeneo', with carriage of Venus, Turin 1750. Museo Civico di Torino.* See Mercedes Viale Ferrero, *La scenografia del '700 e i ratelli Galliari,* Pozzo, Turin 1961.

70 ALESSANDRO GALLI-BIBIENA *Harbour scene, c. 1760.* A ship of state is in port and a throne stands ready to receive a royal visitor. There is an impression of light and air. The symmetry of the pergola is belied by the asymmetrical focus on the throne.

71–72 DROTTNINGHOLM *Stage set attributed to Jean Louis Desprez, late eighteenth century.* A formal park with a palace in the background. Desprez (1743–1804) was a pupil of François Blondel.

73 ČESKY KRUMLOV *Wings for park and hall scenes, late eighteenth century.* Probably by the theatrical designers to the imperial court in Vienna, Johann Wetschel and Leo Merkel. The wings representing a park are painted a clear green with delicate red vases. The slits in the floor show that a third set of wings could have been used.

74 GRIPSHOLM *Stage cellar.* Shows the late eighteenth century machinery for moving the wings, with ropes coiled round a wooden drum.

75 DROTTNINGHOLM *Undercarriage of the wings.* The carriages for the four sets of wings run on wooden rails.

76 VICENZA *Teatro Olimpico, back view of the permanent set.* Cf. Pl. 67.

77 DROTTNINGHOLM *Grid.* A network of ropes and pulleys allows the mechanical changing of flies and sets and the lowering of flying machines.

78 ČESKY KRUMLOV *Stage cellar.* The undercarriages for the wings and the drum date from c. 1766. The machinery here, as at Gripsholm and Drottningholm, is still in working order.

79–82 DIESSEN AM AMMERSEE. *Klosterkirche (Church of St Mary in the former convent of Augustine canons), high altar.* Designed by François de Cuvilliés, the elder, in 1738. The panel over the high altar can be lowered and behind it are a stage and three pairs of painted shutters. With the addition of models the Nativity, Crucifixion and Resurrection can be shown at Christmas and Easter. This theatrical device is accentuated by the pillars, grouped like pairs of wings, on either side of the altar.

83 ROHR *(near Rottenburg, Lower Bavaria) Stiftskirche (Church of the Assumption in the former convent of Augustine canons), high altar.* Built by Ägid Quirin Asam, dedicated 1722. The altar is

built like a stage over the presbytery. The dramatic lighting pours in from the sides, through the pairs of pillars. The apostles stand in attitudes of theatrical amazement around the marble sarcophagus, while the Virgin is borne up to heaven by angels. The spacious, sweeping gesture is echoed by the figures of God the Father and Christ. Just as the mechanism of the flying machines in the theatres was invisible, so here the figures appear to float in the air, supported by carefully concealed iron rods.

84 WELTENBURG AN DER DONAU *Klosterkirche (Church of St Martin and St George in the Benedictine monastery), high altar.* Built by Cosmas Damian Asam, altar dedicated 1721. Totally theatrical in effect, with a proscenium frame of pilasters, twisted columns, entablature and segmental pediments. St George appears like a *deus ex machina* against the light flooding from the background to slay the dragon and rescue the princess. Again, sweeping gestures, and the armour and trappings gleam brilliantly. The space in the background is given the illusion of greater depth by perspective painting.

85 SALZBURG *Rock theatre in the park of Schloss Hellbrunn, 1617.* This, the oldest open-air theatre north of the Alps and one of the oldest in the world, was hollowed out of rock which had already been quarried for the building of the palace by Marcus Sitticus von Hohenems in 1617. Two smaller grottos on either side were also hollowed out, probably for the orchestra and dressing rooms. The wall on the right was built during the seventeenth century. The bare rock walls have openings for the entrances of the performers. Small holes show that decorative hangings were suspended from wooden pegs. This theatre was the scene of the earliest performances of opera north of the Alps, including Monteverdi's *Orfeo.*

86 HANOVER *'Hedge theatre' in park of Herrenhausen c. 1690.* The gardens were first laid out in 1666 for the summer residence of the Electors of Hanover, and added to in 1680 on the accession of Duke Ernest Augustus. This theatre was planted between 1689 and 1692. The perspective effect of the rows of hedges is emphasized by the rows of statues, which were also in the original seventeenth century plan. The overall plan was dictated by the requirements of symmetry in the garden as a whole.

87 LUDOVICO OTTAVIO BURNACINI *Design for garden theatre with avenue of statues. Second half of the seventeenth century.* Shows similarities to both the Herrenhausen and Schwetzingen theatres. It lay in the very nature of this kind of theatre that it should be unchangingly green and unadaptable, but it could provide a framework for more conventional scenery of canvas flats and statuary. In this sketch it is enlivened by the cascade in the background.

88 FLORENCE *Amphitheatre in the Boboli gardens, seventeenth century.* A large arena for tournaments and processions is surrounded by a horseshoe-shaped stone amphitheatre. A broad path leads upwards out of the horseshoe, lined by statues and with steps that could be negotiated by horses. The other end of the arena is enclosed by the Palazzo Pitti as the main grandstand.

89 BAYREUTH *Ruin theatre in the park of the Eremitage, 1743.* A 'Roman ruin' built by the French architect Joseph Saint-Pierre for the Margravine Wilhelmine for open-air performances of operas and pastorals. See Erich Bachmann, *Eremitage Bayreuth, Ämtlicher Führer,* Munich, 1963.

90 BURG ZWERNITZ *(Franconia) Sans Pareil, Ruin theatre, 1766 to 1767.*

91 JOHANN GOTTFRIED KOEPPEL *Sans Pareil Ruin theatre, c. 1790.* It is interesting to compare the present-day state of this other pseudo-ruin with Koeppel's drawing, published in 1793. Built in 1746 to 1747, also for the Margravine Wilhelmine, probably also by Saint-Pierre. A pervasive atmosphere of melancholy and the consciousness of mortality. As a theatre, comparable to that in the Lazienki park in Warsaw (*Pls 94–6*).

92 J. A. OTH *Plan of the gardens at Veitshöchheim, near Würzburg c. 1770*. From the collection of plans of the Bayerische Verwaltung der Staatlichen Schlösser, Gärten und Seen, Munich.

93 VEITSHÖCHHEIM '*Hedge theatre*'. This garden was laid out by J. P. Mayer between 1763 and 1779 for Prince Bishop Adam Friedrich von Seinsheim. The theatre dates from 1767–68. The acting area lies between the six pairs of hedges, which increase the apparent depth by being planted with their ends progressively closer together. Originally, statues of *commedia dell'arte* figures by Ferdinand Dietz stood by them, but these are now lost.

94–96 WARSAW *Open-air theatre in the Lazienki park*. Built 1790, from plans by Domenico Merlini, this ruin theatre, now restored, is a monument of eighteenth-century sensibility, like those in the park of the Bayreuth Eremitage and the Sans Pareil garden. See H. Kindermann, *Theatergeschichte Europas*, vol. V, p. 600, for a reproduction of a painting by Z. Vogel showing its original state.

97 SCHWETZINGEN *Open-air theatre in palace park, 1775–77*. Laid out by Nicolas de Pigage (1723–96), chief architect and director of gardens to the Elector Palatine. The hedges have gone, but the small hill, surmounted by a temple, with a cascade and steps, still encloses the scene. (Cf. *Pl. 87*.) There were seats for a small court audience beyond the *orchestra*, the sunken space flanked by Peter Anton Verschaffelt's sphinxes.

98–101 VICENZA *Teatro Olimpico, 1580–84*. Designed by Palladio (1508–80), completed by Scamozzi (1552–1616). The auditorium is half an oval in shape, with the ends of the curving rows of seats and the orchestra coming right up to the stage itself. Above the central arch in the set are two inscribed panels, one with the words HOC OPUS and a schematic drawing of an amphitheatre, and the lower declaring 'By their virtue and genius the Olympian Academy raised this theatre upon its foundations in 1584'. The set and the auditorium are decorated with statues of heroes, generals, scholars and leading citizens who contributed to the building of the theatre; there are also heroic deeds from Roman history, like Mucius Scaevola's test of courage, and Greek mythology, like the reliefs on the set showing the tasks of Hercules.

102–104 SABBIONETA *Teatro Olimpico, 1588*. See also plate XI. Built by Scamozzi for Vespasiano Gonzaga, Duke of Mantua. A small, horseshoe-shaped theatre with a wide proscenium. The stage occupies about a third of the total length. The seats and the set on the stage are modern.

105 PARMA *Teatro Farnese, 1618–19. Model in the theatre museum at Drottningholm*. Length 65", breadth 53", height 24". In this model, the rows of seats come right down to the floor, an idea of Aleotti's that probably dates from before the completion of the actual building. The figures – French, late seventeenth century, painted on sheet copper – and the model scenery of about the same period, were brought to Sweden by the Swedish collector, Count Gustav Tessin. See Agne Beijer, 'Neues zum Teatro Olimpico' in *Maske und Kothurn* vol. I, 1955, pts 1/2, p. 103 ff.

106 PARMA *Teatro Farnese, 1618–19*, before its destruction in the Second World War. Cf. ill. before p. 161.

108 CASERTA *near Naples, Palace theatre, 1752–59*. Built by Luigi Vanvitelli (1700–73) for the Bourbon King Charles VII of Naples, later Charles III of Spain.

109 HVAR, *Yugoslavia, Civic theatre, 1612*. Renovated 1803. Originally there were no seats.

110 VENICE *Teatro San Benedetto (1755–56) seen during a ball in 1782. Engraving by Antonio Baratta (1724–87). Theatermuseum, Munich*. Built 1755, opened 1756, renamed Teatro Rossini in 1868, completely altered 1952. The decoration of the theatre for this *Ridotto* in honour of a Russian Grand Duke and Duchess was by Antonio Mauro.

111–13 VENICE *Teatro La Fenice, 1790–92*. Designed by Giovanni Antonio Selva. Renovated 1837 by Tommaso and Giovanni Battista Meduna.

114 PADUA *Teatro Grande, 1748–51*. Designed by Antonio Cugini. Renovated in the nineteenth and twentieth centuries. Bell-shaped auditorium.

115 VERONA *Teatro Filarmonico, 1717–20. Coloured engravings*. Built by Francesco Galli-Bibiena. A bell-shaped auditorium with tiers of both boxes and open galleries.

117–121 BOLOGNA *Teatro Communale, 1756–63*. Built by Antonio Galli-Bibiena, opened by Gluck's *Il Trionfo di Clelia*. Bologna was part of the Papal States until 1796, which explains the lack of a royal box. Antonio Galli-Bibiena also designed the Teatro Scientifico in Mantua, opened in 1769. With a bell-shaped auditorium and little balconies projecting from each box it resembles the Teatro Communale. See *L'Architettura*, no. 126, vol. 11, April 1966, p. 822 ff.

122–23 VIENNA *Grosser Redoutensaal, with stage, and tapestry (showing a rustic feast at the sign of the Half-Moon)*. Maria Theresa had the Redoutensäle built for small-scale entertainments that did not need elaborate stage machinery.
The tapestries on the right-hand side of the room depict rural jollity, work, dancing, celebrations and eating. Those on the opposite wall show court recreations: flirting, card games, Blind Man's Buff and dancing to the music of the tambourine and flute in contrast to the barrel-organ and bagpipes which accompany the peasants.

124–28 VIENNA *Schlosstheater Schönbrunn, the imperial private theatre, 1766–67*. Maria Theresa commissioned the design of a theatre for Schönbrunn in 1747 from Nicolaus Pacazzi, the busiest architect in Austria in her reign. He built the theatre in the Theresianum in Vienna and the theatre in Laxenburg in 1753, and re-built the Kärntnertor theatre between 1761 and 1763. (This last was first built in 1710 by Antonio Beduzzi, who also designed the theatrical high altar in the monastery church at Melk.) The Schönbrunn theatre was built under the supervision of Ferdinand von Hohenberg (1732–1816). (See p. 218.) In 1926 the original proscenium arch was moved back to make room for more seats and a metal safety curtain decorated *à la chinoise* was installed. The theatre has been restored since the Second World War.

129 GREIN AN DER DONAU *Civic theatre, 1791*. Small auditorium with a gallery and one box at the side. The seats can be barred and locked. The paintwork has been renovated. (See p. 219.)

130 LAMBACH *(Upper Austria) Theatre of the monastery school, c. 1770*. The only surviving monastery theatre in Austria. Decorated by Johann Turetscher. This illustration shows one side of the proscenium arch.

131–32 ČESKY KRUMLOV *Theatre in the Schwarzenberg palace, 1766. Cf. pl. 73*.

133 PRAGUE *Ständetheater, 1781–83. Sepia wash, c. 1830. City Museum, Prague*. The new German-language national theatre was founded by Count Franz Anton von Nostiz-Rheineck, designed by Count von Künigl and built by Anton Hafenecker. Opened on 21 April 1783 with Lessing's *Emilia Galotti*. The *Gothaer Theaterkalender* of 1783 describes it as having 52 boxes, a spacious *parterre* and a comfortable gallery. Over the years it has been completely altered.

134 PRAGUE *Former tennis court*. Built by Bonifaz Wolmut in 1568. Typical of many disused royal tennis courts which were converted into theatres during the baroque period.

135 MOSCOW *Ostankino palace theatre. Late eighteenth century*. One of the many theatres built in Russian country houses for performances by companies of serfs.

136–37 MOSCOW *Façades of the pleasance in the Kremlin*. Czar Alexey Mihailovich banned all worldly pleasures in 1648, but in 1670 he had a court theatre built in his summer residence Preobratse yuskoye, and engaged actors in 1672. Boyar Milolavsky built a pleasance in the Kremlin in 1652, which passed to the Czar in 1679. The theatre, of which only the façades remain, was built in 1673.

138 MOSCOW *General view of palace and park of Sailo Konskova. Unsigned copper engraving*. Inscription: 'General view of Sailo Konskova, near Moscow, belonging to His Excellency Count P. B. de Sheremettov, from the south side of the lake.' The list of buildings includes church, kitchen, grotto, menagerie, Italian house, theatre, Dutch house, Hermitage, carousel, orangery and round pavilion.

139 MADRID *Coliseo del Principe, 1766. Engraving by Manuel Salvador Carmona, after a painting by Luis Paret y Alcazár. Academía de San Fernando, Madrid*.

140 VERSAILLES *Mme de Pompadour in Lully's 'Acis et Galatée', in the small theatre 1749. Engraving by Cochin fils*. Theatres were built in the Grande Écurie at Versailles for the celebrations at the wedding of Louis XV and Maria Josepha of Saxony in 1747.

141–50 VERSAILLES *Opéra, 1767–70*. Built for Louis XV by Ange-Jacques Gabriel (1698–1782). Completed in barely two years in time for the marriage of the future Louis XVI and Marie Antoinette of Austria. Reliefs and carvings by Augustin Pajou (1730–1809), painted decorations by Louis Jacques Durameau.
The balustrade of the first tier is decorated with Greek gods and goddesses: Zeus, Hera, Ares, Aphrodite, Poseidon, Ceres, Pallas Athene, Hermes, Artemis, Apollo, Cybele and Pluto. Between these reliefs are medallions representing the nine Muses, made of wood, like the whole room. The king used the middle one of the three screened boxes on private visits to the theatre, and the balcony on official, formal occasions. The shape of the auditorium is shown clearly by the ceiling, a horseshoe enclosing an oval painting by Durameau of Apollo, accompanied by Aphrodite and Eros, who are distributing laurel wreaths to the Muses, while cherubs flit about the sky.
The reliefs around the second tier represent pleasures; the one shown below this box (*Pl. 147*) is music. The sculptures in the foyer are also by Pajou (*Pl. 150*): *Youth and Health* at the end, *Apollo* on the left.
See Rose Marie Langlois, *L'Opéra de Versailles*, Pierre Horay, Paris, 1958.

151-57 BORDEAUX *Grand Théâtre, 1773-80.* Architect Victor Louis. Opened 7 April 1780 with a performance of Racine's *Athalie.*

When it was built the portico (*Pl. 151*) did not stand above steps on a raised platform, but carriages and litters could be brought right up to the entrance, so that spectators were protected from the weather. In the *gouache* by Bazire in the Musée des Arts Décoratifs in Bordeaux and in the lithograph by F. d'Andiran in the Archives Municipales de Bordeaux, the ground is banked up to the plinth of the pillars. In the woodcut of 1871 in the Archives Municipales the portico stands on steps, which is more impressive but less practical. Above the twelve pillars are statues of the Muses, Hera, Pallas Athene and Aphrodite, which have been restored. Four of the originals were by Pierre-François Berruer. The Grand Foyer (*Pl. 152*) has been altered. The divisions of the ceilings are original, but the portraits of composers, the plaster emblems and the paintings on the ceiling were added in the nineteenth century.

The bust in the Foyer d'Hiver (*Pl. 153*) is of Victor Louis, and there is a portrait of him in the room as well. The dome over the staircase (*Pl. 154*) makes a central light impracticable. It was designed to be lit by chandeliers.

The circular shape of the auditorium (*Pl. 155*) is repeated in the ceiling. The original ceiling decoration was by Jean Baptiste Claude Robin. It has been renovated, along with the rest of the paintwork in the auditorium, which was originally ivory and blue.

See F. A. Boisson, *Les douze colonnes de Louis, l'histoire inconnue du Grand Théâtre de Bordeaux,* Éditions d'Aquitaine, Bordeaux.

158-59 GRIPSHOLM *Castle theatre, 1782.* Built for Gustav III by Erik Palmstedt on the site of a former chapel. Semi-circular auditorium, walls panelled with mirrors, fluted, gilded pillars. The drawn curtain is a *trompe-l'oeil* painting.

160 DROTTINGHOLM *Palace theatre, 1766.* Built by Carl Frederik Adelcrantz. About thirty complete sets of scenery have been preserved, as well as the stage machinery. *Cf. Pls 71, 72, and 77,* and Plate XIII. See Gustav Hilleström, *Das Schlosstheater von Drottningholm,* Stockholm 1958.

161 OTTOBEUREN *Theatre in the Benedictine monastery, 1725.* The barrel vault is painted to represent a gallery with balconies. Originally the stage probably had six sets of wings. See W. Klemm, 'Benediktinisches Barocktheater in Südbayern, insbesondere des Reichsstiftes Ottobeuren' in *Studien und Mitteilungen zur Geschichte des Benediktinerordens und seiner Zweige,* 1938.

162 and **164** FRANCESCO GALLI-BIBIENA *Two sketches for an opera house, Vienna 1704.* These may well have inspired the interior of the Markgräfliches Opernhaus at Bayreuth.

163, 165-75 BAYREUTH *Markgräfliches Opernhaus, 1744-68.* Interior designed by Guiseppe Galli-Bibiena, completed by his son Carlo. Sophia (*Pl. 172*) was one of the Christian names of the Margravine Wilhelmina.

176 SCHWETZINGEN *Schlosstheater, 1752.* Built by Nicolas de Pigage, enlarged in 1762. Ceiling painted in 1937. Opened with *Il figlio delle selve* by Ignaz Holzbauer. The screened boxes on either side of the stage were formerly trumpeters' boxes (for which information I am indebted to Herr W. Karrer of Schwetzingen) and were also used by the actors while awaiting their cues. Today they hold central heating radiators. Some of the original rollers, drums and winches for moving scenery are preserved.

177-85 MUNICH *Altes Residenztheater, 1750-53.* Original design by Lorenzo Quaglio, built by François de Cuvilliés. Opened with Ferrandini's *Il Catone in Utica* on 12 October 1753. Destroyed in the Second World War, but the salvaged remains were incorporated in a replica built on a different site in the Residenz. See ills. on pp. 181, 183. François de Cuvilliés (1695-1768) came from Soignés in Hainault, and first went to Munich as court dwarf. Elector Maximilian II Emanuel had him trained by François Blondel at the Académie Royale in Paris. At the height of his career he was commissioned to build the Residenztheater by Max III Joseph in 1750. His architectural assistants were Carl Albert von Lespilliéz and François de Cuvilliés, the younger. Adam Pichler, the court joiner, prepared all the woodwork, the panels and the cartouches for the carvings by Joachim Dietrich and Johann Baptist Straub. The painted ceiling by Johann Baptist Zimmermann has been irreparably destroyed.

186-87 POTSDAM *Theatre in the Neues Palais, 1763-69.* Built by Johann Gottfried Büring and Heinrich Ludewig Manger for Frederick II, on the upper floor of the south wing of the palace. The decoration of the pillars recalls Büring's Chinese Pavilion (*cf. Pl. 14*).

188-190 LUDWIGSBURG *Palace theatre, 1730, re-decorated 1810.* Built in the outer east wing of the palace by Donato Giuseppe Frisoni (1683-1735) and painted by Giuseppe Baroffio, for Duke Everard Louis of Württemberg and his mistress, Countess Wilhelmine of Gräfenitz. In 1810 the baroque interior was pulled out and the theatre was re-built in a lyre-shape with a classical decoration, by Friedrich Nicolaus Thouret, Court Master Builder (1767-1845). See Richard Schmidt, *Schloss Ludwigsburg,* Callwey, Munich, n. d.

191 COBLENZ *Stadttheater, 1787.* Built by Grahé and decorated in a cool, classical style.

Colour plates

I ANTOINE PESNE *The dancer La Barbarina. c. 1745.* Verwaltung der ehem. Staatlichen Schlösser und Gärten, Berlin. Barbarina Campanini, known as La Barbarina (1721-99), was celebrated throughout Europe. This portrait was painted while she was at the court of Frederick II of Prussia from 1744 to 1748. In 1749 she married the son of the Prussian Staatskanzler von Cocceji, and was ennobled in 1789. She is dancing here, in front of statuary in a park, dressed as a shepherdess with a leopard skin and a tambourine, in one of the intermezzi that were so popular at the time, consisting of ballet and pantomime and performed between the acts of an opera.

II ISRAEL SYLVESTRE *Versailles: 'Plaisirs de l'Isle enchantée', 1664. Engraving.* Shows the third day of the festivity. 'Théâtre dressé au milieu du grand Estang representant l'Isle d'Alcina ou paroissoit son Palais enchanté sortant d'un petit Rocher dans lequel fut dansé un Ballet de plusieurs entrés et après quoy ce Palais fut consumé par un feu d'artifice representant le rupture de l'enchantement après la fuite de Roger'. ('Theatre erected in the middle of the pond representing the island of Alcina, where her enchanted palace appeared from out of a small rock, in which was danced a ballet of several scenes and after that this palace was consumed by a firework display representing the breaking of the spell after the flight of Roger.')
Cf. the spectacle on the lake of La Favorita in Vienna, c. 1660, in ills. after p. 8 and on p. 11.

III GEORGES DESMARÉES *Maximilian III Joseph, Elector of Bavaria, and his theatre comptroller, Count Seeau, 1775. Residenzmuseum, Munich.* It was Maximilian III who ordered the building of the Altes Residenztheater; he is here drinking a cup of chocolate while talking to his comptroller.

IV JEAN HONORÉ FRAGONARD *Festivity at St Cloud. Puppet theatre, c. 1775. Private collection, Paris.* A sketch for a painting commissioned by the Duc de Penthièvre. A party in a garden, with a marionette theatre. The play was probably performed in dumb-show while the man with the stick acted as narrator. Fragonard (1732-1806) was a pupil of Chardin and Boucher, spent some time in Rome and settled in Paris in 1761.

V JOSEF LEDERER *Fresco in the Maskensaal' Česky Krumlov, 1748.* See also *Pls 63, 131 and 132.*

VI LINZER KASPERL *Marionette, eighteenth century. Oberösterreichisches Landesmuseum, Linz.* Hardly any of the vast numbers of eighteenth century marionettes have survived, and other puppet are very difficult to date. This figure is made to be seen from below, with the feet and legs very small in proportion to the head. Eyes and lower jaw movable.

VII FRANZ ANTON BUSTELLI *Julia and Pantalone.* Modern castings from 18th century moulds. The original models are in the Bayerisches Nationalmuseum, Munich. See also the note on *Pl. 52.* The figures in this set are so designed that any two form a pair. The love story of Isabella and Ottavio is one of the stock themes of the *commedia dell'arte,* involving her *confidante* Julia and the jealous Pantalone.

VIII GIOVANNI BATTISTA TIEPOLO *Rinaldo under the spell of Armida. 1751-53. Bayerische Staatsgemäldesammlungen, Munich.* Painted for the Würzburg Residenz. It illustrates an episode of Tasso's *Gerusalemme liberata,* which was used repeatedly as a source of material for French and Italian opera.

IX LUDWIGSBURG *Curtain in the palace theatre, mid-eighteenth century.* Apollo and the nine Muses and their attributes in an Arcadian landscape. This curtain was made for the theatre at Teinach (1770) and came to this theatre, on the outskirts of Stuttgart, on 1779.

X DROTTNINGHOLM *Set.* A rocky landscape with clouds. Possibly by the French designer Jean Louis Desprez, or perhaps by Jacob Mörck, who also worked at Drottningholm during Gustav III's reign. See also *Pls. 71-72.*

XI SABBIONETA *Teatro Olimpico, 1588.* See also *Pls. 102-104* and the notes on them.

XII VERSAILLES *L'Opéra, 1767-70.* Part of the third tier. Ceiling panels painted by Louis Jean Durameau, depicting the *amours* of the gods. See also *Pls. 141-50.*

XIII DROTTNINGHOLM *Auditorium with royal box.* The front part of the auditorium with the royal box. The very wide, deep proscenium arch makes the transition from stage to auditorium more gradual than usual. See *Pls. 71, 72, 77* and *160.*

XIV BAYREUTH *Markgräfliches Opernhaus. 1744-48. Ceiling.* Richly decorated, coffered ceiling, with panels in *grisaille* and *trompe l'œil.* The central painting is of Apollo and the Muses, a theme which is taken up all over the theatre. See *Pls. 162-75.*

XV BAYREUTH *Markgräfliches Opernhaus. Trumpeters' box.* The trumpeters announced the beginning of performances and, of course, the entrance of the Margrave. See *Pls 162-75,* Plate XIV.

XVI MUNICH *Altes Residenztheater, by François de Cuvilliés, 1750-53.* See *Pls. 177-85.*

Illustrations in the Text

After p.8

LUDOVICO OTTAVIO BURNACINI *Ballet on the lake, La Favorita, Vienna c. 1660.* The inscription dedicates the festivity to the *Sacra Real Maestà*, the emperor Leopold I, who is seated beneath the canopy with the court in a curving row behind him. The seats of the musicians, on either side of the lake, are also arranged in curves.

P. 9

ANON. *Carousel, Paris, early seventeenth century.* A carousel began with fanfares. In the early seventeenth century, faces were still hidden by leather masks, the horses' trappings were quite plain and the men wore scarves as the only decorative feature of their costumes.

P. 10

JACQUES CALLOT *'La guerra di bellezza', Florence, Carnival 1616.* Callot (1592–1635) worked as an engraver in Rome from 1909, then went to the court of Tuscany in 1611 as an etcher. His drawings of scenes from the lives of the common people are famous. His chief works include *Les Misères de la guerre, Capricci, Les Gueux,* and *Balli,* a series of drawings of *commedia dell' arte* characters. (See p. 33.)

In this illustration an oval arena has been constructed in the main square of the city. The manoeuvres of individuals and groups of riders form carefully executed patterns. The floats with transformation machinery to change their decorations, were designed by Giulio Parigi. Inscription: TEATRO FATTO IN FIRENZE NELLA FESTE A CAVALLO PER LA VENUTA DEL SERMO PRINCIPE D'URBNO *Qui fecero 42 Cavalieri diuerse abbanamenti e dipoi un balletto ci si vido ancora una battaglia a piedi di 300 persone, oltre i carri e l'altra gente par diuersi servittj. Julius Parigij Inv., Callot delineavit et F.* ('Spectacle made in Florence at the equestrian celebrations for the visit of the Most Serene Prince of Urbino. 42 knights performed various exercises and then a ballet; here may be seen also a battle on foot of 300 people, as well as the carts and other attendants.')

ISRAEL SYLVESTRE *'Plaisirs de l'Isle enchantée', Versailles 1664, published Paris 1673.* Inscription: *Première journée. Comparse des quatre saisons, avec leur suitte de concertans, et porteurs de presens et la Machine de Pan et de Diana, avec leur suitte de Concertans, et de bergers portans les plats pendant le recit des uns et des autres devant le Roy, et les Reynes.* ('First day: Dumbshow of the four seasons, accompanied by musicians and bearers of gifts; the machine of Pan and Diana, with a chorus, and shepherds bearing dishes before the king and the queens, during the recitals.') The four seasons ride on a stallion, an elephant, a camel and a bear. An artificial grotto was lowered by machinery, and contained Pan, Diana and their followers.

Second day inscription: *Concerts de musique sous une feuillée faite en forme de salon, ornée de fleurs, dans le jardin de Trianon.* ('Musical concerts in an arbour made in the shape of a room and decorated with flowers, in the garden of the Trianon.') The musicians are in the boxes, while the rows of seats for the audience are turned away from them to face the real centre of attraction, the king and the two queens, Anne of Austria and Maria Theresa.

P. 11

LUDOVICO OTTAVIO BURNACINI *Ballet on the lake of La Favorita, Vienna, c. 1660.* A platform floating on the lake with pillars, hedges, trees and statuary arranged to give 'infinite' depth. *Cf.* p. 8 and Alcina's enchanted island at Versailles, in colour Plate II.

ISRAEL SYLVESTRE AND FRANÇOIS CHAUVEAU *The Duc de Guise in carousel costume as 'King of the Americans'; drummer and trumpeter of the Indies', in the Quadrille des Nations, Cour du Louvre, Paris 1662.* Bibliothèque Nationale, Paris. The Duc de Guise

wears a very magnificent tilting costume. By this date, costumes and caparisons were extremely elaborate; crests were sometimes over six foot tall. Snakes and animals' heads were supposed to ward off mishaps. The splendidly dressed musicians played an important part in the *Course de Testes et de Barques.* Israel Sylvestre and François Chauveau published a series of engravings of this carousel some time later, perhaps after hearing of the equestrian ballet held in the Vienna Hofburg in 1667.

P. 13

CARLO PASETTI *Equestrian ballet in the Hofburg, Vienna 1667.* Scene from the spectacular *Contesa dell'aria e dell'acqua.* The *Argo* is surrounded by the carriages of the four elements, Fire, Water, Air and Earth in the *'maggior cortile dell'Imperial Residenza da Vienna'.*

P. 15

JEAN LE PAUTRE. *'Alceste', by Lully and Quinault, in the Cour de Marbre, Versailles 1676.* Inscription: *Première Journée. Alceste Tragédie en musique, ornée d'entrées de Ballet, représentée à Versailles dans la cour de marbre du Chateau éclairé depuis le haut jusqu'en bas d'une infinité de lumières.* ('First day. *Alcestis,* a tragedy in music with balletic interludes, performed at Versailles, in the Marble courtyard of the palace, lit from ground to roof with innumerable lights.') The *mise-en-scène* was by Carlo Vigarani. The multicoloured lighting was particularly remarkable.

P. 21

ANON. *Hobby horse ballet by children. Vienna, seventeenth century.* The children would all have been of noble birth.

M. BODENEHR *Ballet scene from 'Camillo Generoso', Dresden 1693.* The open-air theatre was designed and decorated by Martin Kletzel. Learning to dance was part of the education of every nobleman or noblewoman; dancers were expected to master a considerable range of steps and figures.

P. 23

GIUSEPPE GALLI-BIBIENA *Scene from 'Costanza e Fortezza', Prague 1723.* Open-air theatre on the Hradčany. The emperor and empress are seated on a dais beneath a canopy. The towers on either side of the orchestra hold the chorus. The stage set consists of wings and either three-dimensional structures in the background or a painted backcloth. *Costanza e Fortezza* was a *Festa teatrale per musica* in three acts, by Pietro Pariati, with music by Johann Josef Fux and ballet music by Nicola Matteis.

After p. 32

Peepshow picture showing 'Théâtres de la foire' in the Place Vendôme, Paris eighteenth century. Bibliothèque Nationale, Paris. The stage around which the spectators are crowding is very simple. Three musicians and a barrel organ provide the interludes, two actors are playing a scene, and a couple are at the back, waiting for their entrance. There is no scenery. The inscription reads:

Le monde n'est que tromperie	*Chacun iou' son personage*
Ou moins charlatanerie	*Tel se pense plus que luy saige*
Nous agitons notre cerveau	*qui est plus que luy, charlatan*
Comme TABARIN son chapeau.	*Messieurs Dieu nous donne bon an.*
('The world is illusion	All the world's a stage
Or delusion	You think yourself more sage
We scratch our pate	Than he when you're more of a showman
And Tabarin brings round the plate.	A good New Year to all, good yeomen!)

P. 33

JACQUES CALLOT *Commedia dell'arte.* From the series of *Balli,* various scenes and characters of the *commedia dell'arte.* Here, the stage already has curtains and some primitive scenery.

P. 35

F. CHAUVEL AND N. COCHIN *Fair at Guibray, near Falaise 1685. Detail.* A fair, or market, was an obvious place for the travelling players to set up their stage.

P. 37

PETRUS SCHENK *Carnival on the Piazza Navona, Rome 1708. Detail.* After the Circus Agonalis had fallen into disrepair, the Piazza Navona was the setting not only for tournaments, processions and regattas (cf. *pl. 6*), but also for carnivals and performances by travelling players. There are two stages set up in this picture, and a ballad singer stands beside the fountain, pointing to the illustrations to his song.

P. 38

J. PFEFFEL *Festival decoration in the large hall of the Winterreitschule, by Giuseppe Galli-Bibiena, Vienna, 1744.* 'View of the great hall in which Her Majesty the Queen gave a splendid ball on 12 January 1744 on the occasion of the marriage of her Most Serene Highness, the Archduchess her sister, to the Serene prince, Charles of Lorraine'.

P. 39

BONARD *Frontispiece and title page from 'Théâtre de la foire' vol. V, Amsterdam, 1726.* The set is more ambitious than any seen on the stages of the travelling companies at provincial fairs. The plays, written by Lesage, Piron, Panard etc., were so highly thought of that they could be published, with illustrations and notes by Lesage and D'Orneval, in ten volumes between 1722 and 1734.

P. 40

German theatre as used by strolling players in the mid-seventeenth century. Deutsche Schaubühne, Strasbourg 1655, was a collection of plays, edited and translated by Isaac Clauss, of the kind that were performed by travelling companies in Germany at that time. The scene illustrated is from a play of murder and intrigue (*Haupt- und Staatsaktion*), a far cry from the witty harlequinades of the *théâtres de la foire.* While a corpse lies in the foreground, Amor is hurrying down to bless the lovers. The stage can be divided in two by a curtain. The spectators are seated.

Before p. 45

JEAN MICHEL MOREAU LE JEUNE *The private box.* From *Monument du Costume, 1789 (Cf. Pl. 13).* The young actress in the costume of a shepherdess has been brought to the two gallants in the box by a bawd. A blind can be pulled down in front of the box, and there is also a net curtain so that the occupants can see, but not be seen.

P. 45

JACQUES CALLOT *Players on the road. First half of the seventeenth century.* Inscription:
Ces pauvres gueux plein de bonaventures
Ne portent rien que des choses futures.
('These poor beggars, full of hopes, have nothing in their pockets but things to come.')

P. 46

ANON. *Rustic musicians from the ballet 'Les Fées des forêts de St Germain', Paris 1625.* Watercolour. Cabinet des Estampes, Bibliothèque Nationale, Paris. This ballet was danced at the Louvre on 11 February 1625. The musicians are playing horns and lutes. Madame Musica, girt with a lyre, bells and lutes, has more musicians hidden under her skirts.

P. 47

DANIEL RABEL *Costumes: Servant, Fairy, Innkeeper's wife. France, early seventeenth century.* Musée Carnavalet, Paris. These water colour designs are ascribed to Rabel. The simple figures have no elaborate details, but are distinguished by typical attributes: a light, keys, a purse, an apron, jugs and buskins.

P. 48

JEAN BÉRAIN *Costumes: Neptune, Diana, Zeus.* Bibliothèque Municipale, Versailles (Neptune); Bibliothèque de l'Opéra, Paris (Diana, Zeus). Jean Bérain (1637–1711), French architect and designer, was Dessinateur du Cabinet du Roy, and furnished designs for festivities, court mourning ceremonies, firework displays, the interiors of royal palaces and scenery and costumes for the stage. These costumes are much more sumptuous than Rabel's at the beginning of the seventeenth century. Ornaments, tucks, laces and elaborate head-dresses obscure the characterizing attributes: crowns, eagle, bow and arrow. See *Oeuvre de Jean Bérain, recueillie par les soins du sieur Thuret*, Paris 1911.

P. 49

JEAN LE PAUTRE *Dancer of the Opéra, Paris seventeenth century. Cabinet des Estampes, Bibliothèque Nationale, Paris.* In spite of her gypsy tambourine, this dancer's long skirts and formal dress would have prevented her from performing any very lively steps.

P. 50

FRANCISCUS LANG *Poses from 'Dissertatio de actione scenica', 1727.* A treatise on performance, written for the theatres of the religious schools, which performed plays in Latin.
Left: 'Of the position of the limbs, arms and fingers.'
Centre: 'How to make an entrance.'
Right: 'How to express feelings in silence.'

P. 51

GÉRARD DE LAIRESSE *Polite and vulgar manners from 'Groot Schilderboek', Amsterdam 1707.* An artist of repute, Gérard de Lairesse (1644–1711) lost his sight in 1689, so the illustrations to his treatise on gesture and expression were drawn by someone else on his instructions. These illustrations are from the chapter 'Of attributes and of what movements of limbs are commended in the expression of emotions.' They show 'how to use glass and spoon and how not to' and 'how to stand gracefully and becomingly, and how one ought not to stand'. See also *Maske und Kothurn*, vol. 1, 1955, nos 1/2, p. 140 ff.

P. 61

C. DAUPHIN AND J. THOURNEYSEN *French actor at the court of Munich, c. 1675.* Philippe Millot from Lyon, a member of the company of French actors engaged by Henrietta Adelaide of Savoy, wife of the Elector Ferdinand Maria, between 1671 and 1676. Rich costume of the period, with lace, ribbons and large feathered hat.

JOHANN MESSELREUTHER *Actor and actress in Roman costume, Bayreuth eighteenth century.* Messelreuther, a chamberlain at the court of Bayreuth, published his costume designs for the stage and court festivities in *Neu-eröffneter Masquensaal*. These are stiff and pompous, less elegant than French costumes.

P. 63

LOUIS RENÉ BOQUET *Costumes for the ballet 'Medusa'. Bibliothèque de l'Opéra, Paris.* Boquet (1717–1814), a pupil of Boucher, was one of the most talented of French costume designers. There are still large numbers of his light and graceful original drawings in Paris and Warsaw. He designed the costumes for the opening performances in the Versailles Opéra.

P. 64

JOSEPH LANGE *'Alexander and Campaspe', ballet by J. G. Noverre, Vienna 1773.* This engraving by Mansfeld was the frontispiece of the *Almanach des Theaters in Wien, 1774 (cf. p. 101).* The 'grand heroic pantomime-ballet', sub-titled 'The victory of Alexander over himself', was first performed at the Theater an der Burg on 12 April 1773. The heroine (with spear) was a great princess, so wore a long skirt, even in a ballet. In his day Jean Georges Noverre was the most important ballet master and choreographer in Europe. From successes in Paris he went on to be a soloist at the court of Frederick II of Prussia, and worked in London, Lyon, Vienna, Milan and at the court of Württemberg. He wrote the scenarios for his ballets, mostly tragedies, himself; the sets and costumes were always refined and graceful.

P. 65

JACQUES CALLOT *Young lover from the commedia dell'arte, Paris early seventeenth century.* The juvenile lead still wears plain breeches and a short doublet. He is shown here in front of a stage with perspective scenery.

P. 66

Théâtre Italien: the Commedia dell'arte in France. Published in Paris by F. Guerard. During the seventeenth century the *commedia dell'arte* became naturalized in France. The character of Pierrot evolved and the use of masks died out almost completely.

P. 67

ANON. *Catherine Biancholelli, of the Comédie Italienne, Paris, as Columbine. Bibliothèque de l'Arsenal, Paris.* One of the most famous soubrettes in the Comédie Italienne, and daughter of Domenico Biancholelli (1640–1688), a famous Italian Arlecchino, who developed the part in France to the more refined Arlequin. Columbine's costume is very grand; with her fan, jewels, headdress and long skirts, she bears very little resemblance to a servant any more.

P. 68

JOHANN JAKOB SCHÜBLER *Scene from German improvized comedy, Augsburg c. 1720.* The rather lengthy title of this play, published in Augsburg, *c.* 1720, is 'The triumph of Love, hotly burning but skilfully hid, over the watchfulness of Pantaloon, or, Harlequin, the living picture and ludicrous Cupid'. The scenario of this scene runs: 'As the evening draws on, having received a message, Isabella goes into the garden and finds her lover, Cynthio, hidden in the pavilion. By evil chance, her unwelcome suitor, Captain Rodomondo, following the music played on the Lute by Prigatella, also comes into the garden, hoping to be welcome to Isabella. But not only is the worthy Captain mocked by Columbine, but Isabella orders him not to trouble her again and finally, Harlequin repays the blows he received on the Captain's account in the Doctor's house, in good measure.'

P. 77

Théâtre Italien: Arlecchino discovered in the Seraglio, Paris c. 1690. Theatermuseum, Munich. A scene from *Arlequin Grand Visir.* In the Seraglio, the male characters wear some kind of authentic national dress, but the women are in French court dress. The illustration is accompanied by an explanation in verse (*cf.* p. 68).

Pp. 78–79

MARTIN ENGELBRECHT *Commedia dell'arte characters, late eighteenth. Theatermuseum, Munich.* Scaramouche, Harlequin and Mezzetino have altered very little since the seventeenth century (*cf.* p. 66), but the women and the lovers are dressed *à la mode.*

P. 80

ANON. *Josef Martin Menninger as Hans Wurst.* The Viennese principal (1733–93) wears a typical costume, with conical hat, ruff, waistcoat, braces and short coat.

MARTIN ENGELBRECHT *Hans Wurst, the Salzburg pork butcher. Augsburg, c. 1720, coloured copper engraving.* Hans Wurst carries the insignia of his original trade.

Before p. 89

FRANCIS HAYMAN *Scene from Shakespeare's 'A Midsummer Night's Dream'. Engraving by Hubert-François Bourguignon, dit Gravelot.* From the six volume edition of Shakespeare's works, Oxford 1743–44, edited by Sir Thomas Hanmer. Shakespeare was rediscovered for the stage in the middle of the eighteenth century.

P. 89

Title page of 'Mirame' by Jean Desmarets de Saint-Sorlin and Cardinal Richelieu, showing proscenium of the theatre in the Palais Cardinal. *Mirame* was the work performed at the opening of this theatre in 1641. The palace became the Palais Royal when Richelieu presented it to Louis XIII. Molière's company played there from 1661 to 1673. It was destroyed by fire in 1763.

P. 90

ANON. *Jean Racine. Copper engraving.* One of France's greatest playwrights, born 21 December 1639 in La Ferté-Milon, died 22 April 1699 in Paris. Member of the Académie Française. Molière's company performed his plays.

P. 91

Title page of Molière's 'L'Amour Médecin', Paris 1666. First edition, with a scene from the play as frontispiece.

P. 93

FRANCOIS BOUCHER *Scene from Molière's 'Le bourgeois gentilhomme'.* From an eighteenth century edition of the play.

P. 94

JOHANN ESAIAS NILSON *Children's company in Augsburg. Engraving.* The Kindertheater von St Sebastian, using stock *commedia dell'arte* characters, with Columbine escaping from the mill with the aid of Harlequin's wiles. Child actors were a feature of the theatre from the sixteenth century, playing to both children and adults.

P. 95

JOHANN ESAIAS NILSON. *Scene from Gottsched's 'Atalanta', 1746. Copper engraving.* Title page of the third part of J. C. Gottsched's *Deutsche Schaubühne*, with a scene from *Atalanta*, 'The coy beauty overcome by coyness'.

P. 96

Title page of Lessing's 'Hamburgische Dramaturgie', Hamburg 1769. First edition. Vignette by J. W. Weil.

P. 97

Title page of Goldoni's 'Il Filosofo di campagna', Venice, 1754. A musical comedy. This edition published on the occasion of the first production by Samuel in the Teatro Grimani in 1754.
Title page of Gozzi's works in a German translation, Berne 1777. Gozzi's fables were translated into many European languages, and were a popular source of material for other writers.

P. 98

Playbill of the 'Electoral Court Comedians' of Saxony, Leipzig 1766. A tragedy, a ballet and a comedy: one evening's programme, presented by Koch's company.

P. 99

Playbill of the 'Electoral Court Comedians' of Saxony, Vienna 1697. This may have been Velten's company. Velten died in Hamburg in 1692, but his company still existed in 1712, when they were in Vienna. The performance began at 3 p.m. in the tennis-court on Himmel-Porter Gasse. The game of royal tennis had lost its former popularity and many tennis courts were converted into theatres.

ANON. *Gotthold Ephraim Lessing. Copper engraving.* The first German playwright of major importance (1729–81).

P. 100

DANIEL CHODOWIECKI *Scenes from Lessing's 'Minna von Barnhelm'. Copper engravings. Minna von Barnhelm* is the earliest comedy still in the modern German repertoire. Chodowiecki (1726 to 1801) was an unusually prolific draughtsman and etcher. He was a noted illustrator of the sentimental bourgeois novels which became all the rage in Europe after Samuel Richardson's *Pamela* and *Clarissa Harlowe.*

P. 101

Title page of 'Almanach des Theaters in Wien', 1774. The frontispiece of this volume is reproduced on p. 64.
Title page of French edition of Pergolesi's 'La Serva Padrona', Paris 1752. This opera was first performed in Naples in 1733. Its first performance in Paris by an Italian company in 1752 caused the outbreak of a pamphlet war between the adherents of French and Italian opera (*La querelle des bouffons*).

P. 102

First page of Monteverdi's manuscript of 'L'Incoronazione di Poppea' (above) and a page by a copyist. L'Incoronazione di Poppea, dramma in musica, 1642, with a libretto by Giovanni Francesco Busenello, is the story of Nero's love for his second wife. The page, reproduced here, by a copyist, bears autograph notes by Monteverdi: *Un tuon più alto* on line 5 and *Ritornello* below line 6. Lines 4, 5, 7 and 8 are the treble parts, lines 6 and 9 the bass part of the *ritornello*. This manuscript, IT.CL. 4. N. 439 of the Biblioteca Nazionale di S. Marco in Venice, was published in facsimile by Fratelli Bocca Editore, Milan, 1938, with an introduction by Giacomo Benvenuti.

P. 104

JEAN BÉRAIN *Frontispiece of libretto of Lully's 'Armide', Paris 1686.* This shows the final scene of the first production of the *Tragédie lyrique, Armide et Renaud*, with a libretto by Quinault based on Tasso's *Gerusalemme liberata*. The sets for the production were also by Bérain. Louis XIV was a keen patron of the Académie royale de Musique, and had published illustrated scores of all the operas it produced.

Playbill for Keiser's 'Das zerstörte Troja', Hamburg 1716. The illustration shows Troy burning on stage, with perspective scenery on a central axis of symmetry. From the most brilliant period of the Hamburg baroque opera.

P. 106

Title page of Handel's 'Julius Caesar', London, 1724.

P. 107

JEAN BÉRAIN *Title page of Lully's 'Phaëton', 1683.* The originals of the illustrations on pp. 106–107 are both in the Bibliothèque du Conservatoire de Musique, Paris.

P. 108

Bilingual playbill for Manfredini's 'Charlemagne', St Petersburg, 1764. On this poster, for a performance of *Carlo Magno* by the court musician Vicenzo Manfredini and the court poet Lazzaroni, in the new imperial theatre in St Petersburg, the names of the composer and librettist are printed very much smaller than that of the imperial patroness. History has confirmed this estimate.

Before p. 117

LUDOVICO OTTAVIO BURNACINI *Set for 'Il Fuoco eterno', Vienna 1674. Engraving by Mathäus Küsel.* Stage and scene are divided into two distinct parts. This was a festival production to celebrate the birth of a daughter to Leopold I and his empress. The music was by Antonio Draghi, the ballet by Santo Ventura, arias by Schmeltzer and the text by Nicolo Minato.

P. 117

ANON. *Mediaeval English 'pageant'.* The stage is erected on a cart in a market-place, and could be moved about the town. The actors were artisans, apprentices and students.

P. 118

Setting for the English mystery 'Mary Magdalene'. The only suggestion of rich decoration would have been by means of tapestries or carpets. In these plays all the emphasis was on the text.

HUBERT CAILLEAU *Simultaneous stages at Valenciennes, 1547. Miniature from a manuscript in the Bibliothèque Nationale, Paris.* The 'mansions' (stage-houses), sets and costumes of the Valenciennes passion play, which lasted twenty five days, were recorded in a series of coloured miniatures. Seventy actors took part. The simultaneous scenes are in a row and are designated '*Paradis, Une salle, Nazareth, Le Temple, Jerusalem, Le Palais, Maison des évêques, La Porte dorée, La mer, Le limbe des pères, L'Enfer*'. The temple, the palace and the Golden Gates are sumptuous Renaissance structures. Limbo and hell spout dramatic flames and devils can also be seen.

P. 119

JOHANNES DE WITT *The Swan theatre, London 1596.* The only contemporary illustration of an Elizabethan theatre, made by a visiting Dutchman. It shows clearly the position of the entrance, the orchestra, the seats, the galleries and the roof. The banner flying on the roof, with the device of a swan, signifies that a performance is in progress. De Witt reported the Swan to be the largest of the four London theatres. It was built of wood and plaster and the pillars supporting the roof were painted to look like marble. There is no scenery on the stage; the actors could

make their entrances only through the two doors at the back of the stage.

GEORGE WESTCOTT *Reconstruction of an Elizabethan theatre. Theatermuseum, Munich.* This reconstruction shows a slightly more elaborate setting, with an upper tier at the back of the stage to be used as windows or a balcony, and curtains to indicate changes of scene. The apron stage becomes narrower towards the front and has a low balustrade.

P. 120

GIACOMO TORELLI *Set for 'Venere gelosa', Venice, 1643. Engraving by Aveline.* Garden scene of great depth with three parallel axes. The positioning of the actors is also strictly symmetrical. This is a design from before Torelli's Parisian triumphs. He was summoned there by Mazarin during the regency of Anne of Austria.

P. 121

JOSEF FURTTENBACH *Stage with periaktoi, From Mannhaffter Kunstspiegel, Ulm, 1663.* Below is a general diagram of a stage, with a curtain in front, then a pit, lower than stage level, for the orchestra, into which, also, the act drop was lowered. Beyond that comes the stage proper, with *telari*, or *periaktoi*, on either side, and at the back another pit to enable ships and carriages to be brought on to the stage, manoeuvred from below, out of the audience's sight. The dotted lines behind the back scene converge on the theoretical vanishing point: the perspective would be so contrived that, to the spectators, the scene would appear to stretch as far as that point. Centre, the *periaktoi* in their actual positions for the scene above. The first *periaktoi* used in Germany were those introduced in the theatre Furttenbach built in Ulm in 1640. He studied in Milan, Genoa and Florence, settled in Ulm in 1626 and began to publish a series of theoretical works. In *Architectura civilis* (1628) he wrote of Italian developments in scenic transformation, hitherto unknown in Germany.

P. 122

'Ludi Caesarei' in the Jesuit theatre, Prague 1617. Inscription: PHASMA DIONYSIACUM PRAGENSE EXHIBITUM S. CAES. M. ANNO MDCXVII. ('The apparition of Dionysus, shown in Prague to his Imperial Majesty, 1617.') The set is strictly symmetrical. The actors have come down to perform a solemn dance in the body of the theatre. The letters against them refer to a key, which names them as members of the most noble families. In the Jesuit theatres, women's roles were played by men.

GIUSEPPE GALLI-BIBIENA *Set for Otway's 'Titus and Berenice', Vienna 1719.* Act II, scene 5: a palace, with diagonal axes. This play was performed on the occasion of the marriage of an Austrian Archduchess to the son of Augustus the Strong of Saxony.

P. 123

NICCOLO SABBATTINI *'Pratica di fabricar scene e machine ne' teatri', Ravenna 1638, and diagrams for sets with one and three streets.* In Book I Sabbattini gives detailed instructions on how much space the stage should occupy and how it should be built. 'The room must be carefully surveyed, including the walls, ceiling, rafters and roof, to be sure that they are capable of supporting the weight of the stage, the machinery and spectators, particularly when royalty are to be present. The floor of the stage should be raked at a slope of one inch in the foot; the boards should fit well together and be nailed down very firmly to prevent the nails coming loose during a Moorish dance. This often does happen, and is very dangerous for the dancers.' He also gives instructions for placing a roof over the stage, for fixing the vanishing point, for incorporating doors and windows in the set, *etc.*

P. 124

JEAN LE PAUTRE *Carlo Vigarani's theatre in the park of Versailles, 1672. Engraving.* The work being performed in this picture is

Lully's *Les Fêtes de l'Amour et de Bacchus.* Vigarani erected a wooden stage in the park and a ceiling to shelter the small audience of the court. He was responsible for the staging of the *Plaisirs de l'Isle enchantée*, for another festivity in the park in 1668 at which Molière's *Georges Dandin* was performed, and for the *mises en scène* of Lully's *Alceste*, Racine's *Iphigénie*, and Molière's *Malade imaginaire*.

P. 125

FERDINANDO AND GIUSEPPE GALLI-BIBIENA. *Set for 'Angelica vincitrice di Alcina', Vienna 14 September 1716. Engraving by F. Distel.* On the forestage is an open space with pillars on either side and upstage is a palace with a complex of halls and corridors. In the audience, the imperial family is seated while the court stands. The libretto of the three-act opera was by Pietro Pariati, the music by Johann Josef Fux and the ballet music by Nicola Mateis.

P. 126

LUDOVICO OTTAVIO BURNACINI *Set for 'Il Pomo d'oro', Vienna, 1668. Engraving by Mathäus Küsel.* A huge stage, set with wings and perspective backcloth, equipped with transformation machinery, flying machines and trapdoors. *Il Pomo d'oro*, with libretto by Francesco Sbarra and music by Marc Antonio Cesti, tells the story of the Judgment of Paris.

P. 127

LUDOVICO OTTAVIO BURNACINI *Stage design, c. 1670.* A splendid example of baroque stage design. Massive Atlantes bestride their conquered foes, and allegorical figures of Justice ride on their shoulders. Symmetrical lines of men and women form an avenue, two couples approach a temple opening before them and fire rains down from heaven.

P. 129

GASPARE AND DOMENICO MAURO *Set for 'Servio Tullio', Munich 1686. Engraving by Michael Wening.* The scene is the staircase of the royal palace in Act II, scene 19 of Agostino Steffani's opera. The intricate pillars on the forestage are three-dimensional; the great staircase in the background gives the illusion of both height and depth.

ANON. *Design for Hell, Germany, seventeenth century.*

L. HUPFFER *Design for a camp, Ansbach 1676.* German scenery of the seventeenth century adheres to the Italian rule of symmetry.

P. 130

NICCOLO SABBATTINI *Cloud machines from 'Pratica di fabricar scene e machine ne' teatri', Ravenna 1638, Book 2, ills 145, 140 and 137.* Sabbattini gives detailed instructions on 'how to lower a cloud directly from the sky', 'another method of lowering a cloud bearing a person on to the stage', 'how to lower a cloud bearing people so that it first appears in the very furthest distance and gradually comes forward as it is lowered, to land in the centre of the stage', *etc.*

P. 132

FERDINANDO AND FRANCESCO GALLI-BIBIENA *Set for 'L'Eta dell'oro', Parma 1690.* Large and complex machinery must have been necessary for this transformation, in which a colonnaded hall with heavenly beings in it is being lowered on a cloud on to the stage.

P. 133

ALESSANDRO MAURO *Set for 'Teofane', Dresden 1719.* Opera by Pallavicini and Lotti, performed at the wedding celebrations for the Crown Prince and Maria Josefa of Austria. By now the central axis of symmetry was on the way out. A group of buildings in the background prevents the need for distant perspectives. The very fact that the scenery is less solid and is pierced by the gaps between the pillars gives the impression of three-dimensional depth.

P. 134

Cloud machine from Diderot's 'Encyclopédie'. Shows the support in the stage roof and the pulleys for raising and lowering the clouds.

The left inset shows a rather spacious prison into which the clouds were lowered before they opened to reveal a divine deliverer. The right inset shows the chariot of Medea.

D'HERMAND *Flying apparatus, early eighteenth century*. The pulleys are hidden by clouds, the counterweights are at the side of the stage.

P. 135

JEAN BÉRAIN *Phaëton's chariot, Paris 1685. Bibliothèque Nationale, Paris*. Designed for Lully's opera, *La Chute de Phaëton*.

JEAN BÉRAIN *Cloud apparatus with billowing action, Paris 1685*. The fan-shaped framework allowed variations of thickness and transparency.

Pp. 136–37

NICCOLO SABBATTINI *Diagrams from 'Pratica di fabricar scene e machine ne' teatri'*. The metal cylinders, suspended on pulleys over candles or oil lamps, enabled the stage to be darkened without actually extinguishing the lights. The torch stands in a pot of magnesium. A sharp blow or puff of air sends the powder flying up, to burn with a coloured flame.

P. 138

GIUSEPPE GALLI-BIBIENA *Design for a garden with fountain*. Behind six pairs of wings, the scene is enclosed by a curved horizon and painted perspectives. The vertical line and central position of the fountain emphasize the axes of symmetry.

GIUSEPPE GALLI-BIBIENA *Island for 'Angelica vincitrice', Vienna 1716*. See also p. 125. This scene, with monsters and a sea-battle, was staged on a lake of the Favorita palace.

JEAN BÉRAIN *Harbour scene*. Bérain has observed the rule of symmetry in the side scene, but the ships and fortress in the background are placed asymmetrically.

P. 139

Diagram of the wings in the theatre at Drottningholm, near Stockholm 1766. Reproduced from Agne Beijer, *Drottningholm*, Stockholm, 1950. See also Pls 74 and 77.

GIOVANNI BATTISTA PIRANESI. *Set with staircase, Rome 1743. Engraving by the designer*. Asymmetrical set with curved horizon.

P. 140

CHARLES COYPEL *Theatre in the Palais Royal in Molière's day, Paris late seventeenth century. Bibliothèque de l'Arsenal, Paris*. There are seats for the spectators on the stage, but none in the *parterre*. The house curtain is almost without decoration.

Before p. 161

PARMA *Proscenium of the Teatro Farnese, 1618–19. Engraving by Paolo Fontanesi*. The inscription states that the theatre was dedicated to Bellona and the Muses in 1618. See also P. 164 and Pls 105–6.

P. 161

FLORENCE *Theatre in the Uffizi 1616. Engraving by Jacques Callot*. Shows the theatre during a performance of the ballet *La Liberazione di Tireno*, in the interlude of *Gigante Tifeo*, with sets by Giulio Parigi. This huge theatre was built between 1585 and 1586 by Bernardo Buontalenti (1536–1608) for really large-scale spectacles. Climbing rows of seats line three sides of the room. Steps lead down from the stage, so that the action could overflow into the auditorium. There is a gallery above the seats, with balconies between the pillars.

P. 162

ANDREA POZZO *Diagram for a theatre with five tiers, from 'Prospettiva de' pittori e architetti', 1693–1700*. The type of theatre in which, in addition to the tiers, the *parterre* itself contained steeply rising rows of seats, like an amphitheatre, and exemplified by the Dresden opera house of 1718 (*cf* P. 180). Pozzo gives a full description in his book.

P. 164

JOSEF FURTTENBACH *Plan and elevation of a theatre with four stages, 1650*. The auditorium would have turned to face each stage in turn. There is a comparable arrangement in the theatre in Česky Krumlov.

PARMA *Teatro Farnese, ground plan, 1618–9*. Shows the horseshoe shape of the auditorium. See also ill. before p. 61 and *Pls 105–6*.

P. 167

NAPLES *Theatre in the Palazzo Reale, c. 1750*. Shows a surprising similarity to the theatre in the Palais Royal, 100 years earlier (cf. p. 172). The seats are so arranged that the audience's attention is centred on the prince. The decoration is by Vinzenzo dal Ré.

P. 168

NAPLES *Teatro San Carlo, 1737, Section and plan*. Built 1737 by G. A. Medrano. The longitudinal section shows the theatre decked for a ball by Vinzenzo dal Ré. Steps lead down from the royal box to the floor. See p. 210. The plan, shows the stage to be deeper than the auditorium.

VIENNA *The first opera house, 1652*. Designed by Giovanni Burnacini. The numbers against the dancers refer to a key giving the names of the aristocratic cast in this production of *La Gara* by Antonio Bertali and Alberto Viminia. This theatre stood on the site in the Hofburg occupied today by the Österreichische Nationalbibliothek.

P. 169

GERMANY *Public theatre, c. 1785*. Straight plays, being cheaper to mount than opera, remained the more usual entertainment for the general public. Simple sliding wings, like those still to be seen in the monastery theatre in Lambach (see fl. 130).

P. 170

VIENNA *Opernhaus auf der Cortina, 1666–68*.

P. 171

MELCHIOR KUSEL *Title page of Cesti's 'Il pomo d'oro', showing the proscenium of the Opernhaus auf der Cortina, Vienna 1667*. This opera house was built by Ludovico Ottavio Burnacini and intended to house the more spectacular entertainments devised for the wedding celebrations of Leopold I and Margareta of Spain, but was not ready in time. Three tiers run round the rectangular room. A broad proscenium space lies between the orchestra and the royal dais. The theatre was destroyed during the Turkish siege in 1683.

P. 172

PARIS *Theatre in the Palais Royal, 1641*. From *L'Ancien théâtre en images: L'Ancien théâtre de Richelieu et de Molière, d'après Van Lochum*. Anne of Austria, Louis XIII, the Dauphin (Louis XIV) and Cardinal Richelieu, a little behind, are seated, while the court stands in the galleries. This theatre was built by Jacques Le Mercier (*c.* 1585–1654). See also the picture of the proscenium on p. 89

PARIS *Plan of the Salle de l'Opéra in the Palais Royal (at the level of the first tier), 1770*. Moliere began to alter Richelieu's theatre in 1671, replacing the stage machinery and cutting off the corners of the auditorium. Instead of a canopy a proper ceiling was made and a tier of boxes added. That theatre was burnt down in 1763. The horseshoe-shaped theatre in this plan, designed by M. Moreau, was altogether the sixth to be built in the Palais Royal; it held 2500 spectators, and was destroyed by fire in 1781.

PARIS *Plan of the Théâtre de l'Odéon, 1779–82*. Built by Charles de Wailly and J. W. Peyre. Burnt down in 1799. The present theatre dates from 1880.

P. 173

PARIS *Théâtre de la Porte Saint Martin, after 1781*. Built in less than three months by Nicolas Lenoir (1726–1810). It was the eighth opera house in Paris.

P. 174

LONDON *Sadlers' Wells theatre (1765), as it was in 1792. Drawing by R. C. Andrews*. Built on a site previously occupied by a wooden music hall.

P. 175

LONDON *Old Theatre Royal, Drury Lane, in 1792. Drawing by Bartholomew Howlett, engraved by Capon*. This theatre was enlarged by Sheridan in 1791 to hold 3600 spectators. There was a safety curtain with metal panels, and a huge water tank under the roof. In spite of these precautions the theatre burned down and had to be re-built by Henry Holland in 1794.

P. 176–7

SALLAY and SERVANDONI *A theatre during a masked ball, cross-section and longitudinal section, London eighteenth century*. Drawn by Gabriel Sallay and Giovanni Niccolo Servandoni. From *L'Art pratique, recueil de documents choisis dans les ouvrages*, Leipzig and Paris 1887, no. 59.

P. 178

AMSTERDAM *Nieuwe Schouwburg, 1774*. Designed by J. E. Witte, sculpture by A. Ziesenis. The façade is severe and classical and the interios decoration is also restrained. The floor is tiled, and there are seats in the *parterre* where, in the earlier theatre, there had only been standing room. The walls between the boxes are cut back so as not to disturb the line of the tiers.

P. 179

BRUNSWICK *Festsaal in castle of Dankwarderode, 1642. Universitätsbibliothek, Göttingen*. A performance of *Neu erfundenes Freudenspiel, genannt Friedenssieg*, with text by Georg Schottelius and music by Sophia Elizabeth of Mecklenburg-Güstrow. Fortuna's carriage is surrounded by various characters: Dazzled Reason, Hope, Mars, Iron Necessity, Despair, Cupid, a Frenchman, a Turk and a Spaniard.

MUNICH *Opernhaus am Salvatorplatz, 1654, royal box 1685*. Built by Francesco Santurini and Max Schinnagl, the box by Domenico and Gaspare Mauro. This is believed to be the earliest court opera house in Germany built for that purpose only.

P. 180

DRESDEN *Neues Opernhaus, 1718–9*. Designed by Daniel Pöppelmann (1662–1736), sculpture and moulded decoration by Balthasar Permoser (1651–1732). A horseshoe-shaped theatre in which the tiers of boxes reach round to the proscenium, with the end boxes given architectural emphasis by their protuberant balustrades. There are also boxes on the stage itself, though the spectators are not able to hinder the action as in earlier theatres where seats were placed on the stage. Pöppelmann also built the opera house in Warsaw.

P. 181

MUNICH *Plan of the Altes Residenztheater, 1750–53*. Built by François de Cuvilliés. Plan drawn at some date before 1770.

P. 183

MUNICH *Section drawing of the Altes Residenztheater*. Engraving by Valerian Funck, published in *L'Architecture Bavaroise*, 1771, based on drawings by Cuvilliés of a masked ball held on 14 January 1765. The note at the bottom of the engraving runs 'The basic colour of the boxes is white with gilded ornaments. The drapes on the second tier are of red imitation velvet with gold fringes. The royal box is panelled with mirrors. The interior of the boxes is painted with arabesques on a lilac background.' The machinery seen below the floor was for raising it to the level of the stage.

Bibliography

Seventeenth- and eighteenth-century works

GENERAL

D'Aubignac, Hédelin, *La Pratique du Théâtre*, 1657.

De Beauchamps, P. F. Godard, *Recherches sur les théâtres de France, depuis l'année 1161 jusqu' à présent*, Paris 1735.

Cecchini, P. M., *Breve discorso intorno alle Comedie, comedianti e spettatori*, Vicenza 1614.

Charpentier, L., *Causes de la décadence du goût sur le théâtre*, Paris 1768.

Chetwood, W. R., *A General History of the Stage*, London 1749.

Histoire universelle des théâtres de toutes les nations, 13 vol. Paris 1779–1781.

Léris, A. de, *Dictionnaire portatif historique et littéraire des théâtres*, Paris 1763.

Mouhy, *Abrégé de l'Histoire du Théâtre Français*, 3 Vol., Paris 1780.

Napoli-Signorelli, P., *Storia critica de' Teatri antichi e moderni*, 6 vol. Napoli 1787/90.

Origny, H. J. B., *Annales du théâtre Italien*, 3 vol. Paris 1788.

Parfaict, F. et C., *Dictionnaire des théâtres de Paris*, 6 vol., Paris 1756.

Riccoboni, L., *Réflexions historiques et critiques sur les différente théâtres d'Europe*, Paris 1740.

Le Grand, *Divertissement Royal de Versailles, Sujet de la Comédie qui se doit faire à la grande Fête de Versailles*, Paris 1668.

Les plaisirs de l'Isle enanchtée ... faites par le Roy à Versailles 1664, Paris 1673.

Theatrum ceremoniale historico politicum oder Historischer und politischer Schauplatz aller ceremonien ... Leipzig 1719–20.

Pöllnitz, Karl Ludwig Freiherr von, *La Saxe galante*, Amsterdam 1737.

Schönhaar, W. F., *Ausführliche Beschreibung des zu Bayreuth im September 1748 vorgegangenen Hochfürstlichen Beylagers*, Stuttgart 1749.

Uriot, *Beschreibung der Feyerlichkeiten, welche bey Gelegenheit des Geburtstagsfestes Sr. Hzgl. Durchl. des Herzogs zu Württemberg und Teck ... angestellet worden*, Stuttgart 1764.

PLAYERS AND COSTUMES

Habits des costume pour l'éxécution des ballets de M. Noverre, dessinés par M. Boquet, premier dessinateur des Menus Plaisirs du Roi, Musée de l'Opéra, Paris.

Charnois, J. Ch., *Recherches sur les costumes et sur les théâtres de toutes les nations*, Paris 1790.

Dhannataire, J.-N., *Observations sur l'art du comédien*, Paris 1775.

Engel, J. J., *Ideen zu einer Mimik*, Berlin 1785/1786.

Hill, A., *Essay on the Art of Acting*, London 1745.

Lairesse, Gérard de, *Groot Schilderboek*, Amsterdam 1707.

Lang, Franziskus, *Dissertatio de actione scenica*, Munich 1727.

Le Faucheur, *Traité de l'Action ou de la Prononciation et du Geste*, Paris 1686.

Le Vacher de Charnois: *Recherches sur les costumes et sur les théâtres de toutes les nations*, Paris 1790.

Mylius, C., *Versuch eines Beweises, dass die Schauspielkunst eine freye Kunst sey*, Stuttgart 1750.

Rémond de Sainte-Albine, *Le Comédien*, Paris 1747.

Schlegel, A. W., *Von der Würde und Majestät des Ausdrucks im Trauerspiel*, 1764.

Sticotti, *Garrick et les acteurs anglais*, Paris 1769.

PLAYS AND OPERAS

Almanach des Theaters in Wien, 1774 etc.

Arteaga, Stefano, *Le Rivoluzioni del Teatro musicale Italiano*, 1783.

Bodmer, J. J., *Kritische Betrachtungen und freye Untersuchungen zum Aufnehmen und zur Verbesserung der deutschen Schaubühne. Mit einer Zuschrift an die Frau Neuberin*, Berne 1743.

Desprez de Boissy, *Lettres sur les spectacles*, Paris 1771.

Cahusac, Louis de, *De la danse ancienne et moderne*, 1754.

Clémont, C. F., *Principes de choréographie ou l'Art d'écrire et de lire la Danse par caractères demonstratifs*, Paris 1771.

Gherardi, E., *Le théâtre italien, ou Recueil de toutes les scènes françoises qui ont été jouées sur le Théâtre Italien de Bourgogne*, Geneva 1695.

Gottsched, J. C., *Nötiger Vorrat zur Geschichte der deutschen dramatischen Dichtkunst*, Leipzig 1757–65.

Groppo, *Catalogo di tutti i drammi per musica recitati nei Teatri di Venezia dal 1627 al 1745*, Venice 1753.

Lesage, A. R., *Théâtre espagnol*, 1700.

Lessing, G. E., *Hamburgische Dramaturgie*, Hamburg 1767 to 68.

Menestrier, C. F., *Des réprésentations en musique anciennes et modernes*, Paris 1681.

Menestrier, C. F., *Des ballets anciens et modernes, selon les Régles du Théâtre*, Paris 1682.

Müller, J. H. F., *Genaue Nachrichten von beyden k. k. Schaubühnen in Wien und den vorzüglichsten Theatern in den übrigen k. u. k. Erbländern*, Vienne 1772.

Noverre, J. G., *Lettres sur la danse et sur les Ballets*, Lyons 1760.

Parfaict, F. et C., *Mémoires pour servir à l'histoire des spectacles de la Foire*, Paris 1743.

Parfaict, Fr. et Cl., *Histoire de l'ancien théâtre italien depuis son origine en France, jusqu'a sa suppression en l'année 1679*, Paris 1753; *Histoire du Théâtre françois depuis son origine jusqu'à présent*, Paris 1734–49.

Reichardt, J. R., *Über die deutsche komische Oper*, Leipzig 1774.

Riccoboni, L., *Observations sur la comédie et sur le génie de Molière*, Paris 1736.

Rousseau, Jean-Jacques, *Lettre sur les spectacles*, 1758.

Rubin, D. Conte, *Dei Teatri* Milan 1754.

Schink, J. F., *Dramatische und andere Skizzen nebst Briefen über das Theaterwesen zu Wien*, Vienna 1783.

Schellheim, H. v., *Wienerische Dramaturgie*, Wien 1775.

Schlegel, J. E., *Gedanken zur Aufnahme des dänischen Theaters*, 1764.

Taubert, G., *Rechtschaffener Tantzmeister oder gründliche Erklärung der Frantzösischen Tantz-Kunst*, Leipzig 1717.

ARCHITECTURE

Blondel, Jacques-F., *Architecture Française*, 1752.

Dubreuil, Jean, *La Perspective Pratique*, Paris 1642 (1639?).

Dumont, G. M., *Parallèle des plans, des plus belles salles de spectacles d'Italie et de France avec des détails de machines théâtrales*, Paris 1777.

Fabris, J., *Instruction in der theatralischen Architectur und Mechanique*, 1760.

Furttenbach, Joseph, *Architectura civilis*, Ulm 1628.

Furttenbach, Joseph, *Architectura recreationis*, Ulm 1640.

Galli-Bibiena, Ferdinando, *Architettura civile preparata sulla geometria e ridotta alle prospettive*, Parma 1711.

Galli-Bibiena, Giuseppe – J.A. Pfeffel, *Architetture e prospettive, dedicate alla Maesta di Carlo VI.*, Augsburg 1740.

Pozzo, Andrea, *Prospettiva de'Pittori et Architetti*, Rome 1692 to 1700.

Sabbattini, Niccolò, *Pratica di fabricar scene e machine ne'teatri*, Ravenna 1638.

Serlio, Sebastiano, *Architettura*, 1545.

Troili, Giulio, *Paradossi per praticare la prospettiva senza saperla*, 1672.

Wilkes, Thomas, *A General View of the Stage*, London 1759.

Some works since 1950

GENERAL

Alewyn, R. – K. Sälzle, *Das grosse Welttheater. Die Epoche der höfischen Feste*, Hamburg 1959.

Apollonio, M., *Storia del Teatro Italiano*, 2 vol. Florence 1958.

Beijer, A., 'Le théâtre en Suède jusqu'à la mort de Gustave III', *Revue d'Histoire du Théâtre*, 1956, pp. 140ff.

Bragaglia, A.G., *Storia del Teatro Popolare Romano*, Rome 1958.

Chambers, E.K., *The Elizabethan Stage*, 4 vol. Oxford 1951.

Cohen, G., *Etudes d'histoire du Théâtre en France au Moyen-Age et à la Renaissance*, Paris 1956.

Cronica, A., *Teatro Serbo-Croato*, Milano 1955.

Deierkauf-Holsboer, S.W., *Le théâtre du Marais*, 2 vol. Paris 1954.

El Teatro: Enciclopedia del Arte Escenico, Barcelona 1957.

Enciclopedia dello spettacolo, Roma 1954ff.

Estreicher, R.K., *Die Theater in Polen*, Warsaw 1953.

Evreinoff, N., *Histoire du Théâtre Russe*, Paris 1947.

Hadamovsky, F., *Das Hoftheater Leopolds I. und das Kostümwerk des 1. Burnacini*, Wien 1948.

Hadamovsky, F., *Barocktheater am Wiener Kaiserhof (1625–1740)*, Vienna 1955.

Hilleström, G., *Theatre and Ballet in Sweden*, Stockholm 1953.

Kaiser, H., *Barocktheater in Darmstadt*, Darmstadt 1951.

Kindermann, H., *Theatergeschichte Europas. Band II: Das Theater der Renaissance*, Salzburg 1959; *Band III: Das Theater der Barockzeit*, 1959; *Band IV: Von der Aufklärung bis zur Romantik*, 1961; *Band V: Von der Aufklärung zur Romantik 2. Teil*, 1962. Incorporates comprehensive bibliography.

Kindermann, H. – M. Dietrich, *Dreihundert Jahre österreichisches Bühnenbild*, Wien 1959.

Lagrave, H., *Théâtre et public à Paris au XVIII. siècle. (1715–89)*, Thèse, Paris 1958.

Lanson, G., 'Mémoire de Mahelot, Laurent et les autres décorateurs de L'Hôtel de Bourgogne', *Revue d'Histoire Littéraire de la France*, 1953.

Lennep, W. van, *The London Stage 1660–1800*, 5 vol. Illinois Univ. Press 1960ff.

Moussinac, L., *Le Théâtre des origines à nos jours*, Paris 1957.

Nagler, A.M., *Sources of Theatrical History*, New York 1952.

Rosenfeld, S., *The Theatres of London, Fairs in the Eightennth Century*, Cambridge 1960.

Rosenfeld, S., *Foreign theatrical companies in Great Britain in the Seventeenth and Eighteenth centuries*, London 1955.

Schwanbeck, G., *Bibliographie der deutschsprachigen Hochschulschriften zur Theaterwissenschaft von 1885–1952. Schriften der Gesellschaft für Theatergeschichte, Band 58*, Berlin 1956.

Southern, R., *Seven Ages of Theatre*, London 1962.

Schöne, Günter, *Tausend Jahre Deutsches Theater*, Munich 1963.

Stamm, R., *Geschichte des englischen Theaters*, Berne 1951.

Toschi, P., *Le origini del teatro italiano*, Turin 1955.

Valbuena, Prat. A., *Historia del Teatro Español*, Barcelona 1956.

Veinstein, A., *Bibliothèques et Musées des Arts du Spectacle dans le Monde*, Paris 1960.

PLAYERS AND COSTUMES

Beijer, A., 'Quelques documents sur les farceurs français et italiens', *Revue d'Histoire du Théâtre*, 1957.

Calendoni, G., *L'Attore. Storia d'un arte*, Rome 1959.

Chourlin, O., *Histoire du costume de théâtre et de ballet aux XVIIe et XVIIIe siècles*. Thèse, Paris 1959.

Duchartre, P., *La Commedia dell'arte et ses enfants*, Paris 1955.

Heuzey, J., 'Du costume et de la décoration tragique au XVIIe siècle', *Revue d'Histoire du Théâtre*, 1960.

Kommerell, M., *Über die Commedia dell'arte*, Frankfurt am Main 1952.

Oman, C., *David Garrick*, London 1958.

Pandolfi, V., *La Commedia dell'arte*, 2 vol., Firenze 1957.

Schulz, G., *Die Entwicklung des Schauspielerengagements in Deutschland vom 17. bis zum 19. Jahrhundert*, Berlin 1956.

Schwanbeck, G., 'Sozialprobleme der Schauspielerin im Ablauf dreier Jahrhunderte', *Theater und Drama*, Band 18, Berlin 1957.

Tieghem, Ph. von, *Les grands Comédiens (1400–1900)*, Paris 1960.

PLAYS AND OPERAS

Adel, K., *Das Jesuitendrama in Österreich*, Vienna 1957.

Albert, A.A., *Christoph Willibald Gluck*, Munich 1959.

Balcar, A.J., *Das Ballett. Eine kleine Kulturgeschichte*, München 1957.

Braham, G.C., *Eighteenth-century Adaption of Shakespearean Tragedy*, Berkeley 1956.

Bray, R., *Molière Homme de Théâtre*, Paris 1954.

Carrieri, R., *La danza in Italia*, Milan.

Christout, M.-F., 'Les Ballets Mascarades des Fées de la Forê de Saint-Germain et de la Douairière de Billebahaut et l'œuvre de Daniel Rabel', *Revue d'Histoire du Théâtre*, 1961.

Deutsch, O.E.,*Handel, Documentary Biography*, London 1955.

Huber, W., *Das Textbuch der frühdeutschen Oper*, Diss. Munich 1957.

Komma, K.M., *Musikgeschichte in Bildern*, Stuttgart 1961.

Manifold, J.S., *Music in English drama from Shakespeare to Purcell*, London 1956.

Mann, O., *Geschichte des deutschen Dramas*, Stuttgart 1960.

Pandolfi, V., *Il Teatro drammatico di tutto il mondo dalle origine a oggi*, 2 vol. Rome 1959.

Rommel, O., *Die Alt-Wiener Volkskomödie*, Vienna 1952.

Tenschert, R., *Chr. W. Gluck, der grosse Reformator der Oper*, Olten 1951.

Tiénot, Y., *Rameau*, Paris 1954.

Towneley-Worsthorne, S., *Venetian Opera in the Seventeenth Century*, Oxford 1954.

Tschulik, N., *W.A. Mozart*, Vienna 1955.

Wild, R., *L'art du Ballet des origines à nos jours*, Paris 1952.

Wolff, H.Ch., *Die Barockoper in Hamburg (1678–1738)*, 2 Bände Wolfenbüttel 1957.

ARCHITECTURE

Abel, P., *Bühnenbildentwürfe des 18. Jahrhunderts. – Katalog der Bibliothek der Akademie der bildenden Künste*, Vienna 1956.

Aloi, R., *Architettura per lo spettacolo*, Milano 1959.

Beijer, A., 'Vigarani et Bérain au Palais Royal', *Revue d'Histoire du Théâtre*, 1956.

Bjurstroem, P., 'Servandoni, décorateur de théâtre' *Revue d'histoire du Théâtre*, 1954.

Bjurstroem, P., *Giacomo Torelli and Baroque Stage Design*, Stockholm 1961.

Bourbel, N., 'L'Etablissement et la construction de l'Hôtel des Comédiens Français, Ancienne Comédie', *Revue d'Histoire du Théâtre*, 1955.

Christout, M.F., *Les mises en scène de Jacomo Torelli en France. Estampes, documents*. Thèse, Paris 1957.

De Dainville, F., 'Lieux de théâtre et salles des actions dans les collèges de Jésuites de l'ancienne France', *Revue d'Histoire du Théâtre*, 1950.

De Dainville, F., 'Décoration Théâtrale dans les collèges de Jésuites au XVIIe siècle', *Revue d'Histoire du Théâtre*, 1951.

Frenzel, H.A., 'Brandenburgisch-preussische Schlosstheater', *Schriften der Gesellschaft für Theatergeschichte, Band 59*, Berlin 1959.

Ferrero, Mercedes Viale, *La scenografia dell'700 e i fratelli Galliari*.

Hadamovsky, F., *Die Familie Galli-Bibiena in Wien. Leben und Werk für das Theater*, Vienna 1962.

Hampe, M., *Die Entwicklung der Bühnendekoration von der Kulissenbühne zum Rundhorizontsystem*. Diss. Wien 1961.

Horn-Monval, M., 'La Grande Machinerie Théâtrale et ses Origines', *Revue d'Histoire du Théâtre*, Paris 1957.

Hodges, C.W., *The Globe Restored. A Study of the Elizabethan Theatre*, London 1933.

Jappy, M.A., *L'Opéra Royal de Versailles*, Versailles 1958.

Lejeaux, J., 'Les décors de théâtres dans les Collèges de Jesuites', *Revue d'Histoire du Théâtre*, 1955.

Lejeune, A. et Wolf, St., *Les quinze Salles de l'Opéra de Paris 1669–1955*, Paris 1955.

Lennep, W. van, *The London Stage 1660–1800*, 5 vol. Illinois Univ. Press, 1960f.

Marie, A., 'La Salle du Théâtre du Château de Fontainebleau', *Revue d'Histoire du Théâtre*, 1951.

Marie, A., 'Les Théâtres du Château de Versailles', *Revue d'Histoire du Théâtre*, 1951.

Nagler, A.M., *Shakespeare's Stage*, New Haven 1958.

Niehaus, W., *Die Theatermaler Quaglio. Ein Beitrag zur Geschichte des Bühnenbildes im 18. und 19. Jahrhundert*, Diss. Munich 1957.

Rudloff-Hille, G., *Barocktheater im Zwinger*, Dresden 1954.

Schuberth, O., *Das Bühnenbild, Geschichte, Gestalt, Technik*, Munich 1955.

Stadler, E., 'Die Raumgestaltung im barocken Theater' (R. Stamm, *Die Kunstformen des Barockzeitalters*), Munich 1956.

Southern, R., *The Open Stage*, London 1953.

PERIODICAL PUBLICATIONS

Estudios escenicos. Quadernos del Instituto del Teatro, Barcelona.

Jahrbuch der Schweizerischen Gesellschaft für Theaterkultur, Einsiedeln.

Jahrbuch der Gesellschaft für Wiener Theaterforschung, Vienna.

Maske und Kothurn.

Revue d'Histoire du Théâtre, Paris.

Rivista di Studi Teatrali.

Die Schaubühne, Emsdetten.

Schriften der Gesellschaft für Theatergeschichte, Berlin.

Schweizer Theaterjahrbuch.

Theatergeschichtliche Forschungen, Hamburg.

Theatre Research, Recherches théâtrales, Rome.

The Theatre Annual.

Sources of Illustrations

Alinari, Florence, Pls 106, 107, 108.

BASF-Kalender p. 35.

Bayerische Versicherungskammer Pls I, III, XVI.

Bulloz, Paris, Pls 1, 16, 48, 50, pp. 9, 10, 11, 45, 65, 66.

Giraudon, Paris, Pls 3, 7, 8, 19, 45, 46, 47, 55, pp. 32 (after), 44 (after), 46, 47, 48, 63, 67, 89, 90, 104, 106, 107, 135.

Dr Alfred Kroth, Munich Pls 135, 136, 137.

Verlag Otto Müller, Salzburg, p. 108.

Kremlin Museum, Moscow, Pls 43, 44, 138.

Österreichische Nationalbibliothek, Vienna, Pls 2, 11, 20, 21, 22, 23, 24, 37, pp. 8 (after), 11.

Prestel Verlag, Munich, Pl. II.

Theatermuseum, Munich, Pls 10, 15, 17, 18, 33, 36, 56, 100, 115, 116; pp. 14, 15, 21, 23, 33, 37, 38, 40, 61, 80, 94, 95, 98, 99, 100, 104, 117, 118, 119, 120, 122.

Turisticko Drustvo, Hvar, Pl. 109.

The Age of Rococo (Thames and Hudson / Verlag Georg D. W. Callwey), Pls 5, 6, 13, 34, 35, 38, 39, 51, 52, 54, 57, 61, 64, 66, 70, IV, VIII; pp. 88 (after), 96, 97, 101 (right).

All other photographs by Helga Schmidt-Glassner.

Index

Upright figures: page numbers. *Italic figures: monochrome plates.* Roman numerals: colour plates